PIONEERS OF
MODERN GRAPHIC DESIGN

A COMPLETE HISTORY

JEREMY AYNSLEY

MITCHELL
BEAZLEY

For Agnes and Hugh

First published in Great Britain in 2001 in hardback as *A Century of Graphic Design*
by Mitchell Beazley, an imprint of Octopus Publishing Group Ltd,
2–4 Heron Quays, London E14 4JP.

Copyright © 2001 Octopus Publishing Group Ltd.
This paperback edition copyright © 2004 Octopus Publishing Group Ltd.

Executive Editor	Mark Fletcher
Art Directors	Vivienne Brar, Geoff Borin
Managing Editor	John Jervis
Graphic Design	Damian Jaques
Editor	Richard Dawes
Proof Reader	Christine Davis
Picture Research	Claire Gouldstone
Production	Nancy Roberts, Alex Wiltshire
Index	Hilary Bird

ISBN 1-84000-939-X

A CIP record for this book is available from the British Library

Set in Meta and Bell Gothic

Colour reproduction by Sang Choy International Pte. Ltd
Produced by Toppan Printing Co. (HK) Ltd

Printed and bound in Hong Kong

CONTENTS

6 Introduction

A NEW PROFESSION

16 Peter Behrens
18 Henry van de Velde
20 Will Bradley
22 The New Poster
26 Graphics for Retail
28 The Suffrage Movement
30 Eric Gill
32 Wiener Werkstätte
36 Charles Rennie Mackintosh

THE NEW DESIGN EXPERIMENT

42 Italian Futurism
44 World War I Posters
46 E. McKnight Kauffer
50 A.M. Cassandre
54 De Stijl
56 El Lissitzky
58 Alexander Rodchenko
60 Bauhaus
64 László Moholy-Nagy
66 Herbert Bayer
68 Jan Tschichold
70 The Ring
74 Photomontage
78 Alexey Brodovitch
80 Art Deco
84 Studio Boggeri
86 Karel Teige
88 Ladislav Sutnar
90 Hendrik Werkman
92 National Identity

142 Henryk Tomaszewski
144 Jazz Covers

POP, SUBVERSION AND ALTERNATIVES

150 Massin
152 Push Pin Studio
156 Herb Lubalin
158 Pop in the High Street
160 Psychedelic Graphics
162 The Underground Press
164 Chinese Graphic Design
166 Roman Cieslewicz
168 Cuban Posters
170 Grapus

LATE MODERN AND POSTMODERNISM

176 Pentagram
180 Wim Crouwel
182 Jan van Toorn
184 Gert Dumbar
186 Hard Werken
188 Muriel Cooper
190 Wolfgang Weingart
192 Dan Friedman
194 Bruno Monguzzi
196 Ikko Tanaka
198 Jamie Reid

DESIGN IN THE DIGITAL ERA

204 April Greiman
206 Style Magazines
210 Javier Mariscal
212 Vaughan Oliver
214 Cranbrook Academy of Art
216 Emigre

MID-CENTURY MODERN

98 Hermann Zapf
100 Max Bill
102 Herbert Matter
104 Saul Bass
106 Paul Rand
110 Cipe Pineles
112 Lester Beall
114 Leo Lionni
116 Bernard Villemot
118 Abram Games
120 F.H.K. Henrion
122 Design Magazines
124 Josef Müller-Brockmann
126 Bruno Munari
128 Olle Eksell
130 Design for Transportation
134 Ivan Chermayeff
136 Massimo Vignelli
138 Robert Brownjohn
140 Yusaku Kamekura

218 Tibor Kalman
220 Erik Spiekermann
222 Neville Brody
224 Why Not Associates
228 Jonathan Barnbrook
230 Eiko Ishioka
232 David Carson
234 Ott + Stein
236 Sheila Levrant de Bretteville
238 Adbusters
240 Design/Writing/Research
242 Cyan

INFORMATION

244 Bibliography
248 Museums and Design Collections
249 Glossary
250 Index
255 Acknowledgments

INTRODUCTION

Visual communication is an inextricable part of human history. It has existed as long as there has been the need to make marks or leave traces, to communicate through signs and symbols rather than the spoken word. In the contemporary world the activity of organizing signs and symbols, or words and images, for public exchange is recognized as graphic design – a specialist area of the broader field of design.

Some histories of graphic design begin with prehistoric cave paintings and go on to consider, along the way, Egyptian hieroglyphics, Chinese calligraphy, medieval manuscripts and type design of the eighteenth century. This book concentrates on twentieth-century graphic design, which started with the division of labour brought about by industrialization.

Today graphic design embraces printed material from the smallest ephemeral item – a stamp, label or ticket – to publication design in the form of the interiors and exteriors of books and magazines. It also includes poster and advertising design, as well as trademarks, logos and symbols. Then there are extensive systems of information design – signage in the built environment, exhibitions and corporate identities for companies, all often developed in close association with architectural practices. Graphic designers can also be involved in multi-media design, whether in areas of traditional print media or in screen-based design for film, computer and television.

GRAPHIC DESIGN DEFINED

It is believed that the American typographer William Addison Dwiggins first coined the term "graphic design" in 1922, in order to distinguish different kinds of design for printing. Before this the mechanization of printing processes had coincided with the emergence of advertising as a major form of print culture to propel the market for goods. In the mid- and late nineteenth century the demands of a mass market had encouraged a proliferation of specialist hand-workers to supply the printing presses. These workers were responsible for a wide range of illustrations executed in a variety of figurative styles in wood engraving as well as in the more recent techniques of lithography and photogravure. At first the graphic arts were closely aligned to their technical base in craft skills. Later, however, the need to coordinate activities and to advise a client on the best appropriate solution, led to a separation between plan and execution. The intermediary was the graphic designer – someone who would receive instructions from a client, devise drawings and plans and then instruct technicians, typesetters and printers to realize the designs.

The enthusiasm captured in this photograph speaks of the optimism at the Bauhaus school of art, design and architecture. Established at the end of World War I in Weimar under the direction of the architect Walter Gropius, it became a seedbed for new design, including many exploratory ideas about modern graphic and typographic design.

The designers discussed in this book worked in a variety of contexts. Some, such as Will Bradley, Eric Gill, Hermann Zapf, Herb Lubalin, Erik Spiekermann and Jonathan Barnbrook, have been employed by type foundries, applying their specialist knowledge of calligraphy, lettering and typography to devise new typefaces or adapt existing ones for changing technologies. Others were taken on by a particular company. This was so for Peter Behrens, artistic adviser to AEG, the world's largest electrical company before 1914; or Massin, art director for the French publisher Gallimard for 20 years in the middle of the century. Still others joined advertising agencies, but by far the most common model was that of the independent designer. Most designers featured in this book established their own studios, while others formed partnerships. In both cases the individual designers' names acted as a form of shorthand label for a group of staff, equipped with a variety of skills suited to the interdisciplinary nature of graphic design.

COMMERCIALIZATION

In the early years the expression "commercial graphics" had pejorative connotations. It imposed a hierarchy in which the fine arts, apparently not associated with commerce, stood above the applied arts, which were at the service of commerce. Towards the end of the century such assumptions became hard to sustain, as it was by now clear that all arts are part of an economic system. However, much energy had to be spent convincing the public that the activities of graphic design were worthy of attention.

Professionalization of graphic design involved establishing organizations for its promotion. The lead came in different ways from Europe and the United States. In the latter the American Institute of Graphic Arts (AIGA) was founded in New York in 1914, making it the oldest organization concerned to promote the activities of the "graphic arts". Many of the designers in this book have been high-profile members of the AIGA and recipients of its gold medals, among them Ivan Chermayeff, Seymour Chwast and Massimo Vignelli. The aims of the AIGA were to improve standards through debate, education and good practice. Advertising was a particularly sensitive area, where visual excess and false claims had led the public to distrust it as "quackery". It was decided that to give awards and to treat advertising as art would improve the situation by bestowing greater significance on the activity. Advertising was of prime interest to the Art Directors Club, founded in New York in 1920. An annual exhibition and publication served to promote the best of creative standards in design and art direction. Again, many of the designers in this book were elected to the Art Directors Club Hall of Fame in recognition of their achievements.

In Europe the century opened with many publications devoted to the poster, at that time the most visible and prestigious genre of graphic art. In Paris Roger Marx published the periodical *Les Maîtres de L'Affiche* from 1895, including the work of famous painters who were also designing lithographic posters for theatre, concerts and consumer goods. He championed their collection by museums and private enthusiasts. This was followed by the publication in England of *The Poster* (1898–1901) and in Germany of *Das Plakat* (1910–21).

During the interwar years more specialized publications indicated that graphic design was gaining strength. Journals such as *Arts et Métiers Graphiques* (1927–39) and *Gebrauchsgraphik* (1924–44) took a wide interest in book, poster and exhibition design. It was not until after 1945 that the term "graphic design" was broadly adopted to define the educational and professional activity – a stage when degree courses in Graphic Design and Illustration were established in many parts of the world. During the period a generation of international magazines reviewed graphic design, among the most prominent being *Graphis* (1944–) and *Neue Graphik* (1958–65) from Switzerland, *Print* (1940–) from the United States and *Typographica* (1958–65) from Britain. This increasing awareness of graphic design coincided with major technological change. Design for film and television demanded an

Moser, a member of the Vienna Secession, made the magazine a central motif in this poster exhorting the public to take the *Illustrierte Zeitung*. The decorative design is typical of the Secessionist style. An important element is the woman's dress, which reflects the aim of Secessionist designers to harmonize the domestic interior, women's clothing and graphic design.

8

Kamekura was among the first Japanese designers to introduce modernism to his country and to subsequently become an internationally recognized graphic designer. The poster exploits the apparent simplicity of two symbols: the red sun of the Japanese flag and the five rings of the Olympic symbol, both anchored by the words "Tokyo 1964".

emphasis on systems. "Visual communication" became preferred as an all-embracing term that avoided the underlying assumption that graphic design activities were necessarily for print on paper.

When the Apple Macintosh computer was launched in 1984 it opened up graphic design to a much wider group of users, who were now equipped to develop the new field of desktop publishing. The impact of the computer is further discussed in the section "Design in the Digital Age". From this time changes in typography and graphic design reflected a renewed excitement about the interaction between typography and other forms of artistic expression, as articles in magazines such as *Emigre* (1982–) and *Eye* (1991–) revealed. Instead of adhering to the earlier, over-reductive definition of the graphic designer as a problem-solver, this recent movement interpreted typography and graphic design as part of a wider cultural practice with references in film, music, style, fashion and fine art.

REVIEWING A CENTURY

This book employs recognized thematic headings to define graphic design in common with other fields of artistic and design activity. Accordingly, style labels such as Futurism, Constructivism, Surrealism, New York School, Pop and postmodernism are used as markers to indicate how graphic design is part of a broader visual and artistic language.

The century opened with the idea of graphic design as "A New Profession". Initiatives were made to improve the standard of design for print in the Design Reform movement in Europe and the USA. Pioneering individuals moved from painting or architecture to define what graphic design might be. The second section, "The New Design and Artistic Experiment", explores the extremely rich cultural activities of the interwar years and the impact of modernism in design and architecture on graphic design. At this time many trained artists abandoned easel painting in their belief that design could be democratic. The Bauhaus, the school of design and architecture that ran for a relatively short period from 1919 in Weimar until its closure in Berlin in 1933, epitomized this belief. The school was a seedbed of ideas that informed subsequent design for communication.

The section "Mid-Century Modern" covers the consolidation of modernism as the official style for graphic design at a time of worldwide political disarray. Modern sans-serif typefaces, photographic illustration and ideas from modern art were all thought of as strategies that would encourage international communication. As an approach, modernism informed the commissioning by art directors for clients in publishing, advertising and publicity design for multinational companies. Escaping the totalitarianism of Europe in the 1930s, many modernist graphic designers crossed the Atlantic, including Sutnar, Moholy-Nagy, Lionni, Bayer and Teige, and helped to introduce the style to the increasingly sophisticated and professional atmosphere of corporate America. After World War II modernism was re-exported to the rest of the world, partly perceived as an American phenomenon, with important centres forming most notably in Japan and Switzerland.

ALTERNATIVE VOICES

In a professional sense, graphic design has been largely a product of the "first world" and is profoundly associated with an industrial and commercial base. Many of the celebrated figures in this book have worked for national and international companies, their work a participation in the global economy. There are also independent voices, exceptions who refused to play this role. The Constructivist designers El Lissitzky and Alexander Rodchenko were both involved in the great experiment to find a graphic language suited to a new communist society in the Soviet Union during the experimental years under Lenin in the early 1920s. In later decades Polish, Cuban and Chinese graphic design, discussed in the section "Pop, Subversions and Alternatives", did not conform to the model of Western-style industrial graphics, with its concern to sustain market values. Designers in these countries, a number of them at odds with the dominant political system, turned instead to graphic design as a form of cultural enrichment.

Many graphic designers in the West have likewise been unhappy with the model of acquiescence and support for the political status quo that was evident throughout the century. In the 1960s social and political unrest was manifest in the

Emigre Fonts, based in California, is a digital type foundry, typeface distributor and publisher founded in 1984 in response to the introduction of the Apple Macintosh computer. The company grew quickly, making available, by the end of the century, 157 original typeface designs by many contemporary designers. It was just one part of the highly significant intervention of VanderLans and Licko in contemporary graphic design.

10

Booklet for Emigre fonts, 1999

This poster displays many characteristic ideas of the French graphic design collective Grapus, who were committed to work of an engaged, political nature. Gerry-Chambertin, a well-known brand of champagne, is cross-referred to an image of a Molotov cocktail in an announcement for a play performed by the radical Theatre of the Red Hat. Details of the performance are given in an urgent, scribbled style.

underground press and in moves to found alternative societies. In a political reaction against capitalism, the work of John Heartfield, the famous German designer of the Weimar era who used photomontage as a political weapon in his struggle against the rise of Nazism, took on renewed significance. The French collective Grapus grew out of the climate of political radicalism in the Paris of 1968, accepting commissions only from groups whose causes they supported and producing work that extended the principles of collage and montage. Also springing from the radicalization of the New Left, feminist design practice encouraged alternative approaches to graphic design, including site-specific installations based on social issues, as in the work of the American designer Sheila Levrant de Bretteville.

Much graphic design of the 1980s and 1990s turned to academic debate on the character of word and image, informed by French cultural theory, semiology and post-structuralism. The phrase "typography as discourse" usefully summarizes this emphasis on meaning and the subsequent exploration of the linguistic character of design.

LATE MODERN AND POSTMODERN
The choice facing the graphic designer in the late twentieth century seemed to be at least twofold. Many designers retained the idea that graphic design could improve the visual environment. This outlook, usually described as "late modern", represented continuity with the founding aims of graphic design. Meanwhile postmodernists, by contrast, suggested that there had been a category redefinition, that a fundamental break with modernism had occurred. They chose to celebrate pluralism of style and diversity of audience in reaction against what they perceived to be the over-reductive tendency of previous design. As the century closed, this critical perspective was mirrored in a collaboration between the Canadian-based "cultural jammers" Adbusters, led by Kalle Lasn, and the British graphic designer Jonathan Barnbrook. Asked to create a huge billboard for the annual AIGA conference in Las Vegas, attended by 3000 designers, they selected a text by the American graphic designer Tibor Kalman: "Designers, stay away from corporations that want you to tell lies for them."

Taking stock at the beginning of a new century, it becomes clear that graphic design is a well-established genre of design with its own set of intellectual debates, its own culture of journalism and criticism, and a thriving, active response to the changing demands of new technology. Graphic design continues to fulfil important social and cultural roles, while also offering a space for reflection, contestation and subversion.

11

A NEW PROFESSION

A NEW PROFESSION

Graphic design was a new profession for a new century. Its emergence was underpinned by major technological changes, and while these had their roots in the previous century, it was only at the beginning of the twentieth century that their implications for the design process were realized.

For a modern communication system to emerge, an infrastructure of mechanized printing, ink and paper manufacture and specialist machinery for folding, binding and stapling was necessary. This was prompted by a huge change in the pattern of life of urban populations in the late nineteenth century that may be summarized as a collective move to modernity. The migration of people to towns and cities to find industrialized work, the growth of railway networks and the steady increase in the mass market for consumer goods were linked to other important changes. Modern communications became dependent on reproduction, at first through print and later in the century through radio, television and film. Books, magazines, posters and advertisements began to be produced on an unprecedented scale, for instruction, education and entertainment. This led, for economic and practical reasons, to the concentration of large-scale printing houses in cities.

The responsibility to train young workers for the graphic trades and industries had previously belonged to the guilds, but now trade schools and colleges of art and design took on the task. The model of design education was largely based on what was known as the "South Kensington system", named after the area of London where the British government established the School of Design in 1837. A network of similar "branch schools" was subsequently set up in manufacturing towns and cities throughout the country. Matters of taste and aesthetics were taught alongside technical skills. An understanding of ornament was considered fundamental to all branches of design and the best way to reform taste. Most active in this campaign were Henry Cole, the founder in 1853 of the South Kensington Museum (later the Victoria and Albert Museum), William Morris, Owen Jones and John Ruskin. Their influence was felt across many parts of Europe, where similar arts and crafts schools and museums were soon established.

The example of William Morris is indispensable to an understanding of the Arts and Crafts movement between 1890 and 1914. An all-round designer, Morris worked in textiles, wallpapers and furniture, and made an important contribution to printing. The aesthetic of Morris and his followers was drawn from medieval arts and showed a preference for natural motifs and colours, figuration and high pattern. In 1891, towards the end of his life, Morris established, with T.J. Cobden-Sanderson,

Poster by Louis John Rhead for *New York Sunday Press*, 'Winter Tales for Winter Nights", 1896

Rhead's design is characteristic of the introduction of Arts and Crafts ideals to the modern commercial poster. Emphasis on the harmony of the composition is achieved through the choice of coloured inks and the arm reaching into the text.

the Kelmscott Press to publish limited editions. He advocated hand-set type, woodcut illustrations and decorated initials, all integrated to embody the "book beautiful". A flurry of small private presses sprang up all over Britain, Europe and the USA. But while Morris was against the machine for what he saw as its degradation of human labour and the impoverishment of design, not all his followers denied themselves the opportunity to work with mechanized processes. Many carried out his aesthetic principles but adapted them to mechanical reproduction.

A fundamental reform of design could only be possible if the typefaces available at foundries were improved. In this advance the way was led by Germany, where a designer such as Peter Behrens would be commissioned by major companies to design several important new typefaces. A similar pattern followed in the United States with Will Bradley, Bruce Rogers and Frederic Goudy and in Britain with Eric Gill, Edward Johnston and others.

If one leading impulse for the emergence of graphic design came from the Arts and Crafts reform of typography, another came from the poster movement. Here connections between the graphic and fine arts were emphasized. As it emerged, the new poster shared a visual language with Symbolism, Art Nouveau and the Secession, all movements that stressed links between the various fine and applied arts. Reacting against neoclassical and neo-baroque historicism, these versions of the "new art" veered towards new techniques and materials, advocating an aesthetic simplicity. In the field of posters the technique of lithography was particularly important as it offered artists the opportunity to visit print workshops and draw directly on the especially prepared stone. In some cases artists integrated their own lettering into designs for posters, bringing aesthetic harmony to the medium.

The sense of composition among designers in Europe and America was profoundly affected by their interest in the visual arts of Japan. The asymmetry of Japanese woodblock prints, their flat colour, emphasis on single female figures and balance between foreground and background excited modern designers.

A series of international exhibitions provided a venue for much comparison and competition between the various nations' art industries, and posters were a central part of these events. The exhibitions in Paris in 1900, Turin in 1902, St Louis in 1904 and Brussels in 1908 simultaneously encouraged national distinctiveness and international awareness.

By 1914 the book and poster arts were about to be subsumed into a greater whole: graphic design. With the outbreak of World War I, however, this synthesis was delayed and the full emergence of the graphic designer would have to wait until the 1920s.

Peter Behrens, a self-taught architect and designer, was a prolific and outstanding figure of the German Jugendstil movement at the beginning of the twentieth century.

Originally from Hamburg, Behrens studied painting in Munich. Inspired by the British Arts and Crafts reform ideals of William Morris and others, he designed a villa in Darmstadt's artists' colony in 1902. This was praised as a "Gesamtkunstwerk", a total work of art, conforming to the contemporary ideal that all aspects of design should be given equal attention and be coordinated in the same style. The same principle was to inform much of his later work.

In the field of graphic design Behrens was most important for his early Symbolist prints published in small art journals, his typeface designs and his work for the Berlin electrical manufacturer AEG. All of this was largely undertaken between 1900 and 1914; after World War I Behrens worked mainly as an architect. In the belief that, with the turn of the century, the arts were in need of regeneration, German type foundries commissioned Behrens to design typefaces which would express the new spirit of the age. It was also hoped that these might help put German industry on a competitive footing with France. Controversially, against the German tradition of setting texts in Gothic script, Behrens was keen to base designs on roman typefaces. He inflected these with calligraphic qualities more associated with German lettering. The first of the designs was Behrens-Schrift of 1902, a distinctive, elongated letterform compatible with Jugendstil decoration. Kursiv followed in 1906, and Behrens-Antiqua was available in 1908. The latter, a "roman in a German spirit", was used extensively in Behrens's designs for AEG.

⊖ 1868–1940
⊖ Important figure in German Arts and Crafts movement and linked with Jugendstil
⊖ Trained as painter in Karlsruhe and Düsseldorf
⊖ Artistic adviser to AEG electrical company
⊖ Pioneer industrial designer with later career as architect

Booklet for Gebrüder Klingspor type foundry, 1908

Behrens-Antiqua (Roman) typeface, designed for the Klingspor type foundry, was an elegant typeface that Behrens later used in his own designs. New typefaces were announced internationally through booklets such as this.

In 1907 Behrens was appointed artistic director to AEG, a major manufacturer of generators, cables, light bulbs, arc lamps and other electrical goods for domestic and industrial use. This was among the most celebrated appointments in design history, as it heralded the birth of the corporate identity. Behrens's responsibilities grew from overseeing trade pamphlets and advertising to organizing displays at international exhibitions. He redesigned AEG's trademark as a hexagonal motif, reminiscent of a honeycomb, which he then applied to the designs of new products, such as electric kettles, fans and lamps. This led to a visual consistency in all AEG goods, which brought instant recognition by the consumer. Extensive use of Behrens-Antiqua gave the company's identity a clean, sober appearance and brought AEG praise for its systematic ordering of product information. Behrens's architectural office in Berlin also oversaw the construction of new factories and workers' housing for AEG.

The classicism of Behrens's designs, with their striking use of symmetry, geometry and strong black and white contrasts, was praised for giving AEG a look which was artistic yet rational. This approach became associated with much modern German design for the rest of the century.

The Deutsche Werkbund's exhibition in Cologne in 1914 was an important climax to the organization's initiatives to display the outstanding aesthetic qualities of German industrial goods. On the eve of World War I, however, Behrens's design was considered too aggressive and withdrawn, to be replaced by a more moderate design by Fritz Ehmcke.

17

This design develops from an arrangement of concentric circular motifs around a strong central axis, suggesting the radiation of light provided by electricity. Behrens took up the post of artistic director to AEG (Allgemeine Elektrizitäts Gesellschaft) of Berlin in 1907. As well as designing the products themselves, he was responsible for the entire graphic output of this major industrial company.

Frontispiece for Nietzsche's book *Ecce Homo*, 1908

Van de Velde took great care in his selection of typefaces, chapter initials, paper, inks and binding. He designed many of the ornamental panels and letterforms for Nietzsche's *Ecce Homo*, published by Insel Verlag of Leipzig in 1908, and for a larger companion volume, *Also Sprach Zarathustra*.

Poster for Tropon, 1898

Van de Velde designed this poster for Tropon egg-white concentrate in 1898. It was celebrated as the first application of Art Nouveau for a readily available commercial product.

18

→ 1863–1957
→ Leading Belgian Art Nouveau designer who lived in Germany 1904–17
→ Important theory of line and ornament in applied art and design
→ Art Nouveau posters and book designs

Henry Van de Velde, whose career was established before the full emergence of graphic design, is best known as a designer and architect. Born in Belgium, he spent much of his career in Germany, where, from early in the twentieth century, his teaching played an important role in the foundation of modernism. In the field of graphic art he designed posters, packaging and books in the Art Nouveau style.

Van de Velde studied painting at Antwerp Academy from 1881 to 1884 and then under Carolus Duran in Paris. After settling in Brussels he joined the post-impressionist group Les Vingt, who, inspired by Gauguin and his contemporaries, were interested in applying the new aesthetic ideas of Symbolism to the applied arts.

Van de Velde was an articulate designer who, throughout a long career, wrote a considerable number of essays and offered many statements about his work. In 1894 his essay "Déblaiement de l'Art" (Clearing the Way for Art) made a plea for the unity of the arts. Typically for an artist of his generation, he was influenced by the writings of John Ruskin and the wallpaper and textile designs of William Morris.

In 1895 Van de Velde built his own house in Uccle, near Brussels, in which his design principles were tested in a variety of disciplines. Through exhibitions, he was introduced to a wide public and he was commissioned by Samuel Bing to design part of his new gallery, L'Art Nouveau, which promoted the latest style in Paris. Later he designed the interior of the Maison Moderne for Bing's rival, Julius Meier-Graefe.

Stained-glass panels, Brussels, 1894

In Van de Velde's early work there were strong similarities between his use of line and ornament in graphic design and in the other kinds of design he executed, such as these stained-glass panels for the Maison P. Otlet in Brussels. This work also points the way to a later stage in his career, when he became an important architect and interior designer.

In his early paintings and prints Van de Velde developed the abstract potential of organic lines in ornament. He was especially interested in the way a line could convey energy and force while defining both negative and positive space.

In 1904 Van de Velde was appointed Professor of the School of Applied Arts (later the Bauhaus; see pp60–3) in Weimar, Germany, in a new building to his design. While in Weimar he was also associated with Count Harry Kessler, for whose Cranach Press he designed some important limited editions of the philosophical works of Friedrich Nietzsche. In keeping with their content, the design of the books embraced more than the simple organization of the text. Nietzsche, basing his ideas on the coming together of artistic forms in opera, advocated the idea of the *Gesamtkunstwerk*, the

principle that all the components of an artwork can cohere within a greater whole. If Van de Velde's book designs represented a response to Morris's medievalizing aesthetic, they also suggested a systematic approach to the entire design process that was highly influential for twentieth-century design.

Van de Velde made clear his fundamental position on design in a famous debate with the German architect Hermann Muthesius which took place at the Cologne Deutsche Werkbund exhibition in 1914. Muthesius advocated standardization in design, whereas he supported individual artistic autonomy. Van de Velde's later architectural career, in Belgium, the Netherlands and Switzerland, saw the completion of several major projects, most notably the library of Ghent University and the Kröller-Müller Museum in Otterlo.

WILL BRADLEY

In the designs Bradley produced in 1904–5 for the American Type Founders Co.'s series of monthly magazines *The Printer Man's Joy*, he drew on his deep knowledge of early English and American Colonial woodcuts.

Cover for magazine *The Printer Man's Joy*, 1905

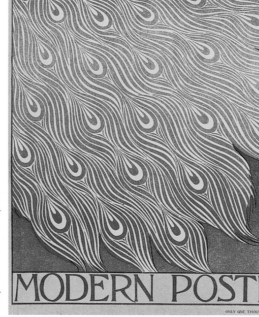

Poster, "The Modern Poster", 1895

Bradley is associated with the first flowering of Art Nouveau in America. The shared sources of the style were Japanese prints and the English graphic artist Aubrey Beardsley, whose work was known through *The Studio*, an illustrated magazine of fine and applied art. Bradley's use of this style is exemplified by this poster, published by Scribner's Sons in 1895.

20

⊕ 1868–1964
⊕ Influential American Art Nouveau typographer and poster artist
⊕ Self-taught in design
⊕ Pioneer of artistic printing in United States
⊕ Decorative illustrations in magazines and books

Printing and the graphic arts underwent rapid change in the United States in the late nineteenth century. Will Bradley, more than anyone, took the ideas of the Arts and Crafts movement, the new style of Art Nouveau and a strong interest in Japanese design and assimilated them into American graphic design to prepare it for the new century.

Bradley was born in Boston but grew up in Michigan, where he was introduced to the skills of printing at an early age. Apprenticed at the age of 12 to a general printer, he later became a foreman of the local newspaper. He was therefore self-taught in matters of design. His ideas and inspiration were drawn from his own magazines and books, and from reading in libraries about Japanese prints and the theories of decoration of Owen Jones and Christopher Dresser. The most profound inspiration came from William Morris, whose founding of a private press and use of nature as a basis for ornament made a great impression on the young Bradley.

By 1886 Bradley had moved to Chicago, a thriving commercial city in the midst of reconstruction after the great fire of 1871, and in 1893 the venue of the World's Columbian Exposition. He established himself in the specialist community of typographers and printers, designing covers for Chicago's foremost trade journal, *The Inland Printer*, among other publications.

Bradley's illustrative style depended on asymmetric, curvilinear ornament with contrasting black and white areas. The year 1894 marked the beginning of Art Nouveau in America, and Bradley and Edward Penfield became its most recognizable exponents. Bradley's main

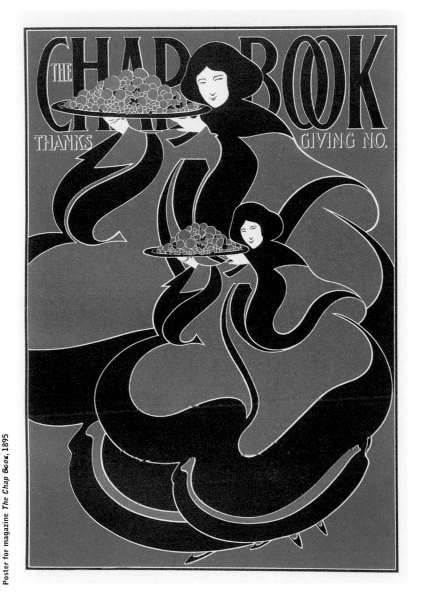

Poster for magazine *The Chap Book*, 1895

Bradley's design for this poster for the leading American publishers Stone & Kimball uses contrasting asymmetrical and curvilinear forms of flat colour. The company was noted for commissioning fine printing and graphic design.

work was for magazines, designing both covers and interiors. He also designed several posters for publishers and other commercial companies in the new style, often depicting the fashionable new woman in natural surroundings. His first book commission, for Herbert Stone at Harvard University Press in 1894, was to design the cover, title page, page decorations and a poster for *When Hearts Are Trumps*, a volume of verse by Tom Hall.

The technique of colour lithography for printing large-scale posters was being rapidly improved in the last decades of the nineteenth century, and a poster craze swept the United States. The fashion for acquiring posters, especially by the French artists Bonnard, Chéret, Steinlen, Toulouse Lautrec and others, prepared the ground for Bradley's designs, which received favourable reviews as exemplars of the new style.

Bradley was also a serious typographer, and he founded his own press, The Wayside Press, on moving to Springfield, Massachusetts, in 1894. He published his own writings in *Bradley: His Book*, an art and literary magazine. Here he showed a broader interest in the history of printing than was possible in the flat graphic work. He was a keen advocate of the use of Caslon typeface and studied early Colonial printing. These influences emerged in *The Chap Books*, a series of 12 journals published for the American Type Founders Co. in 1904–5 as "a campaign of type display and publicity".

In later life Bradley became art editor of a series of prestigious magazines. Between 1910 and 1915 he worked on *Good Housekeeping*, *Metropolitan*, *Success*, *Pearson's* and the *National Post*, and then for William Randolph Hearst before retiring in 1925.

THE NEW POSTER

The modern artistic poster was an invention of the last years of the nineteenth century. Before this, letterpress posters for bill-posting in the streets had emphasized the text, and goods had been sold or events advertised by using the principal means of persuasion: words, set in a wide variety of typefaces.

The technique of lithography encouraged changes. Lithographic printing is described as an autographic medium because what is printed is a direct record of the lines drawn by the hand of the lithographic artist or master printer. The process, invented by the German Alois Senefelder between 1796 and 1799, involves drawing in chalk on a flat surface; this was initially done on a specially prepared stone and later on flat rubber sheets that were compatible with mechanized presses. Artists could visit the printers, either to instruct the master printers or to work directly on the lithographic plates. Lithography attracted artists, who valued the mark-making qualities of the medium. The new poster was also distinctive in that it allowed the copy-line, or text, and pictorial schemes to be integrated in an artistic whole. This was the case in Paris, for example, where designers and artists such as Jules Chéret, Théophile-Alexandre Steinlen, Henri de Toulouse-Lautrec and Pierre Bonnard devised lettering that enhanced their pictorial compositions.

The identity of the poster depended on the close association between the graphic and commercial arts. In the 1880s and 1890s posters were just as likely to be used to advertise a portfolio of prints or a concert as they were to sell bicycles, sewing machines or soap. This new and powerful status was celebrated by the poster's advocates as part of the modernity of contemporary life, but equally it was strongly criticized by its detractors, who believed that fine art was endangered by commerce.

Colour lithography also offered tremendous possibilities for verisimilitude, and the technique was used for sophisticated reproductions. The most celebrated example of this was an advertisement for Pear's soap, which popularized the painting *Bubbles* by the Royal Academician John Everett Millais when it was converted into a poster in 1886. Such pictorialism became commonplace in posters advertising transportation (see pp130–3) and many other industrial or domestic goods.

From the 1870s a proliferation of illustrated posters could be seen in the streets of major towns and cities in Europe and North America, announcing theatrical performances and musicals, branded foodstuffs, new forms of travel, domestic goods and clothing. In response to the welter of styles on display, designers associated with the fine arts or in association with the Arts and Crafts reform movement developed new styles of "artistic" poster, in the hope that these would stand out from the rest. In France there was a close association between painters and poster art, whereas in the Netherlands, Germany and Belgium it was more often designers and architects who turned to poster design, seeking to instil values of good taste and appropriateness of form and typography.

As early as 1881 the *Magazine of Art* suggested that visitors to the cities could witness "the street as art galleries". By implication, posters became a means to disseminate visual ideas to those unfamiliar with the art gallery. This idea would remain for decades a leitmotif in commentaries on graphic art and design, and often provided an incentive to improve the quality of designs.

However, not everyone was so enthusiastic about the spread of printed images across the town and countryside. In London in the 1890s, for example, the Society for Checking the Abuse of Public Advertising met to monitor issues of artistic style and the location of posters. They held the view that these modes of persuasion were too forceful, and that outdoor advertisements presented a form of visual pollution. In many French and German cities this problem was addressed by using poster columns to encourage an orderly and artistic display.

To further the promotion of the poster a number of magazines were also launched around this time, including *Les Maîtres de L'Affiche* in France (1895), *The Poster* in Britain (1898) and *Das Plakat* in Germany (1910). The spread of posters was also fuelled by private collectors and societies, and examples began to be acquired by the print collections of major museums of the decorative arts.

The poster boom led the acerbic Austrian writer Karl Krauss to comment in 1909: "Is there life beyond the poster?" – a comment strangely prescient of postmodern debates about whether there is life beyond the media.

The date of appearance of publications dedicated to the poster reflected the respective degree of commitment

This poster designed by Steinlen for the Parisian lithographic printer Charles Verneau, equates modernity with contemporary graphic styles to celebrate the colourful variety of street life.

23

Transatlantic ocean liners were a popular subject for prestigious chromo-lithographic posters. In this case, the design is arranged as a triptych with frame, a format more often used for painted altarpieces.

THE NEW POSTER

MAISON FONDÉE EN 1851

PARAPLUIE-REVEL

LYON   (FRANCE)

VERITAS VERITAS VERITAS

The very best umbrella manufacturer
Established 1851

Marque déposée   MADE IN FRANCE   Trade Mark

Cappiello, a prolific poster artist based in France, specialized in posters which, like this example (left), interpreted the power of the brand for an international market. He linked the first generation of Art Nouveau designs with the modern interwar poster.

A photograph of a street scene in the United States in the 1930s (below) shows the haphazard juxtaposition of posters on billboards and buildings that was characteristic of the period. After World War II television took an ever-increasing share of advertising.

of countries to innovation and development of the form. First came Japan and France in the 1870s, while Britain, Belgium and the United States followed in the 1890s. Germany, by contrast, did not gain recognition for contributing to the history of the poster until the early twentieth century, with Jugendstil designs and the Berlin poster school. The latter, a loose affiliation of poster designers who tended to work for the same art printers, Hollerbaum and Schmidt, came to be defined by a shared approach. They produced the *Sachplakat* – literally, "object poster" – in which a single, highly lit object was depicted in a manner that emphasized the product's brand name. Such an approach could be used internationally, as it crossed linguistic boundaries.

One of Germany's most popular poster artists was Ludwig Hohlwein (1874–1949), who worked in a similar style in Munich. This tradition was continued between the wars by various poster artists, notably Leonetto Cappiello (1875–1924), who designed more than 3000 examples.

The geography of poster art continued to shift for the rest of the century. By the late 1920s Switzerland was acknowledged as "the classic country of poster advertising". In France the Alliance Graphique of A.M. Cassandre (see pp50–2), Jean Carlu, Charles Loupot and Paul Colin continued the dialogue between fine and graphic art. These *affichistes* worked in the convention of highly individualized, autograph styles of posters, employing a wide repertoire of graphic ingenuity. During the second half of the century, however, the poster gave way in many parts of the world to advertising in wider-reaching media, such as radio and television. Notable exceptions were China (see pp 164–5), Poland (see pp166–7) and Cuba (see pp168–9), where distinct poster traditions evolved, often for particular artistic or political reasons.

Poster by Ludwig Hohlwein for Riquet Mammut-Kakao, 1920

Ludwig Hohlwein was the most successful poster designer in Germany during the interwar period. His strong figurative style depended on striking contrasts and silhouettes, as in this advertisement for cocoa.

25

Lucian Bernhard pioneered the *Sachplakat*, or "object poster", in the early years of the twentieth century. The formula depended on a straightforward iconic juxtaposition of name and object.

Poster by Lucian Bernhard for Stiller, 1908

GRAPHICS FOR RETAIL

For most consumers at the beginning of the twentieth century by far the most usual way to come across graphic design was when shopping. During the last quarter of the nineteenth century and the first quarter of the twentieth, huge changes in the ways goods were prepared and presented for sale were introduced. Whether customers were aware of it or not, manufacturers, distributors, retailers and advertisers were involved in a process of specialization that permanently altered the way we encounter goods.

Before 1914 a designer was sometimes involved in this change, although in most cases designers remained anonymous and were not recognized as individuals. Packaging was nothing new. The Chinese are known to have had labels 2000 years ago. Engraved labels for textiles exist from the sixteenth century and patent medicine bottles carrying the maker's name moulded into the glass were used in the eighteenth century. All acted as guarantees of quality, promising that the customer would receive goods free from contamination.

However, the change in scale of distribution brought about by industrialization and the railways accelerated new techniques of salesmanship. Singer stamped its name on its sewing machines in the 1850s as sales increased across the United States. Over the following years more mundane goods, such as soaps and biscuits, appeared with imprints of their company or signets and trademarks. The move to encourage trademarks began with the Union des Fabricants in Paris in 1872. Five years later the United States Trade Mark Association was formed.

In the area of foodstuffs, technology enabled goods previously sold loose as staples to be packaged hygienically in ways that could withstand distribution. The paper-bag machine was patented in 1852 by Francis Wolle, who went on to supply America through the Paper Bag Machine Company. Machines for printing and embossing designs on metal for decorated tins were developed in the 1860s, followed by cardboard technologies and automatic canning and bottle-making. Aluminium foil was invented in 1910 and cellophane in 1913.

Manufacturers stressed that the label or package was not just an advertisement but an integral part of the object as a newly defined commodity. Goods sold by middlemen were given names, or "brands", that were not those of the distributor or the manufacturer. Among the earliest was Ivory soap for Procter & Gamble in 1881.

Until Art Deco (see pp80–3) in the 1920s the modernity of goods was not always the obvious sales strategy. Instead associations with tradition and quality appeared most noticeably in advertisements for new products. References to products' success in the universal exhibitions attested to their value. The "science" of advertising and the psychology of marketing were introduced to university syllabuses in the early 1900s in the Unites States, where journals such as *Profitable Advertising* and *The Inland Printer* covered the conjunction of interests of the printer, retailer and advertiser. It was not until the interwar period that an equivalent specialist press emerged in Europe.

Designs for the British grocery retailer J. Sainsbury show a coordinated approach to the shop front in place by the early century. Graphic design was also applied to packaging and delivery bicycles.

Exterior of J. Sainsbury, Romford branch, c.1905

Boots Number Seven was an inexpensive range of cosmetics introduced by Boots, the British high-street chemist, at the height of the popularization of make-up. The package design, by Barringer, Wallis and Manners Ltd, emphasized the tradition of the company as well as asserting the modernity of this brand.

In 1888 the American entrepreneur Asa Candler bought the recipe and name of the drink Coca-Cola. The bold calligraphic trademark and the bottle's distinctive shape enhanced its identity. The original designer of the bottle is unknown, but the industrial designer Raymond Loewy later modified the shape.

A uniform approach to this product's identity, embracing both bottle and box, illustrates the professionalization of packaging design that had occurred by the middle of the century. Once a design was deemed successful, it could be retained with only minor modification for many years, asserting the enduring strength of the brand in the marketplace.

THE SUFFRAGE MOVEMENT

The campaign for women's suffrage in Britain intensified greatly between 1907 and 1914, raising awareness that to gain the vote was an essential stage in the development of female emancipation. The movement was the first identifiable stage in the twentieth century when women as a group defined representation and questioned social convention through popular graphic means. The visual arts, and in particular banners, posters and leaflets, were a central part of the strategy for campaigners, and the forms of visual representation employed reveal the complex nature of the struggle.

The Reform Act of 1832 had seen the enfranchisement of middle-class men, or one-fifth of the population. In spite of attempts by several groups in the second half of the nineteenth century, an equivalent recognition of the rights of women was resisted by successive governments, even when further Acts in 1867 and 1884 increased representation to the majority of men. Among the most famous campaigners were Millicent Fawcett, who was president of the National Union of Women's Suffrage Societies (NUWSS) from 1897, and Emmeline Pankhurst, who founded the Women's Social and Political Union (WSPU) in 1903. A third group, the Women's Freedom League (WFL), emerged when the NUWSS split in 1907.

The situation for women remained unchanged after years of struggle and attempts to lobby members of political parties were always diverted, but the campaign escalated until many forms of direct action were taken. The WSPU was the militant group. In 1905, at an election meeting at the Manchester Free Trade Hall, Christabel Pankhurst and Annie Kenney disrupted events by heckling. The *Daily Mail* invented the term "suffragette" as a diminutive of the suffragist, and even though the name was initially disparaging, it stuck and was adopted to describe those who believed in "deeds not words".

No single designer represents the full variety of strategies among the Suffragette artists. Instead designs reflect a complex set of circumstances and their work ranges from Pre-Raphaelite depictions of women, to representations similar to contemporary advertising or children's illustrations, and imitations of popular prints

from chap books. In response anti-suffrage campaigns used similar graphic strategies to provoke ridicule. Middle-class women had gained access to arts and crafts schools in the last years of the nineteenth century on an unprecedented scale. Therefore there were many skilled and talented women who could join artists' groups.

The Artists' Suffrage League, a suffrage society for professional women, was formed to assist the NUWSS, and gave prizes for posters for the cause. Visual metaphor was abundant in both pro- and anti-Suffrage campaigns. The Suffrage Atelier, All Arts and Crafts Society working for the Enfranchisement of Women", moved from the fine arts to the graphic arts in support of the Women's Freedom League. A guiding principle was the cheapness and appropriateness of the means of reproduction. The WSPU, by contrast, had only a few individual artists associated with its cause, and it preferred direct action and public spectacle.

It was not until 6 February 1918 that the Representation of the People Act became law. All men over the age of 21 received the vote, as well as all women over 30 who were "householders, the wives of householders, university graduates and occupiers of property worth £5 per year". In 1928 women gained the vote on the same basis as men.

Typical of the Suffrage Atelier is the use of a popular graphic form to draw attention to inequality between the sexes. The cartoon format, familiar from magazines, is used to explain differences in inheritance laws for men and women.

HOW THE LAW "PROTECTS THE WIDOWER"

WIDOWER: "My wife has left no will"
LAW: "Then all her property is yours, had you died, she would only have got a third of your property."

Poster by Suffrage Atelier, 1909

The design of this poster allowed it to be adapted to announce the various events of the Artists' Suffrage League. The depiction of the figure draws on the medievalized female beauty associated with the Arts and Crafts movement.

An Artists' Suffrage League postcard depicts a scene adapted from the Mad Hatter's Tea Party, part of Lewis Carroll's book *Alice's Adventures in Wonderland*. As Alice found herself confounded by irrationality, so this message alludes to the paradox confronted by women who were active in the feminist struggle to be given the vote.

- ↪ 1882–1940
- ↪ British sculptor, letter-cutter, typeface designer and illustrator
- ↪ Studied lettering at Central School of Arts and Crafts, London
- ↪ Instilled with Arts and Crafts principles
- ↪ Designed influential Gill Sans typeface
- ↪ Ran private press

Eric Gill was a sculptor, letter-cutter, typeface designer and illustrator, whose most important contribution to graphic design was the typeface Gill Sans, which changed the face of British typography in the mid-twentieth century.

Gill studied lettering at the Central School of Arts and Crafts in London, which, under the directorship of the architect W.R. Lethaby, was an important source of Arts and Crafts ideas. Gill was taught by Edward Johnston, who was responsible for the revival of the art of formal lettering in England. While Johnston emphasized penmanship, Gill applied these ideas to letterforms in stone and established a career as a stone- and letter-cutter.

Gill's life breaks down into periods when he was a member of established artistic and religious communities – he converted to Catholicism in mid-life. These settings provided an important environment for his understanding of the unity of art, spirituality and life. He was at Ditchling, Sussex, from 1907 to 1924, as a member of the Craft Guild of St Joseph and St Dominic; then, from 1924 to 1928, at Capel-y-ffin, in the Black Mountains of south Wales, where a group of artists and craftsmen joined him; and from 1928 at Pigotts, a farmhouse near High Wycombe, Buckinghamshire, where he set up a press with René Hague.

In 1925 Gill was asked by Stanley Morison, typographic adviser to the Monotype Corporation, to design a new typeface. The result was Perpetua, a fine classical alphabet, aspiring to the tradition of Caslon and Baskerville, and its italic variant, Felicity (1925–30). Gill started work in 1927 on a second typeface for Monotype, an adaptation of Johnston's Railway type. Based on the Roman alphabet, it was derived from exact mathematical drawings produced by Gill, although Monotype's mechanical advisers made important modifications, for instance to the ascenders and descenders. More than 20 versions in the Gill Sans series were developed. Like many other sans-serif typefaces, Gill Sans did not work well for text, but it was very effective for forms and timetables and was made famous by the distinctive book covers of the publisher Penguin. Gill's ideas on typography and the graphic arts became known through *An Essay on Typography* (1931) and his *Autobiography* (1940).

Gill had several associations with members of the private-press movement. At Ditchling he collaborated with Hilary Pepler at the St Dominic Press, and later he worked with Robert Gibbings of the Golden Cockerel Press, most notably on *The Four Gospels* of 1931. A celebrated example of the combination of pictorial image, hand-drawn lettering and typography, this was exceptional in his output. Typically Gill's figures have elongated faces and simplified facial character, and his treatment of drapery stresses the linear movement of the designs. The integration of decorated capitals, illustrations and his Golden Cockerel type resulted in his distinctive conservative modernity.

30

Design for book *The Four Gospels*, 1931

The Four Gospels contained 64 illustrations and initial letters from wood engravings by Gill. It was printed by the Golden Cockerel Press in an edition of 500 in 1931.

HAGUE & GILL

8-pt. Light
Of pulling — The puller lays on sheets, lays down the frisket and tympans, runs in and out the carriage, takes up the tympans and frisket, takes off the sheet, and lays it on the heap. All these operations are in general mingled and lost in the name of pulling; and as in pulling, so in beating; for though the beater brayers out the ink, distributes it on

8-pt. Medium
the balls, peruses the heap, &c. yet these operations are lost in the general name of beating. To take a sheet off the heap, he places his body almost straight before the near side of the tympan: but he nimbly twists the upper part of his body a little backwards towards the heap, the better to see that he takes but one sheet

8-pt. Bold
off, which he loosens from the rest of the heap by drawing the back of the nail of his right thumb nimbly over the bottom part of the heap, (but in the reiteration care should be taken to draw the thumb on the margin, or between the gutters, that the sheet may not smear or set off), and receiv-

12-pt. Roman
ing the near end of the sheet with his left hand fingers and thumb, catches it with his right hand about two inches within the further edge of the

14-pt. Roman
sheet, near the upper corner, and about the length of his thumb below the near edge of the sheet, & brings it nimbly to the tympan

18-pt. Roman
and at the same time twists his body again before the tympan, only moving his right foot a little

GILL SANS

12-pt. Italic
from its first station forwards under the coffin plank; and as the sheet is coming to the tympan, (supposing it to be white paper) he nimbly disposes

14-pt. Italic
the fingers of his right hand under the further edge of the sheet near the upper corner: and having the sheet thus in both his hands, lays

18-pt. Italic
the further side and two extreme corners of the sheet down even upon the further side and extreme

24-pt. Italic
further corners of the tympan sheet; but he is careful

24-pt. Roman
that the upper corner of the sheet be first laid even

24-pt. Titling
UPON THE CORNER OF THE TYM

30-pt. Titling
J. JOHNSON'S TYPOGRA PHIA Or Printer's Instructor 1824

36-pt. Titling
PRINTING

HIGH WYCOMBE

A sample sheet of Gill Sans Serif, 1928, showing the changes in the design from 8-point light to 36-point titling. Gill Sans became the most popular sans-serif typeface in Britain between the wars. It was used on timetables, advertisements and, most evocatively, by Penguin Books for the cover designs of its series of paperbacks.

31

This wood engraving is typical of the precision of line in Gill's informal work. Gill moved to Pigotts, near High Wycombe, in 1928 and produced this map to guide visitors. One of the buildings housed the press that Gill established with René Hague. Other buildings included a workshop, where he did sculpture and inscription lettering, and his studio, where he drew and made wood engravings.

WIENER WERKSTATTE

With the approach of the twentieth century, Vienna became the site of a vibrant reaction against the established artistic order. In 1897 the young painter Gustav Klimt, convinced that the time was ripe for a new style, led a group of artists, known as the Vienna Secession, who broke away from the city's Künstlerhaus, a gallery firmly associated with academic and historicist traditions of art.

The group included the architects Josef Hoffmann and Joseph Maria Olbrich and the artist-designers Koloman Moser, Michael Powolny, Alfred Roller and Carl Otto Czeschka. In seeking a consciously new style that was in tune with the avant-garde of other major European cities of the time, the Secessionists were part of an international quest for an appropriate design for the new century. Generally rejecting the overabundance of floral ornament in the contemporary French Art Nouveau, they turned instead to a controlled sense of line and decoration, rich materials and strong references to classical forms and symbolism. This style was epitomized by the Secession exhibition building of 1897–8, designed by Olbrich.

A forum for Secessionist ideas was the journal *Ver Sacrum* (Sacred Spring), which published essays, poems and exhibition commentaries from 1898 until 1903. This journal was a very conscious form of graphic expression. It revealed a highly aestheticized approach to page layout, with the use of metallic and coloured inks, wide borders, and a clear sense of the open page, decorated initials and chapter headings, as well as a variety of papers, including transparent insertions with discreet watermarks and other novel decorative devices.

In 1903 the Wiener Werkstätte (Vienna Workshops) opened as an extension of the Secession. These were led by Josef Hoffmann and Koloman Moser, with the financial assistance of the banker Fritz Wärndorfer, and their declared aim was, in Hoffmann's words, the "pursuit of art and quality in all the crafts". The Werkstätte set out to produce limited lines of furniture, metalwork, textiles, glass and ceramics. Inspiration came in part from the Arts and Crafts movement of William Morris and others, although in Vienna there was a greater sense of luxury than among their British counterparts. In the field of graphic design, the Werkstätte provided companies and individuals with posters and advertisements, logotypes, postcards and bookbinding, winning acclaim in each of these areas.

Secessionist posters advertising the group's work are among the most striking graphic designs of the first decade of the century. Exhibitions were publicized by a highly stylized, decorative design, usually in exaggerated vertical format and showing a female figure with suggestions of richly printed textiles. The lettering and motifs were designed as a unity. In many cases the block-style lettering was partly inspired by that of Charles Rennie Mackintosh (see pp36–7) and the Glasgow Four, who were known through their success at Turin's international exhibition of 1902 and were subsequently commissioned by Wärndorfer to design an interior in Vienna.

However, the distinctive lettering movement in Vienna was mainly attributable to one individual, Rudolf von Larisch, who taught at the city's School of Applied Arts. Many Secessionists were taught by him and others knew his work and his books *Über Zierschriften im Dienste der Kunst* (Ideas on Lettering in Decorative Types in the Service of Art) of 1899 and *Unterricht in Ornamentaler*

Postcard by Oskar Kokoschka, *The Rider*, 1907–8

Several members of the group designed prestigious posters in a distinctive vertical format for the important exhibitions of the Vienna Secession. Here Moser has made the motif of the Art Nouveau woman almost abstract. The design bears comparison with the work of Charles Rennie Mackintosh of the same time.

Poster by Koloman Moser for the Thirteenth Vienna Secession, 1902

Graphic items were available in the Wiener Werkstätte shops, in particular postcard series. Highly decorative designs with full colour and distinctive black outlines, like this example (opposite) by the Austrian-born artist Oskar Kokoschka, often allude to fairy tales.

Cover by Koloman Moser for magazine *Ver Sacrum*, vol. 2, no. 4, 1899

Koloman Moser, a leading figure in the establishment of the Werkstätte, studied painting and then design. *Ver Sacrum* (Sacred Spring) was the cultural magazine that promoted the Vienna Secession and the applied arts. A finely produced publication illustrated by members of the group, it specialized in poetry and aesthetic philosophy as well as promoting the new aesthetic way of life.

Schrift (Instruction in Ornamental Lettering) of 1907. At first he had criticized the Secessionists' posters as illegible. He encouraged them to make their lettering more controlled but without losing its characteristic energy. Among the exercises Larisch taught them was filling a square with the letterform, to help develop a fine sense of figure and ground. The square was a consistent motif in the Secession style, and it appears in, for example, Secessionist stationery and the monogram "WW" of the Wiener Werkstätte. This distinctly linear approach to form was a feature in the decoration of objects across various media, including tableware, textiles and architecture.

In addition to the obviously "designed" graphic works of the Werkstätte, another distinctive form of graphic output was their highly decorative illustrations. Series of woodcut and lithographic prints were published as postcards or book illustrations in richly coloured, dense designs, often of a medievalizing character. Among the most notable of the Werkstätte designers of lithographic prints was Carl Otto Czeschka. The illustrative work produced in Vienna had much in common with the illustrations and prints of artists associated with the Munich Jugendstil. Through these projects, other new artists were introduced to the Viennese group, such as the young early Expressionists Oskar Kokoschka and Egon Schiele, who both went on to become famous painters.

The distinctive graphic designs of the Wiener Werkstätte belong to the years before 1914, and so are part of their first phase. Later, at the height of their success, the Werkstätte were selling designs in many media through shops in Paris and New York, as well as in Vienna. Throughout the 1920s the workshops continued to produce goods in a variety of styles, but, faced with mounting financial difficulties, they closed in 1932.

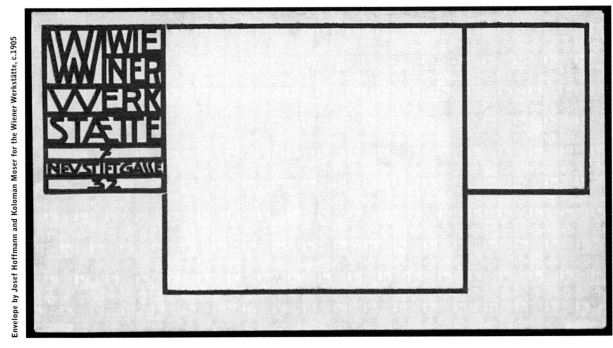

Hoffmann and Moser designed the distinctive identity of the Wiener Werkstätte, which was applied to all items of stationery. It was based on a repeated "W" and the lettering was broad, angular and highly stylized.

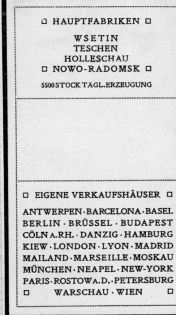

The Kohns were leading manufacturers of modern furniture. Wiener Werkstätte designers took on commissions for fabric and furniture designs for the company as well as designing its publicity material.

Perspective drawing for dining room of House for an Art Lover, 1901

Alexander Koch of Darmstadt published this perspective of a dining room in the Haus eines Kunstfreundes (Art-Lover's House) in 1901. Mackintosh's scheme for the house won first prize in a competition organized by Koch in the magazine *Innen-Dekoration*. The house was built retrospectively in the 1990s in Bellahouston Park, Glasgow. The drawing shows a version of Mackintosh's famous high-back chairs and the recurrent thistle motif.

36

→ 1868–1928
→ Developed individual version of Art Nouveau
→ Stylistic coherence across designs in diverse media
→ Distinctive posters
→ Later career as painter

The Scottish architect and designer Charles Rennie Mackintosh is best known for his furniture and architectural designs. But he also produced graphic art in the form of posters and inscriptions, as well as highly stylized lettering on his architectural drawings. His graphic work played a very important role in broadening recognition of the so-called Glasgow style.

As a young man Mackintosh was apprenticed as a draughtsman to the architect John Hutchison and then to the larger Glasgow practice of Honeyman & Keppie, where he met Herbert MacNair. The pair attended evening classes at the Glasgow School of Art, where the principal, Francis Newbery, introduced them to the sisters Frances and Margaret Macdonald. MacNair and Frances

married in 1899, Mackintosh and Margaret a year later. The two couples established a studio, taking on decorative designs for clocks, embroidery, book illustration, furniture, light fittings and jewellery, and became known as the Glasgow Four.

An important inspiration for the group was *The Studio*, a magazine launched in 1893 to promote new art. In particular they took from the figurative styles of Aubrey Beardsley and Jan Toorop, adapting their attenuated, willowy women with motifs of flowers, often thistles, and gentle greens, greys, pinks and purples.

The style was at its height between 1896 and 1911, a period when Mackintosh was also especially successful as an architect. He won the competition to design a new building for Glasgow School of Art. He also produced designs for houses, a church and a school, as well as

Mackintosh's lettering stressed vertical and square formats, and he made use of unusually high strokes on E, F, R and H, as in this hand-lettered motto of 1901 (above). The compositional feel was close to that of the Vienna Secessionists Josef Hoffmann and Koloman Moser.

Typified by Mackintosh, the Glasgow style used floral motifs and elongated female forms in common with Art Nouveau in other centres. The angularity and stylized geometry of designs like this poster were distinctive (left).

several interior schemes for Miss Cranston's tea rooms in Glasgow, before leaving Scotland and establishing himself as an architect in London. His first contact with London had been during an unsuccessful contribution to the Arts and Crafts exhibition in 1896, when the Glasgow Four received a hostile reception. However, their work was more favourably reviewed elsewhere in Europe.

Mackintosh's graphic work was not as prolific as his other design work, yet it was an important aspect of the Glasgow style, particularly his stylized lettering. His graphic designs combined familiar Art Nouveau motifs, but he also gave them a tautness of line and geometrical emphasis that added to their distinctiveness.

A special issue of the art magazine *Ver Sacrum* was devoted to Glasgow, and Fritz Wärndorfer, the banker sponsor of the Wiener Werkstätte (see pp32–5),

commissioned a music-room interior from Mackintosh. The architect also won a competition, part of Alexander Koch's *Zeitschrift für Innen-Dekoration* in 1901, for the design of the "House of an Art-Lover".

Other contemporary designers applied the Glasgow style more prolifically in areas of book design, illustration and typography. They included Jessie M. King and, most significantly, Talwin Morris, whose extensive work as art director to the major Glasgow publisher Blackie & Son from 1893 was shown alongside that of the Glasgow Four in contemporary European design journals. In many ways the real fulfilment of Mackintosh's lettering came at the end of the century, when Erik Spiekermann and MetaDesign (see pp220–1) created the typeface Glasgow, which was used for the UK's City of Architecture and Design for 1999.

THE NEW DESIGN AND
ARTISTIC EXPERIMENT

After World War I industrial production was severely disrupted and the commercial application of design could not resume at its normal rate. For many designers the conflict had created a tabula rasa on which the world could be built anew. As a result the interwar years witnessed a full integration of experimental artistic ideas within graphic design, and art and design schools became a laboratory for testing the fundamentals of design language.

Before 1914 Italian Futurism had celebrated the coming of war through the apocalyptic vision of machinery and factories colliding in paintings and poems. This dissonance continued in the work of the Dadaists in Zurich, Berlin, Paris, Barcelona and New York. Their manifestos disrupted the conventional syntax of the printed page in what were some of the most experimental typographical arrangements of the time. Futurists and Dadaists explored the principle of simultaneity. In recognition that the eye can take in immediate messages across a page, texts were arranged apparently arbitrarily. One of the Futurist inspirations came from seeing advertising hoardings from a passing train: the equivalent of typography in motion. Raiding the compositor's tray, artists, designers and poets experimented with letterforms and the arrangement of words, emphasizing or distorting meaning.

The end of World War I marked a change in sensibility in art and design. Encouraged by the successful political revolution in Russia of 1917 and several attempted revolutions elsewhere in Europe, many young artists and designers pledged allegiance to the working classes. The hardship of returning soldiers, which was exacerbated by the widespread destruction of the built environment during the war, led to an urgent need for housing. Responding to the crisis, architects embarked on social projects to provide mass housing and functionalist furniture.

International visual communication was also identified as a priority. Designers held that this could encourage international understanding and hoped that abstract geometry, simplified sans-serif typefaces and photography or photomontage could combine as a universal visual language that would transcend differences of culture and class. They came together in groups that ignored national boundaries, as in the 1922 Constructivist Congress in Düsseldorf, to which designers from Romania, Scandinavia, Switzerland, the Netherlands, Germany and the Soviet Union contributed. Such meetings gave rise to small periodicals and reviews, further promoting experimental design ideas.

The most concentrated versions of modernist graphic design were based around the Dutch journal *De Stijl*, and the art and design schools the Bauhaus in Germany and the VKhUTEMAS (Higher State Artistic and Technical Workshops) in Moscow.

This poster for the second part of the film *Die Frau ohne Namen* (The Woman Without a Name) shows all the elements of the "new design" as developed in the 1920s by designers interested in defining a modernist graphic language. Tschichold depicts elements from the narrative, "projected" from a single vanishing point. His choice of typeface, primary red ink and photomontage all mark the design style as distinctively new.

Although the rhetoric of the new graphic design invoked the machine, individual designs were not always a mechanized product. McKnight Kauffer and Cassandre, for example, used the manual airbrush to suggest machine-like precision in their posters.

By far the most popular variant of modern graphic design was Art Deco, a style retrospectively named after the Exposition Internationale des Arts Décoratifs et Industriels Modernes, held in Paris in 1925. Less extreme than the new typography, Art Deco was associated with film, fashion and luxury goods.

Also in France, the psychological meaning of visual language was investigated by the Surrealists after 1924. The juxtaposition of unexpected elements was initially a disruptive strategy intended to expose latent sexuality and psychological unease. However, it could equally be used by graphic designers to intrigue the customer looking at an advertisement and cause surprise at the unexpected, as part of a developing psychology of retailing. Modern ideas of unexpected juxtaposition were especially applicable to fashion photography, and in this spirit Alexey Brodovitch introduced Surrealist photography to the United States through his magazine art direction.

The path of modernism was disrupted and displaced by the advent of totalitarianism in Europe. In 1933, on the coming to power of the National Socialists in Germany, graphic design migrated to Switzerland, or Italy, where Mussolini continued to approve of Futurism. Modernism then moved further afield, most characteristically via Paris and London to the United States. Many of the designers discussed in this chapter took this path, among them Moholy-Nagy, Cassandre, Sutnar, Teige, Matter, Brodovitch, Bayer and Zapf. In New York they were welcomed by the Museum of Modern Art, whose exhibition policy promoted European modernism. Other designers were taken up by sympathetic art directors and quickly appeared as cover artists for high-profile magazines such as *Vogue*, *Harper's Bazaar* and *Fortune*. However, Moholy-Nagy's New Bauhaus school in Chicago was short-lived, closing after a year.

The transfer of the ideas of modernism to the pragmatic, commercial climate of America did not lead to a seamless adoption of all of its principles. The ideological commitment to a new society expressed in Europe during the 1920s had informed many of the aesthetic values of early modernism. However, removed from its original context, the style at times became a set of borrowed mannerisms. Its central characteristics – a tendency towards simplification; use of signs and symbols as visual shorthand; use of a grid; a bright, associative visual language with parallels in modern art – would be transformed in the United States into a visual language for corporations, just as much as for individual design experiment.

ITALIAN FUTURISM

The Futurist movement was announced to the world in a founding manifesto, published in the French newspaper *Le Figaro* on 20 February 1909. Eleven points of action summoned young artists to reject the museum-minded approach to the culture of the past and to embrace modern technology, speed, the machine and war: "a roaring car that seems to ride on grapeshot is more beautiful than the Victory of Samothrace".

The leader of the movement was the Italian writer and poet Filippo Tommaso Marinetti. Visual artists associated with Futurism included Umberto Boccioni, Carlo Carrà, Giacomo Balla and Gino Severini. In painting, for which the movement is best known, the Futurists concentrated on urban subjects, which they depicted through fragmented and facetted forms reminiscent of Cubism. What most distinguished such works was the concern to depict speed and simultaneity through lines of force, repeated motifs and the inclusion of typographical elements, all emblems of a hectic world of advertising, cafés and railway stations.

Marinetti's manifestos were planned as part of a provocative cultural programme. He organized Futurist events in major European cities from 1910 to 1914, when poetry and music recitals accompanied exhibitions of the visual arts. As he made clear in the "Destruction of Syntax" manifesto of 1913, the written and printed word were central to Futurism: "I initiate a typographical revolution aimed at the bestial, nauseating idea of the book of passéist and D'Annunzian verse, on seventeenth-century handmade paper bordered with helmets, Minervas, Apollos, elaborate red initials, vegetables, mythological missal ribbons, epigraphs, and roman numerals. The book must be the Futurist expression of our Futurist thought. Not only that. My revolution is aimed at the so-called typographical harmony of the page, which is contrary to the flux and reflux, the leaps and bursts of style that run through the page."

Later in the same manifesto Marinetti proclaimed: "On the same page, therefore, we will use three or four colours of ink, or even twenty different typefaces if necessary. For example: italics for a series of similar swift sensations, boldface for the violent onomatopoeias, and so on. With this typographical revolution and this multi-coloured variety in the letters I mean to redouble the expressive force of words."

This was the most radical acknowledgement of the possibilities of typographical experiment to alter the understanding of language that had yet been made in the new century. It opened the way for Marinetti and other Futurists metaphorically to raid the compositor's tray for greater impact in a series of small publications. Marinetti's first book, *Zang Tumb Tumb*, published in 1914, was an attempt to convey the Battle of Tripoli in typographic form. He was particularly harsh towards parallel experiments by the French poet Mallarmé, who aimed to break down the conventional syntax of poetic language, dismissing his work as a "precious aesthetic" and "static".

The commercial adoption of Futurism occurred largely in the 1920s, led by Fortunato Depero, who created covers for *Vanity Fair* magazine and advertising design for Campari, as well as his own remarkable typographical experiment, the book *Depero Futurista* (1927).

In this "explosive" novel, published in Milan in 1919, Marinetti, the leader of the Futurists, divided his personality during World War I into eight different souls, which are described in eight chapters.

Cover by Marinetti for his book *8 Anime in una Bomba*, 1919

This is a later version of Marinetti's 1919 text *Words in Freedom*, bound in tin plate to celebrate his enthusiasm for technology. The designer, D'Albisola, was more systematic in his arrangement of text than Marinetti, but nevertheless conveyed an excitement at "typographic architecture" with words overlayed and set in different directions.

Depero joined the Futurists in Rome in 1914. This remarkable book, with a bolted cover, acted as a self-portrayal, showing examples of Depero's designs. Depero employed the typographic dynamism of Futurism in advertisements, posters and magazine covers as well as in artistic manifestos.

WORLD WAR I POSTERS

In the history of graphic design, posters of World War I are usually acknowledged for introducing a new, heightened level of psychological persuasion. The colour lithographic poster had been perfected in the years up to 1914, and before cinema or radio could supersede them, posters were the major form of mass visual propaganda. War posters drew from the visual traditions of their respective countries and consequently indicate strong national styles. But, because they needed to address shared concerns of public morale and war effort, many also indicate common techniques of visual persuasion.

Britain's War Office established the Parliamentary Recruiting Committee (PRC) in August 1914, only weeks after the outbreak of war. The Committee organized the publication of a vast number of posters until conscription was introduced in January 1916 in response to mounting difficulty in encouraging young men to enlist. The output of war posters exceeded the numbers in the commercial advertising campaigns of peacetime. In addition to enlistment posters, the other major form was posters intended to encourage people to contribute to the war effort by buying war bonds.

Although World War I was the first mechanized, technological war, witnessing the introduction of aeroplanes, artillery, tanks and Zeppelins, the emphasis of many posters tended to be on the resulting human situation. Great play was made of the psychological relationships within soldiers' families, or their relationship with future leaders. Among the most famous was "Daddy, What Did YOU do in the Great War?" a poster by Savile Lumley of around 1915 that depicted the domestic scene of a father being questioned by his daughter in the future. It was unquestioningly accepted that all male viewers of the poster would rise to its challenge, with the unambiguous implication that children expected their fathers to fight. Such a strategy of playing on guilt and stereotypes in the public mind would subsequently become formative for advertisers in the interwar years.

Another poster became the prototype of a series of recruitment posters, Alfred Leete's "Your Country Needs You". This was first used as a *London Opinion* magazine cover. The pointing finger and staring eyes of Lord Horatio Kitchener, Britain's Secretary of State for War, asserted a direct one-to-one message. The image was subsequently adapted as a poster for the PRC with the additional words "God Save the King". In the United States a famous version of the poster "I Want You for the US Army" was designed by James Montgomery Flagg, with a depiction of Uncle Sam derived from a self-portrait.

In contrast to the emphasis on figurative and literal depictions in the posters of the Allies, German and Austro-Hungarian posters tended to have simpler designs, derived from the Secessionist and Jugendstil movements. Their posters concentrated on war loans and war bonds. In this area, posters produced for both sides tended to concentrate either on the women and families left at home or on action in the field.

Animal symbolism has a long tradition in the graphic arts and during World War I it provided a familiar visual language to encapsulate stereotypes such as the German eagle, the Gallic cock and the British lion. These appeared in Allied posters, but, curiously, German posters did not feature animal symbolism to a great extent until after the war, when poster designers presented the extreme political opponents by employing exaggerated animal types.

Forceful animal symbolism is used here to represent the perceived dangers of anarchy to Germany, which, after defeat in the war, experienced extreme political turbulence. Based in Munich, the conservative Engelhaard was a painter, poster designer and illustrator and contributed to the satirical journal *Simplicissimus*.

During the war the respected and prolific British artist Frank Brangwyn produced visual propaganda. Some criticized this poster for its candid depiction of one-to-one armed combat.

45

This image was adapted as a recruiting poster carrying the same portrait of Lord Kitchener, Britain's Secretary of State for War. It was a prototype of effective wartime propaganda.

Fred Spear produced this poster (opposite) for the Boston Committee of Public Safety after the sinking of the *Lusitania* by a German submarine. The United States entered the war in April 1917 and posters were used to recruit troops, with an estimated 2,500 different designs issued.

Edward McKnight Kauffer, an American designer who lived for much of his professional life in London, made a major contribution to British graphic design in the interwar years. He was a highly gifted artist who applied his understanding of modern styles of painting, particularly those associated with Paris, in a range of striking designs for important clients.

Kauffer studied for a few months at the Art Institute of Chicago before being sponsored to travel to Paris in 1913. He took the name McKnight in tribute to his sponsor, Professor McKnight of Utah University. In Paris, Kauffer drew in the museums and attended the Académie Moderne. He became immersed in the rapid succession of art movements of Post-Impressionism, Cubism and Futurism. On the outbreak of World War I, however, it became necessary for him to leave France, and he settled in London in 1914.

An overriding interest for Kauffer was the poster, and in 1924 he published a book on the subject, *The Art of the Poster*. His first designs were painted landscapes, adapted as posters to advertise the destinations offered by the London and North Eastern Railway. By contrast, a 1919 poster advertising a newspaper, "Soaring to Success! Daily Herald – the Early Bird", was his first distinctively modern design. In this Kauffer integrated a graphic symbol of flying birds with carefully chosen lettering, all placed in a distinctive vertical format. The design reflected his awareness of Japanese prints. Like many artists and designers of his generation, he was inspired by the simplicity of composition and the striking use of silhouette in such work.

An important challenge for Kauffer, with his strong commitment to modern design, was to identify like-minded people who would commission his work. Unlike many parts of continental Europe, Britain showed little enthusiasm for modernism. An important professional relationship for Kauffer began in 1915, when he first worked for Frank Pick, the publicity manager for London Transport, who was a strong advocate of improved links between art and industry. Through Pick, Kauffer's mature style was introduced to a wide public in the form of travel posters, of which he designed 141 for London Transport. Pick pioneered modern approaches to publicizing transportation services, especially the London Underground. As part of his strategy for the design of stations and trains, he asked Kauffer and other designers familiar with modernism to design posters for display on stations. These stressed the attractions of locations served by the Underground, such as department stores, museums or country walks on the outskirts of the city, as well as the convenience and pleasure of this form of travel.

Kauffer also benefited from the patronage of Jack Beddington, advertising manager of the Shell-Mex and BP petroleum company, and this led him

⊖ 1891–1968
⊖ Important modernist graphic designer
⊖ Trained in Paris
⊖ Understood and adapted Cubism and Futurism to design of posters
⊖ Majority of work in London, including acclaimed transport posters for London Transport and Shell-Mex

46

Poster for London Transport, "Winter Sales Are Best Reached By Underground", 1922

Kauffer had trained in Paris just before designing this poster for London Transport. His familiarity with Cubism shows in the treatment of the drapery and background scene.

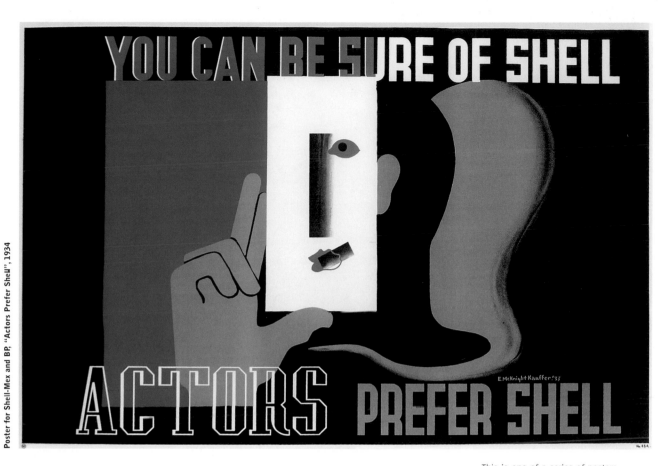

This is one of a series of posters, commissioned by the Shell-Mex and BP petroleum company from designers including Kauffer, which bore the slogan "You Can Be Sure of Shell". While many of the designs were modern, the format reinforced the separation of word and image and therefore ran counter to the hopes of many graphic designers.

47

Kauffer was well aware of developments in the new typography in mainland Europe. Influenced by these, this design uses visual shorthand and direct juxtaposition to convey its message.

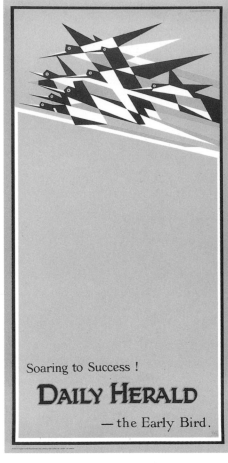

For his first modern poster, for the *Daily Herald* newspaper, Kauffer used an unusual format and a strikingly plain background. The motif was inspired by Japanese prints.

Poster, "Soaring to Success! Daily Herald – the Early Bird", 1919

In the interwar years the Shell-Mex and BP petroleum company commissioned many designers. Kauffer, in particular, was sponsored by the publicity manager, Jack Beddington, and produced posters in several styles.

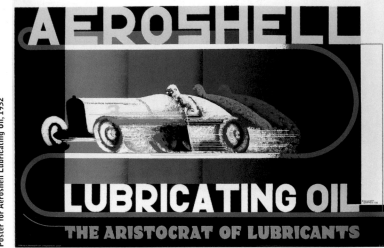

Poster for Aeroshell Lubricating Oil, 1932

48

to design another series of high-profile posters in the 1930s. In this campaign Beddington responded to criticism of advertisers for despoiling the countryside by introducing posters for use on the sides of delivery lorries.

While always concerned to produce modern designs in a variety of styles, Kauffer also felt a deep empathy with England. He expressed this in his romantic interpretations of landscape, which drew on a more traditional sensibility. Kauffer knew many figures from literary circles and designed book jackets for Gerald Meynell of the Westminster Press, Francis Meynell of the Nonesuch Press, and the publisher Faber. This work allowed him to pursue a more private approach to imagery.

In the late 1920s and the 1930s Kauffer continued to produce posters and book covers but also took on designs which offered new opportunities to work three-dimensionally, devising interior designs, theatre sets and shop windows. He also designed rugs for the Royal Wilton

carpet factory with his future wife, Marion Dorn. His association with modern architects led to commissions for photo-murals, in which his fluency with Constructivism and Surrealism was clear. In 1930 he became art director at Lund Humphries, a London publisher firmly committed to the promotion of modernism. He also assisted with a series of design exhibitions, several devoted to newly arrived émigré graphic designers from Europe, among them Jan Tschichold (see pp68–9) and Hans Schleger.

Kauffer's work was shown in an exhibition at the Museum of Modern Art, New York, in 1937, a sign of his international standing. In 1940, soon after the start of World War II, he returned to the United States, where he and Marion Dorn established themselves in New York. He continued to design posters, working for the Museum of Modern Art, New York; the Greek War Relief Association; American Airways, and the New York Subway Advertising Co., as well as for prominent American publishers.

This poster was part of a campaign to encourage passengers to use London Transport to enjoy cultural events. In tune with the increasing interest in neoclassicism among graphic designers and fashion photographers, Kauffer incorporated a Surrealist juxtaposition of a sculptural head and an artist's palette.

Poster for London Transport, "Treat Yourself to Better Play – Music", 1935

Page from specimen book for Peignot typeface, 1937

Peignot was the most popular of the three typefaces Cassandre designed. For this all-purpose typeface he retained the original form in lower and upper cases of many of the letters, inspired by the characters in Carolingian manuscripts.

Poster for Florent pastilles, 1925

Cassandre incorporated Florent's packaging design as a vital element of this early poster. The change in colour of the Florent lettering, from black to white as it crosses the background, was a device he took from Cubist paintings.

50

➔ 1901–68
➔ Epitome of French modern poster designer
➔ Modernist designs for mainstream clients
➔ Designed three typefaces for type foundry and publisher Deberny Peignot of Paris

The career of Adolphe Jean-Marie Mouron, better known as A.M. Cassandre, coincided with the transition, in the 1920s and 1930s, of French commercial art from a strong lithographic poster tradition to a fuller range of graphic design. Of the work of a trio of internationally recognized Parisian poster designers, the others being Paul Colin and Jean Carlu, Cassandre's is the most celebrated. His posters carried familiar French and international brand names and, in many cases, established their visual identity and long-standing resonance.

Born in the Ukraine, Mouron trained as a painter at the École des Beaux Arts and the Académie Julian in Paris immediately after World War I. On designing his first poster he adopted the pseudonym "Cassandre" –

possibly to distinguish his identity as a graphic artist from his other long-term commitment as a painter. Among the first posters Cassandre designed were those for the Parisian furniture store Au Bucheron. When they appeared on the city's streets in 1923, these striking designs were some of the earliest to interpret the ideas of modern painting and to emphasize the typographic arrangement of words as a key element in the design.

Cassandre's career as a graphic designer took off at a time when the Paris art world was still investigating the compositional discoveries of Cubism, Futurism and Purism, and he applied many of the ideas of Picasso, Braque and Léger to his new medium. In all these artistic movements, modern painters had depicted still lifes, portraits or street scenes through the breaking up of conventional perspective. What were called "facetted" forms were used to merge objects in space. The idea of

This famous poster for the popular alcoholic drink Dubonnet appeared in several versions, either as a single image or a series of three. It depends on the spectator understanding the caption, which suggests the gradual change in the man's reaction as he drinks: from Dubo (short for "dubious") to Dubon ("of some good") to Dubonnet.

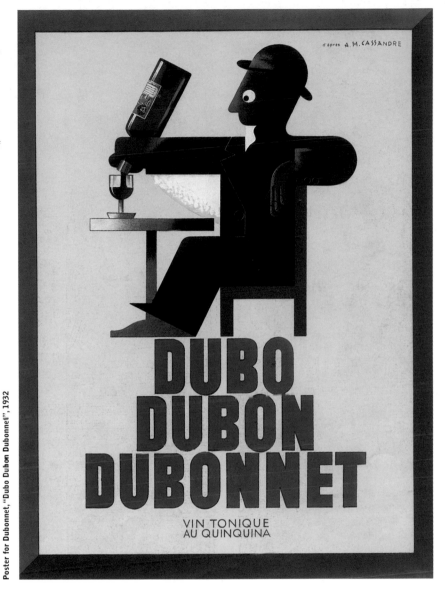

Poster for Dubonnet, "Dubo Dubon Dubonnet", 1932

51

simultaneity, which suggested that the eye can register diverse elements on a canvas at one time, was an important influence on this generation of poster designers. Cassandre's work was also in tune with the simplification of form that characterized much of the design known as *moderne* in the years leading up to the influential Exposition Internationale des Arts Décoratifs et Industriels Modernes held in Paris in 1925.

Cassandre's compositions were derived from a firm geometrical base, more familiar to architecture than graphic design. The Florent poster shown here, for example, is based on a 2:3 rectangle and the diagonal line draws attention to this proportion. The composition is softened and enhanced by a series of repeated motifs, the curves of the tin box and the product's name.

Some of Cassandre's most famous posters – he designed a total of more than 200 – were produced for international railway and shipping lines, including Nord Express, Étoile du Nord (both 1927), Wagons Lits Cook, (1933) and Normandie (1935). These designs show his extreme virtuosity in using elegant symbols as a form of visual shorthand. These he depicted in illusionistic spaces with clever use of shadow, intriguing silhouettes or reversed forms.

Like many of his contemporaries, including the architect Le Corbusier and the painters Léger and Ozenfant, Cassandre stressed the beauty of machines. Echoing Le Corbusier's functionalist declaration that "the house is a machine for living in", Cassandre wrote in 1929 of the poster as the "machine à annoncer" (a machine for announcing). By the 1930s, together with the precise depiction of industrial forms, which he achieved by using an airbrush, Cassandre introduced neoclassical heads or figures into his designs – a

Poster design for magazine *Arts et Métiers Graphiques*, 1928

Poster designers, in collaboration with their printers, often provided posters without lettering. These designs could be offered to potential clients for adaptation to meet their own requirements. The magazine *Arts et Métiers Graphiques* was published by the Parisian type foundry Deberny Peignot, which also developed type designs by Cassandre.

Poster for Grande Quinzaine Internationale de Lawn-Tennis, 1932

Many posters in Cassandre's mature style derive their effectiveness from the use of the airbrush. In this example, advertising the Grand International Lawn Tennis Fortnight staged in Paris in 1932, the tennis ball and net are created by masking the surface and defined by the transition from dark to light.

52

reference to Surrealism and its popularity among contemporary fashion photographers.

In 1927 Cassandre founded an advertising agency, Alliance Graphique in Paris, with Charles Loupot and Maurice Moyrand. At the peak of his activity he was also commissioned by Charles Peignot, of the prestigious type foundry and publisher Deberny Peignot in Paris, to design typefaces. The results, Bifur (1929), Acier Noir (1937) and Peignot (1937), indicate how modern French designers were prepared to stress elegance over functionalism – by contrast with, for example, the Bauhaus (see pp60–3). Cassandre's typefaces are distinctive for their stress on negative and positive space. One of the important sources for their style was the Carolingian lower-case letterforms developed during the tenth century.

An acknowledgement of Cassandre's international significance came in 1936, when the Museum of Modern Art, New York, installed a solo exhibition, making him one of the first graphic designers to be honoured in this way. Following this, he spent the winters of 1937 and 1938 in New York, where he designed covers for the magazines *Fortune* and *Harper's Bazaar*, as well as monthly press advertisements for the Container Corporation of America and advertisements for the agencies Young and Rubicam and N.W. Ayer & Co.

At what might have been the apex of his career, Cassandre appeared uncomfortable with the division of labour in New York publishing, which was more marked than in Europe. He retreated to France and concentrated on stage design and painting, more at ease with the European model of the autonomous graphic artist.

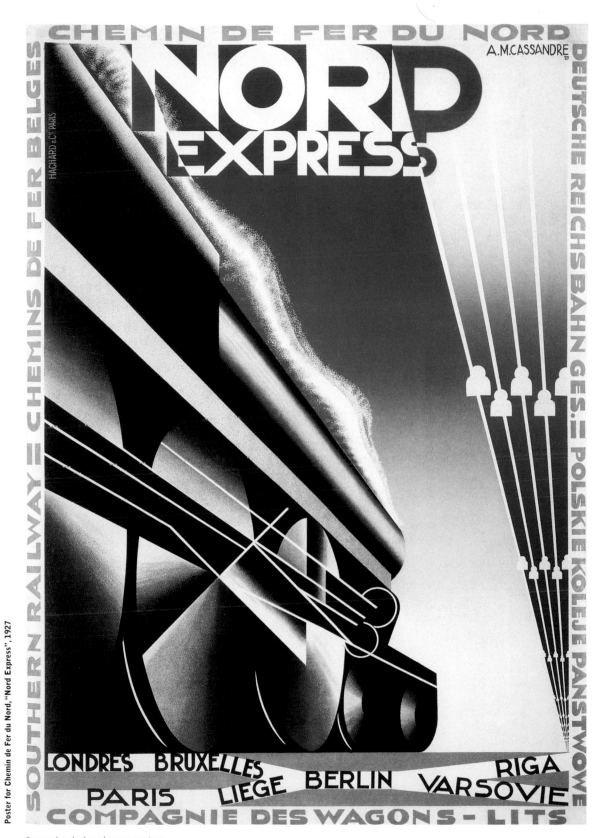

Poster for Chemin de Fer du Nord, "Nord Express", 1927

53

Cassandre designed many posters
advertising travel, notably by luxury train
and ocean liner. This example depends
on the suggestive possibilities of
geometry. Characteristically, it is clearly
signed with the designer's autograph.

DE STIJL

The first poster and manifesto for De Stijl indicated the rectilinear character of the movement's style. The logotype was made up of blocks, and the design suggested an abstract architectural space.

De Stijl was a Dutch avant-garde movement based around the magazine of the same name. Edited by the painter, architect and poet Theo van Doesburg, it ran from 1917 until his death in 1931. The movement had a strong stylistic coherence in its use of primary colours, rectangular forms and asymmetrical composition. The style was most internationally recognized through Piet Mondrian's severe non-figurative paintings of this period.

The roots of De Stijl are often explained as a combination of strong interest in geometry in turn-of-the-century Dutch architectural tradition and an equally dominant cultural and religious heritage of austere, iconoclastic Calvinism.

The movement was initially more oriented towards painting and three-dimensional design. The magazine *De Stijl* was its first typographic experiment. An exercise in the arrangement of block letterforms, the cover suggested an abstract architectural motif. Vilmos Huszar, who designed it, explained that he wanted neither foreground nor background to dominate. At first the typographic style of the interior of the magazine was conventional. It became more adventurous with the experiments of Van Doesburg, who explored visual

typography in the arrangement of poetry. Working under the Dadaist pseudonym of I.K. Bonset, he organized page layouts in which emphasis was given to words through bold type, increased sizes and a loosening of syntax. This was an extension of the "calligrammes" of the French poet Apollinaire. As in Italian Futurism (see pp42–3), typographic experimentation was part of an examination of language. However, unlike at the Bauhaus (see pp60–3), De Stijl designers did not invent their own geometrical type designs, but employed existing sans-serif typefaces.

They maintained contact with avant-gardes elsewhere, especially the Soviet Union and Germany. Van Doesburg's visit to Weimar seemed to have great significance for the new typography of Moholy-Nagy (see pp64–5) and Bayer (see pp66–7), while Soviet design interested De Stijl with its social commitment and range of styles. Of particular importance was the visit of El Lissitzky (see pp56–7).

De Stijl's elementarist principles of primary colour, grids and blocks survived into the late 1920s, but as its graphic designers took on more mainstream commissions these tended to be enlivened by photomontage and looser, associative graphic languages. Examples are Paul Schuitema's work for Berkel weighing machines and Piet Zwart's for the Dutch cable factory NKF and the country's PTT (Postal, Telegraph and Telephone Authority).

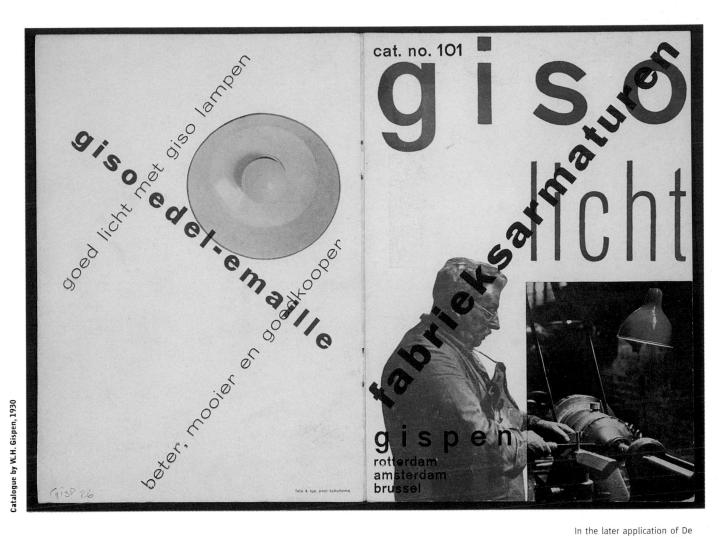

cat. no. 101

giso

licht

giso edel-emaille

goed licht met giso lampen

giso lampen

beter, mooier en goedkooper

foto & typ. paul schuitema

fabrieksarmaturen

gispen
rotterdam
amsterdam
brussel

In the later application of De Stijl ideas to more mainstream commercial and industrial design, new typography and photography were combined. As well as designing the modern light fittings produced by his company, Gispen took on the design of its publicity material.

55

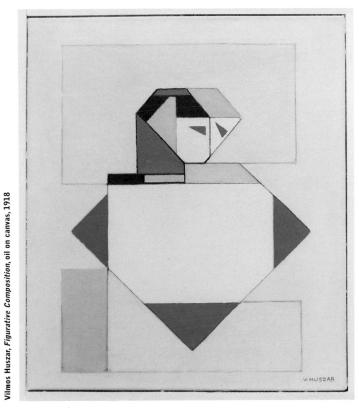

The members of De Stijl were divided into those who used only rectilinear formats, and those, like Vilmos Huszar and Theo van Doesburg, who exploited the potential of the diagonal.

This design for Vladimir
Mayakovsky's volume of poetry
Dlja Golosa (For the Voice) used
the new typography to arrange
each poem and a thumb index
of symbols to identify them.

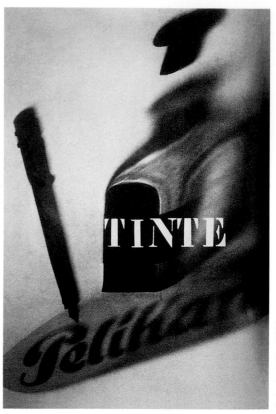

The design of this poster for Pelikan, a
manufacturer of inks based in Hanover,
uses a photogram, an image produced
with photographic materials but
without a camera.

56

➔ 1890–1941
➔ Trained as architectural
engineer in Darmstadt
➔ Leading Soviet
Constructivist designer
➔ Worked as graphic
and exhibition designer
in Germany in 1920s
➔ Pioneered use of
photograms in field of
graphic design

El (Lazar) Lissitzky was one of the most
innovative designers of the early Soviet
avant-garde. His approach was rooted in his
architectural background, and, whether in
graphic design and photography, furniture
and exhibition design or architecture, most
of his designs explored space and abstraction.

Born near Smolensk, Lissitzky studied architectural
engineering in Darmstadt from 1911 and returned to
Russia on the outbreak of the war in 1914. His first
experimental works relate to his Jewish origins and took
the form of secular illustrated scrolls, with a loose,
figurative style of painting. In 1919, on the invitation of
Marc Chagall, he began to teach architecture and graphic
art at the Vitebsk People's Art School. Here he met
Kasimir Malevich, then developing Suprematism: non-

objective, radically abstract paintings of flat colour
intended to have spiritual meaning. Lissitzky responded
with his own abstract paintings, sculptures and room
installations, which he gave the collective title "Proun"
(an acronym for "Project for the Affirmation of the New").

After the Revolution of 1917, Lissitzky, along with
other Constructivist artists and designers, was concerned
to find a new artistic language, developed from Cubism
and Russian Futurism. In a time of high illiteracy,
designers believed that graphic design based on
geometry and simplified Cyrillic script would prove more
accessible for their intended readers. Aiming to take art
into life, Lissitzky used abstract forms floating in space
for a series of posters and book designs in a style often
called Elementarism. Using primary colours and pure
geometry, he believed that this would be a universally

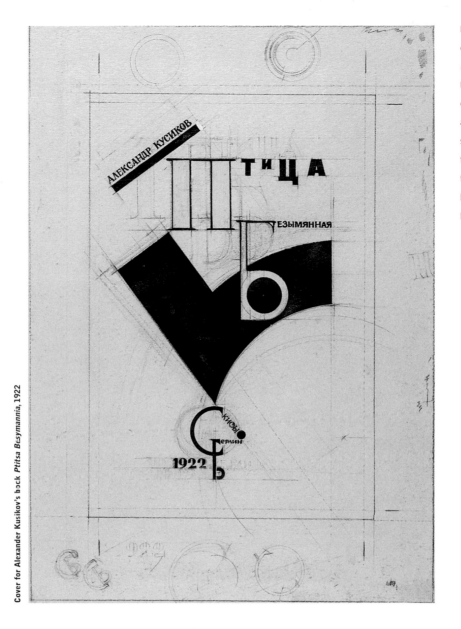

Cover for Alexander Kusikov's book *Ptitsa Besymannia*, 1922

In his design for the collection of poems *Ptitsa Besymannia* (Bird Without a Name), El Lissitzky made use of negative and positive abstract letterforms suggesting a bird's head to form a composition drawn from the title poem. The book was published in 1922 by Deutsche Bücherei, Leipzig.

understood visual language. The famous political poster "Beat the Whites with the Red Wedge" of 1919 used the dynamism of geometric forms and spatial illusion to suggest its narrative political content; a large red triangle pierces a white circle, while splinters of geometric shapes are sent off into space.

Lissitzky worked internationally throughout the 1920s, participating in De Stijl (see pp54–5) events, attending the First Congress of Progressive Artists in Düsseldorf in 1922 and contributing to Kurt Schwitters's magazine *Merz*. He collaborated with poets and playwrights, designing a book of the poems of Mayakovsky, *Dlja Golosa* (For the Voice) and a print portfolio of Meyerhold's play *Victory over the Sun*, both in 1923. In these works Lissitzsky revealed a strong interest in typography as an integrated visual element.

In the late 1920s Lissitzky produced a number of exhibition designs, in particular the Soviet contributions to "Pressa", an international press exhibition in Cologne in 1928, the "Film und Foto" exhibition in Stuttgart in 1929 and the International Hygiene exhibition in Dresden in 1930. In these he applied ideas from Soviet cinema, inspired by Sergei Eisenstein's theory of "montage of attractions". According to this, documentary photography could be assembled on a dramatic scale, projecting images of mass political groups, workers and abstract configurations of machinery. Picture editing now became central to Lissitzky's approach and from 1932, with Russia under Stalin, it was difficult to pursue experimental work. His major activity was to work on *USSR in Construction*, a series of architectural propaganda publications distributed internationally.

ALEXANDER RODCHENKO

➔ 1891–1956
➔ Energetic advocate of
Soviet Constructivism
➔ Studied at art school
in Kazan
➔ Strong, direct style
using basic components
of graphic design
➔ Books, posters and
architectural graphics
➔ Returned to painting
in later life

The work of the Russian Alexander Rodchenko stands out for its vigour and dynamism. His attempt to find a collective way of working for a new society was influential both in its time and on young designers in the late twentieth century.

Rodchenko attended art school in Kazan from 1910 to 1914. He became familiar with the recent avant-garde activities of Russian Futurism and moved to Moscow, where in 1916 he met Vladimir Tatlin, Lyubov Popova and Malevich. All cultural activities were reorganized after the Revolution of 1917. Rodchenko and his contemporaries became important leaders in a new, experimental art that turned to industrial manufacture and production for its inspiration.

In 1918 Rodchenko joined Narkompros (People's Commissariat of Enlightenment) and in 1921 he was appointed to teach on the Basic Course and in the Metalwork Faculty at the VKhUTEMAS, the Higher State Artistic and Technical Workshops, the reformed art school in Moscow. Here students were taught fundamental principles of modern design with an emphasis on materials and formal principles of composition based on abstraction. They were also encouraged to work with the latest technologies. At this point Rodchenko's contributions to exhibitions were hanging constructions made from geometrical parts, and monochrome, non-objective easel paintings in primary colours or black and white, in which he explored line, plane and space.

Prompted by Mikhail Tarabukin and other Constructivist art critics, Rodchenko moved in 1923 from fine art to design, or from the "easel to the machine". In that year he began collaboration with the poet Mayakovsky on posters designed for various government trading organizations. Mayakovsky supplied slogans and Rodchenko developed the visual aspects. To complement the direct and punchy, sometimes humorous, copylines, Rodchenko's designs were composed with strong contrasts of blocks of bold colour. They were often arranged with a strong diagonal emphasis, incorporating readily identifiable images of products and heavy, block typography, rules and underlinings, in what amounted to a Constructivist set of ingredients.

Rodchenko also worked for the theatre and cinema, important areas of cultural agitation at the time. He designed the posters "Kino Pravda" (Cinema Truth) and "Kino Glaz" (Cinema Eye) for the revolutionary documentary film-maker Dziga Vertov as well as the film poster for Sergei Eisenstein's *Battleship Potemkin*. In these designs, as well as in covers for the magazine *Lef* (1923–5) and *Novyi Lef* (1927–8), he made important use of photography and photomontage.

As for other Soviet designers, the changes from the experimental culture of the early years of the Soviet Republic to Stalinist Socialist Realism were difficult for Rodchenko. During the 1930s he worked on the journal *USSR in Construction*, but in his later years he returned to painting.

Rodchenko, like his fellow Soviet Constructivists, was committed to adapting the new design to a public context. His design for painted advertisements for the exterior of Mossel'prom, one of Moscow's major department stores, was an overt confirmation of this.

Painted advertisement for Mossel'prom, 1925

Cover for magazine *Lef*, 1923

The cover for the third number of *Lef*, the magazine of the Left Front of the Arts, shows Rodchenko's use of elementary typography. In this typeface, a simplified version of the Cyrillic alphabet, the upturned "M" serves as a "3". The photomontage conveys a narrative through the use of emblematic images.

Cover for magazine *Kino Glaz*, 1924

With the cover of the sixth number of *Kino Glaz* (Cinema Eye) Rodchenko alerts the reader to the construction of the cinematic process. The staring eye is a self-reflexive motif that draws attention to the act of seeing in viewing through a camera lens, watching a film and reading a poster.

BAUHAUS

The Bauhaus is the best-known school of art, design and architecture of the twentieth century. Among its staff and students were leading pioneers of early modernism in all areas of the arts and crafts, and the impact of their work and ideas has been felt in Europe and the United States for many years.

Intended to represent a fresh start after World War I, the school opened in 1919 under the direction of the architect Walter Gropius, in the buildings of the Weimar Academy of Art. In 1925 it moved to Dessau, a city with stronger industrial links, in new buildings designed by Gropius. After being closed by the government, the Bauhaus, now under Mies van der Rohe, operated in Berlin in 1932–3, until it was closed once again by the Nazis.

Extending the thinking of leading figures in the Arts and Crafts movement in Britain such as William Morris, C.R. Ashbee and W.R. Lethaby, Gropius hoped to reunite the fine and applied arts in the aftermath of the war. He attracted an impressive range of established artists to form the initial staff, including Wassily Kandinsky, Lyonel Feininger and Paul Klee. Although these teachers were not architects, the school's aim was that all students should graduate in architecture, for it was believed that this discipline encapsulated all other areas of art and design. In their first year students pursued the Vorkurs, or foundation course, after which they studied in a workshop dedicated to materials, investigating wood, metal, weaving, ceramics and printing. In fact many graduated as designers in these fields rather than in architecture.

The foundation course, taught initially by Johannes Itten, then László Moholy-Nagy (see pp64–5) after 1923, was crucial in establishing a common approach among the students. Emphasis was placed on examining the formal and physical properties of materials in order to find principles of design that would respect the axiom "truth to materials". Consequently, abstract ideas of texture, volume, form, space, colour, transparency and extension became a shared visual language across diverse media, and helped to shape a recognizable "Bauhaus approach".

One continuing question at the school was how designs could be adopted by industry. The original emphasis on the crafts changed after 1923, when there was a drive to find industrial sponsorship and to view the work carried out in the workshops as prototypes serving industrial manufacture. Some workshops achieved better results than others in this goal, and among the successful items produced were lamps, industrial glass, woven textiles, wallpaper, furniture and graphic designs.

The first printed graphic works reflected the bias towards craft in the school's early years and the output consisted of artists' portfolios, largely of prints by teachers, often in Expressionist styles. By the time of the first major exhibition of all Bauhaus products, held in Weimar in 1923, the catalogue showed the influence of the Dutch De Stijl movement (see pp54–5) and Russian Constructivism. The cover, designed by Herbert Bayer (see pp66–7), and the interior layout, by Moholy-Nagy, used the sans-serif typeface Venus Grotesk, in black and red inks, and the text was arranged in blocks of asymmetrical type. This very modern appearance signalled the beginning of a stable alliance between the "new typography" and the Bauhaus.

The school was extremely successful in self-promotion, publishing a magazine at various stages of its existence and, most importantly, a series of volumes, the Bauhausbücher (Bauhaus books), from 1925. Through both these publications the writings of Bauhaus staff and other international modernist designers and architects were

Cover by Margit Téry for magazine *Utopia: Dokumente der Wirklichkeit*, 1921

Schmidt, a teacher at the Bauhaus, used the motif of the rotary press for the cover of this special issue of a trade magazine for offset lithographic printers, devoted to the graphic work of the school. He schematized a cross section of a machine, devising a cover that reflected the interest in geometry and sans-serif typefaces apparent in the work under review. Offset-Verlag of Leipzig printed the magazine.

Cover by Joost Schmidt for magazine *Offset*, no. 7, 1926

In this lithograph (opposite), an early typographical work by a Bauhaus designer, the lettering is hand-rendered and shows an interest in elementary geometry – each letter is reduced to a half circle or straight line. *Utopia: Dokumente der Wirklichkeit* (Utopia: Documents of Reality) was a short-lived magazine which reflected the early interest of the Bauhaus in spiritual idealism.

Cover by Herbert Bayer for book *Staatliches Bauhaus...,* 1923

In 1923 staff at the Bauhaus were asked to present their work in exhibition, partly to justify the financing of the school. The exhibition marked the transition from experimental craft to a concentration on prototypes for industrial design. The cover of the accompanying book was designed by Herbert Bayer and the interior layout by László Moholy-Nagy.

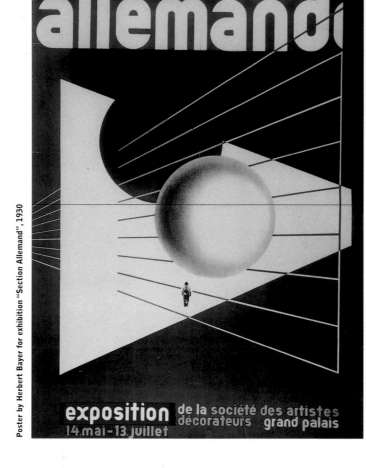

HERBERT BAYER: Abb. 1. Alfabet
„g" und „k" sind noch als
unfertig zu betrachten

Beispiel eines Zeichens
in größerem Maßstab
Präzise optische Wirkung

sturm blond

Abb. 2. Anwendung

Bayer asked his students to design a typeface using straight lines, the circle and a 45-degree angle. He made his version, Universal (above), in the belief that a single-case, sans-serif alphabet would aid international communication.

To considerable acclaim, Bayer designed, with Marcel Breuer and Moholy-Nagy, the poster (left), catalogue and Bauhaus stand for this exhibition. The typeface was his own adaptation of Universal.

disseminated, and in addition a modern typographical style became firmly associated with the school.

In the teaching of graphic design, Moholy-Nagy, Bayer and Joost Schmidt subscribed to the "rationalization" movement, which was popular in modernist circles at the time. All graphic designs were interpreted as "industrial" design, and, in tune with the school's expressed commitment to functionalism, were expected to use sans-serif typefaces, while asymmetry and primary colours were also advocated. Photography and photomontage were the preferred media for illustrations. Paper in DIN, or German Industry Standard, sizes was to be used.

In the late 1920s an awareness of how visual communication was changing, particularly in the United States, prompted lectures on economics, marketing psychology and advertising science to encourage students to think about the non-visual aspects of design. This modern approach to graphic design led to exhibition

design being considered a natural extension of it. Bayer was very successful in this field, devising new methods for displaying furniture and other industrial goods, as well as making original use of photography and typography.

The axiom "form follows function", promoted by Gropius, was intended to show that the school would not adhere slavishly to one style. Nevertheless, it is possible to detect a common Bauhaus approach or style, and indeed its development was perhaps inevitable given the shared curriculum and close exchange between staff and students.

The full implications of the Bauhaus philosophy could not be realized because of the political situation in Germany. Many of the staff emigrated, most to the United States. Among these, Moholy-Nagy became director of the unsuccessful New Bauhaus: American School of Design in Chicago in 1937–8. Over the following years Bayer, Gropius, Josef Albers and Marcel Breuer introduced modernist design principles to the teaching of design in America.

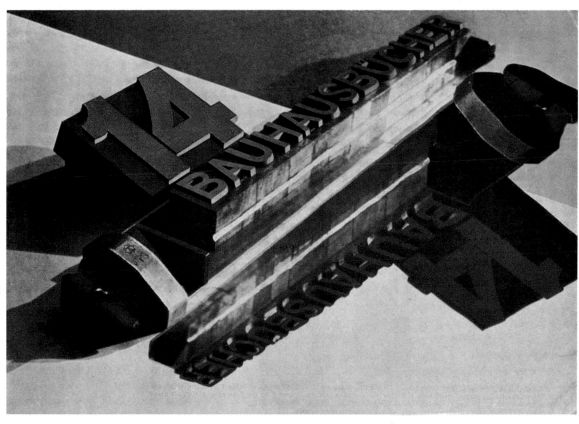

The Bauhaus published a series of books explaining the ideas of its teachers. This design takes the principle of self-reflexiveness – it is made up of a block of type, photographed in reverse – and the message becomes the medium.

The cover for this prospectus showed a part of Moholy-Nagy's *Light-Space Modulator*, an automated sculpture that he had used as the basis of an abstract film, *Light-Play, Black – White – Grey*, in 1930. The New Bauhaus: American School of Design was a short-lived attempt to revive the Bauhaus ideal in the United States, opening in 1937 and closing the following year.

→ 1895–1946
→ Hungarian theorist of graphic design and visual communication
→ Pre-eminent pioneer of "new typography"
→ Teacher at Bauhaus
→ Wrote important books on graphic design
→ Emigrated from Germany 1934 and took ideas to Amsterdam, London and Chicago

László Moholy-Nagy was one of the first abstract artists to move from painting to design for communication, famously taking the step in 1923 of ordering a painting by telephone, using a colour chart and geometric grid to signal the "death of painting".

He was initially part of an avant-garde in Budapest and after World War I was strongly influenced by Soviet Constructivism. He moved to Berlin in 1921 and in 1923 was invited by Walter Gropius to join the Bauhaus (see pp60–3) in Weimar as a professor in the metal workshop. His marked interest in design for print showed when he took charge of the typographic design of many of the school's publications, including, from 1925, the Bauhaus Books series.

With many of his contemporaries, including El Lissitzky (see pp56–7), Herbert Bayer (see pp66–7), Jan Tschichold (see pp68–9) and Kurt Schwitters, Moholy-Nagy advocated a modernist approach to graphic design, known as *die neue typographie* (the new typography). This recommended using lower-case alphabets with inks of primary colours and photographic illustrations, with the aim of creating a universal and democratic medium. His design philosophy was a curious combination of technological determinism, a belief in the social role of design and a mystical preoccupation with the properties of light.

Moholy-Nagy wrote prolifically and in his first book, *Malerei Fotografie Film (Painting Photography Film)*, published in 1925, he predicted the route that communication would take from a single image to a narrative form of film montage. He was interested in extending the possibilities of combining typography with photography in what he called "Typophoto". As well as investigating the possibilities of rendering the familiar strange, through negative and positive photography, he experimented with photograms (camera-less photography) and photomontages (see pp74–7), which were applied in designs for posters, book covers and exhibitions. A common thread in his work was his wish to expose the elements of design by revealing structure, as

64

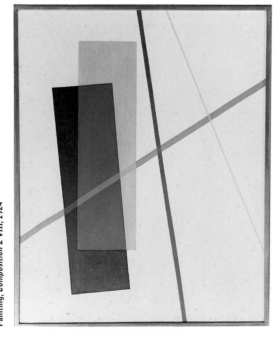

Painting, Composition Z VIII, 1924

Moholy-Nagy's last paintings before he turned exclusively to design, such as *Composition Z VIII*, explored the transparency of geometrical planes. This idea was later resolved in his graphic design.

he did in the advertisement for the Bauhaus Books list in 1925, in which he used the ingredients of typography themselves for the design.

From 1928 until he emigrated to the Netherlands in 1934, Moholy-Nagy was an established designer in Berlin. He showed his work at the German Werkbund contribution to the Société des Artistes Décorateurs in Paris in 1930, an exhibition he co-designed with Gropius and Bayer. In the Netherlands and then England and the USA (where he settled more permanently) he worked on publication design and exhibitions as well as industrial design.

In 1937 Moholy-Nagy became director of the New Bauhaus in Chicago. This failed in 1938 and the following year he founded the School of Design in the city. Despite confronting social and political upheaval throughout his life, Moholy-Nagy was one of the seminal figures in the transmission of modern design of his time.

Cover for magazine *die neue linie*, 1929

Moholy-Nagy was so committed to the new vision embracing the significance of design that he pronounced that the illiterate of the future would be those who could not use a camera. He also relegated verbal language to a position of lesser significance than the visual. This striking design is from the cover of the newly fashionable magazine *die neue linie*, published by Otto Beyer in Leipzig and Berlin.

In his book *Malerei Fotografie Film* Moholy-Nagy asserted that visual communication would move from painting to film. He also displayed great enthusiasm about the use of mechanical reproduction. This cover was developed from a photogram.

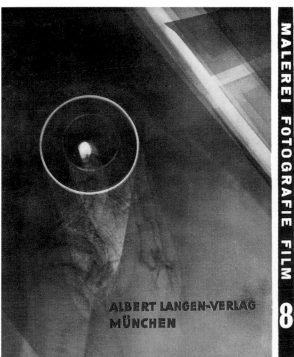

Cover for book *Malerie Fotografie Film*, 1925

➔ 1900–85
➔ Sophisticated graphic designer born in Austria
➔ Student and then teacher at Bauhaus
➔ Early application of modernism to commercial design
➔ Emigrated to United States 1938
➔ Later career as environmental designer and architect

Herbert Bayer took radical European ideas of modernism and transferred them to the context of American corporate culture. In doing so he became one of the first fully recognized international graphic designers.

A prodigious student at the Bauhaus (see pp60–3) in Weimar from 1921 to 1923, Bayer responded to Kandinsky's teaching on colour and Klee's on form by applying their ideas to some of the earliest examples of the "new typography". He was simultaneously interested in the two-dimensional arrangement of abstract motifs and type on the page and in the three-dimensional extension of these ideas in temporary structures such as exhibitions and pavilions.

In 1925 Bayer became a member of staff at the Bauhaus, where his lettering course introduced students to the principles of modern typography. He was an advocate of *Kleinschreibung* (literally, "small writing"), a system of using lower-case letterforms instead of the conventional combination of upper and lower case. For posters, tickets and other designs for display, he tended to use only capitals, whereas for most texts he used only lower case. This was all the more controversial in Germany, where the first letter of every noun is capitalized. Bayer argued that this saved space and money because printers needed to stock only one range of the typefaces, and also that it enhanced international communication. His most celebrated exercise in typography was the Universal typeface of 1926, a design based on the circle, which he applied in subsequent designs, for example in the fashion magazine *die neue linie*.

On leaving the Bauhaus (by now in Dessau) in 1928, Bayer moved to Berlin and worked as a graphic designer and art director, mainly for the Dorland Agency. The term "art director" was new and in this role for German *Vogue* and *die neue linie* Bayer interpreted the American idea of the coordination of all aspects of magazine design. In his striking covers he devised photomontages with surrealist juxtapositions. Bayer's work in Berlin reveals the contradictions of design under National Socialism: although modernism was banned in 1933, he continued to work. Avowedly modernist, he took on major commissions for the design of high-profile exhibitions in Berlin and catalogues promoting the new regime. For these he adapted photomontage techniques to explicitly National Socialist content.

After settling in the United States in 1938, Bayer worked on exhibitions for the Museum of Modern Art, New York, and designed covers for *Harper's Bazaar* and *Fortune* magazines as well as tourist brochures. He also worked for the Container Corporation of America, becoming design adviser in 1946. This large packaging firm's publicity extended to a cultural programme that included sponsorship of the Institute for Humanistic Studies in Colorado, for which Bayer designed the *World Geo-Graphic Atlas* in 1953. This work was a summation of his interests: a sophisticated arrangement of symbols, montaged figures and modern typography.

Emergency currency for Thuringia, 1923

During the rapid inflation of the German Reichsmark in 1918–24, Bayer devised a simplified banknote in which the figures could be easily adapted. Most strikingly for its time, the typeface was Venus sans-serif, whereas all other banknotes were produced in German Fraktur.

die neue linie

August 1938

Cover for magazine *die neue linie*, 1938

On leaving the Bauhaus in 1928 Bayer became art director for the new woman's magazine *die neue linie* as part of his work for the Dorland Agency in Berlin. Remaining in this post until 1938, he adapted montage ideas, making experimental modernist ideas more acceptable to a wider public.

67

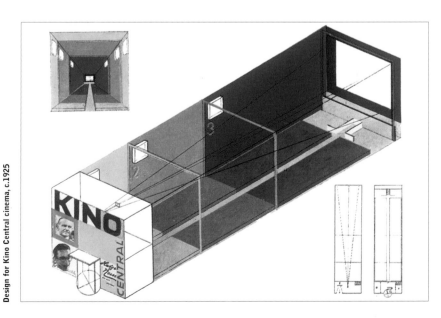

KINO

CENTRAL

Design for Kino Central cinema, c.1925

Bayer retained a strong interest in exhibition and architectural design throughout his career, as in this project for a cinema in Germany. He was attracted to the idea of making typography and graphic design central elements to exteriors of buildings, helping to direct the visitor in an immediate way.

JAN TSCHICHOLD

→ 1902–74
→ Internationally
known as typographic
adviser and designer
of distinction
→ Trained as typographer
in Leipzig
→ Defined "new
typography" in 1920s
→ Initial strong
modernist sympathies
modified by experience
in 1930s

Jan Tschichold was one of the most important typographic and graphic designers of the twentieth century. His career covered the crucial years of early modernism and he contributed to the debate about its application to graphic design.

One of the few designers in this book to receive a full formal education in calligraphy and typography, Tschichold studied from 1919 to 1923 at the Leipzig Academy for Graphic Arts and Book Trades under Walter Tiemann, who introduced him to the principles of classical typography. However, a visit to the 1923 Bauhaus (see pp60–3) exhibition in Weimar impressed the young designer and, as a result of this and his growing familiarity with Soviet Constructivism, he began to apply radical principles associated with these movements. These included asymmetric composition, a reduction of form to its basic geometry, preference for single-case, sans-serif typfaces and the use of photographs as illustrations. Tschichold's most celebrated example of these principles in large graphic form is the series of posters he made for the Munich cinema Phoebus Palast, a job he took while teaching at the German Master Printers' School in the city. Following the ideas of Constructivism, the posters not only make striking visual summaries of each film but also comment on the character of film-making, employing the Constructivist device of self-reflexiveness with a recognition of the camera and the act of projection.

In 1925 Tschichold published his ideas on typographic design in a special issue of the journal *Typographische Mitteilungen*. The publication of *Die Neue Typographie* in 1928 established his long-term significance for international design. Intended as a handbook for practising printers and publishers, it summarized the ideas of modern typography in a short art-historical essay and examined the elements of typographic design, from letterheads and postcards to the design of a whole book. The book had a significant impact on the future of design, even though it was not translated into English until 1985.

After their arrest by the Nazis in 1933, Tschichold and his wife Edith were forced to emigrate to Basle, Switzerland, where he taught at the Arts and Crafts School and worked for the publisher Benno Schwabe. Gradually his style grew less uncompromising. He regarded standardization and a house style for typography as necessary in modern publishing. By contrast with the geometrical austerity of the new typography, he considered a second approach to book design which was defined by harmonious composition using complementary typefaces, symmetry and decorative borders – all elements of neoclassical book design. This he termed "the new traditionalism". Either approach could be used, according to the nature of the design task.

In his later life Tschichold acted as typographic adviser to the publishers Birkhäuser in Basle (1941–6) and Penguin Books in London (1946–9), applying his consistently high standards to systematize book design and corporate identity.

Cover design, lettering and borders for book *The Tragedy of Macbeth*, 1950

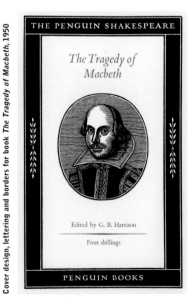

THE PENGUIN SHAKESPEARE

The Tragedy of Macbeth

Edited by G. B. Harrison

Four shillings

PENGUIN BOOKS

Tschichold was typographic adviser to Penguin Books in England between 1947 and 1949, although his influence lasted longer. He revised existing series and introduced elegant solutions for new series. His designs represented his return to what he termed "the new traditionalism". The engraved portrait used in this design is by Reynolds Stone.

unter mitarbeit des schweizerischen photographen-verbandes

gewerbemuseum basel   ausstellung

der berufsphotograph

sein werkzeug — seine arbeiten

8. mai — 6. juni

werktags		14-19	
mittwochs		14-19	19-21
sonntags	10-12	14-19	
eintritt frei			

When the poster was first published, the stunning use of a negative portrait and spare asymmetry made this design for the Gewerbemuseum in Basle, Switzerland, appear extremely modern. Evoking the process of photography, the typography is set in the graded colours of the spectrum.

In sympathy with the Constructivist paintings on display at the Kunsthalle in Basle, this design depends on minimum means. Geometry and the aymmetrical counterbalance of typographical elements are used with the precision and refinement that characterize Tschichold's work.

69

● vom 16. januar bis 14. februar 1937

kunsthalle basel

konstruktivisten

van doesburg
domela
eggeling
gabo
kandinsky
lissitzky
moholy-nagy
mondrian
pevsner
taeuber
vantongerloo
vordemberge
u. a.

THE RING

In 1927 the former Dadaist artist Kurt Schwitters – by then a designer working in Hanover in his own advertising agency, Merz Werbecentrale, set up three years earlier – proposed the formation of a group of like-minded graphic designers. Der Ring Neuer Werbegestalter, or Circle of New Advertising Designers, usually known in English as the Ring, would publish its works collectively, organize exhibitions and promote the new approach to design. Schwitters's model was most likely a group of radical architects, also named Der Ring, who had formed a professional association in Berlin in 1925.

In design and architecture the last years of the 1920s witnessed the high point of the first stage of modernism, and in graphic design this meant the new typography and new photography. Many designers, including Schwitters, had moved from the avant-garde context of experimental graphics to take on more mainstream commissions. Schwitters worked for Günter Wagner of Pelikan inks, for whom he devised striking modernist advertisements, and for the city authority of Hanover, whose corporate identity and stationery he designed.

During the experimental years in art and design, between 1918 and 1924, designers had questioned many of the basic assumptions about order and the hierarchy of composition in graphic design. Dadaist experimentation had dissolved the logical arrangement of word and image, introducing capital and bold letters, and signs and symbols, and breaking up the conventional arrangement of syntax in designs for manifestos. Principles of simultaneity informed the deployment of type across the page. Photomontage (see pp74–7) was also a central element.

With the stabilization of the mark in 1924, Germany and the rest of western Europe experienced relative economic growth until the Wall Street Crash of October 1929. It seemed possible that modernist design could become more than just an artistic experiment limited to the avant-garde studio or the sphere of design teaching, and the Ring turned to the German Werkbund and municipal authorities, as well as to architects and designers, for patronage. By the mid-1920s a move to rationalize this design inventiveness occurred at, for

example, the Bauhaus (see pp60–3). Several new typefaces, in particular sans-serifs, became available, among them the celebrated Futura (1926–8).

Designers in the Ring were keen to advocate standardization in graphic design. In the case of German members, this involved above all the use of Roman instead of Gothic typefaces, a radical step that was criticized by many commentators for being "unGerman", as choice of typeface was considered a part of national identity. There was widespread agreement among members that design could be run more effectively and economically if rules and guidelines were followed, and many advocated using standardized paper sizes. It was also recognized that if designers limited their choice of typefaces to a few, printers would need to stock only those, rather than the usual vast array.

The Ring believed that modern communication should be in lower-case type only, which again avoided the costs of providing a second alphabet. While arguments were put forward on functionalist and economic grounds, it is debatable whether these justifications were sustainable when scrutinized. It was characteristic of the age that science and standardization were invoked to support an aesthetic preference and a new approach to design.

Collage by Kurt Schwitters, *Merz Continental Number 59, 1926*

Gefesselter Blick (The Captured Glance), edited by Heinz and Bodo Rasch in 1931, promoted the ideas of the Ring by presenting 25 short monographs on designers, accompanied by examples of their work. The cover shows a photocollage by Willi Baumeister and a photogram by El Lissitzky.

71

Schwitters ran his own small advertising agency, Werbezentrale (Publicity Centre) in Hanover, undertaking design work for the city. His approach, evident in works such as this postcard, was readily identifiable as the "new typography".

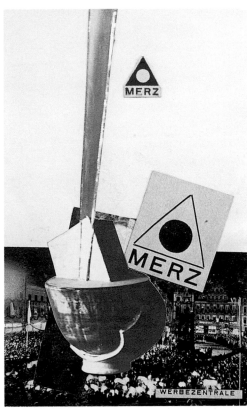

Kurt Schwitters combined design work with an interest in collage. To his collages he gave the name "Merz", an abbreviation of the German word for commerce. He had been criticized by the Berlin Dadaists for being preoccupied with beauty, and compositions of graphic ephemera such as this (opposite) are certainly harmonious in their design.

THE RING

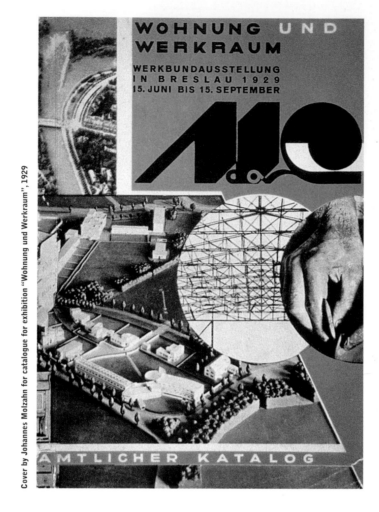

The "Wohnung und Werkraum" (Dwelling and Workplace) exhibition, organized by the Deutsche Werkbund in Breslau in 1929, examined the new architecture for domestic and public use. The cover of the catalogue shows the logo, used on tickets, stamps and the poster, that Molzahn devised for the exhibition.

Schwitters invited contributions from an international pool of designers, and although many members of the Ring were German, there were also Czech, Dutch, French and Swiss members. The full list of 25 contributors was published on the cover of the Ring's only book, *Gefesselter Blick* (The Captured Glance), which was edited by the brothers Heinz and Bodo Rasch in 1931. This gave a short profile of each designer, accompanied by illustrations of their work. Often statements regarding their approach or design philosophy were included, tending to stress their belief in standardization and rationalization and a pursuit of international communication. On a more pragmatic level, the list of contributors' addresses indicated that the book was intended to act as a catalogue, encouraging further commissions of work.

Among the designers in the Ring were those who saw graphic design solely as an activity for the promotion of left-wing political culture, such as the photomontagist John Heartfield, who refused to accept advertising as a viable or moral means of living. Others, including Max Burchartz and Johannes Canis, took on publicity for Germany's metalwork industry, in the belief that the new typography could be a form of progressive, democratic information. The Dutch members Cesar Domela, Paul Schuitema, Mart Stam, Friedrich Vordemberge-Gildewart and Piet Zwart had similarly received commissions from public service companies in the Netherlands, where modernism had less ideological charge than in Germany.

To coincide with the publication of *Gefesselter Blick*, a travelling exhibition was arranged, with venues in Germany, the Netherlands, Switzerland and Scandinavia. In the circumstances of political polarization in central Europe that shortly followed the Ring's pronouncements, the group's aims could not be fulfilled. Many similar goals would be reformulated in the 1950s and 1960s, however, in the pursuit of a utopian international visual language.

Piet Zwart was one of six Dutch members of the Ring. He worked as a graphic designer for a variety of companies and for the "Internationale Tentoonstelling op Filmgebied" (International Film Festival) in The Hague. A continuation of the design principles of De Stijl, his work showed an interest in dynamic asymmetry.

Max Burchartz was one of the first designers to apply the principles of experimental photomontage to the catalogue for a major industrial client, in this case the metalwork industry of Germany's Ruhr district.

PHOTOMONTAGE

Photomontage played an important role in both fine art and commercial art during the twentieth century. Making composite images from cutting and pasting photographs has probably been carried out by amateurs as well as professionals since shortly after the invention of photography in the 1830s, but the new century's renewed interest in subverting photographic statements by imaginative juxtaposition led to the popular use of the technique. For example, during World War I soldiers in the field adapted picture postcards to send to their families.

The implications of photomontage travelled quickly from the radical artistic experiments of the early twentieth century to mainstream graphic communication. Its origins as an avant-garde artistic activity have been much contested. One account comes from the Dadaist Raoul Hausmann, who wrote in *Courrier Dada*: "I also needed a name for this technique, and in agreement with George Grosz, John Heartfield, Johannes Baader, and Hannah Höch, we decided to call these works photomontages. This term translates our aversion at playing the artist, and, thinking of ourselves as engineers (hence our preference for workmen's overalls) we meant to construct, to assemble [*montieren*] our works." (Translated by Dawn Ades, in *Photomontage*, Thames and Hudson, London, 1976.)

The "invention" of photomontage as described above suggests that it was perceived as a revolutionary break from the preoccupations with authorship traditionally associated with the fine arts. This idea gains poignancy when we consider that Hausmann was writing during World War I. In his description photomontage was an extension of collage, the activity of pasting together ready-made images to create a new pictorial reality, as practised by Picasso, Braque and other Cubists and Futurists before 1914. By 1918, in war-torn Europe, many artists wished to align themselves with the working class and to advocate artistic and political revolution. In this changed context, photomontage, derived from a machine-made image, was deemed more appropriate than collage, as a way of taking the industrial into the world of art. At first dismissed as absurdist images, many Dadaist photomontages appear to have been serious reflections on the impact of war.

Injustice, social upheaval, feminism and revolutionary politics were all addressed, as the work of Hannah Höch, who, like Hausmann, was active in Dada in Berlin, reveals.

After the initial period of Dadaist experiment, photomontage was adapted to construct more systematic images of utopian societies, particularly in revolutionary Soviet Union. Avoiding past artistic languages, which in their view were contaminated by their association with Tsarist Russia, Soviet designers such as Gustav Klutsis, El Lissitzky (see pp56–7) and Alexander Rodchenko (see pp58–9) turned to photomontage instead.

John Heartfield, another member of the Berlin Dada group, also adapted his original style of photomontage as absurd disruption to mount a systematic attack on the growing power of the National Socialist Party in Germany during the 1920s and 1930s. German by birth, Heartfield anglicized his name, Herzfelde, in protest at his country's belligerence during World War I. He continued his political activities during the Weimar Republic of 1919–33, using photomontage "as a weapon of the class war". He moved from Cubist and Futurist arrangement of images, which suggested chaotic simultaneity, to a more programmatic

Poster by Cesar Domela for exhibition "Fotomontage", 1931

The painter and designer Cesar Domela revealed the process of film editing for this poster (opposite).

In photomontages like this (above), Höch subverted meanings through rupture and juxtaposition.

PHOTOMONTAGE

Klutsis and many other Soviet Constructivist designers turned to photomontage in the early 1920s in the belief that it represented a new democratic language. Lenin is shown striding across a modern world.

This photomontage parodies a speech in which Hermann Goering stated: "Iron always makes a country strong, butter and lard make people fat."

arrangement of elements to create numerous designs for book and magazine covers as well as posters. Heartfield's most remarkable series were his covers for the workers' weekly illustrated magazine *Arbeiter Illustrierte Zeitung*. From 1930 to 1938 he contributed over 200 photographic covers in which he exposed National Socialist policies, using models, enacted scenes and clever juxtapositions, airbrushed to appear seamless. Many of the covers worked following a dialectical principle, inspired by Heartfield's colleague the playwright Bertolt Brecht. According to this, an initial statement is contradicted, often through a montage of absurd elements that relies on humour or irony, leaving the viewer to complete the message.

In Europe political photomontage could be used to celebrate a new society just as much as to criticize reactionary regimes. At the height of its popularity, in the late 1920s, the technique was also the subject of several exhibitions that stressed its experimental, avant-garde nature, thereby aligning it to modernism.

In the United States photomontage took on an extra dimension – for selling goods. It proved a popular and effective way for advertisers to produce "before and after" shots. In addition, the "magical" properties of products could be enhanced by dynamic visual styles based on the tricks of cut and paste. Such techniques became familiar and soon returned to Europe through advertising agencies, which at the time were growing increasingly international.

During the Great Depression photographers used photomontage in exhibitions and publications, notably for the Farm Security Administration, an agency of President Roosevelt's "New Deal". The public use of photomontage continued after the outbreak of World War II, when the federal government commissioned large-scale photo-murals to promote solidarity, patriotism and national unity.

Photo-mural by Edwin Rosskam, "Buy Defense Bonds and Stamps Now!", 1941

"THAT GOVERNMENT··BY THE PEOPLE SHALL NOT PERISH FROM THE EARTH"

THAT WE MAY DEFEND THE LAND WE LOVE

THAT THESE MAY FACE A FUTURE UNAFRAID

THAT WE MAY BUILD FOR A BETTER WORLD

BUY DEFENSE BONDS AND STAMPS NOW!

A huge photo-mural in Grand Central Station, New York, for the Treasury Department shows how the US government used modern techniques of persuasion as part of the war effort.

77

Photomontage by John Heartfield for magazine *Arbeiter Illustrierte Zeitung*, 16 October 1932

A·I·Z

DER SINN DES HITLERGRUSSES:

Motto:
MILLIONEN
STEHEN
HINTER MIR!

Kleiner Mann bittet um große Gaben

Heartfield's design for the weekly communist magazine *Arbeiter Illustrierte Zeitung* carries the legend "Der Sinn der Hitlergrusses: Kleiner Mann bittet um große Gaben" (The meaning of the Hitler salute: a small man asks for large gifts). His clever juxtaposition of the two figures and a dramatic sense of scale convey with immediacy the message that Hitler's campaign was funded by large financial concerns. The motto "Millions Stand Behind Me" adds a further ironic twist.

ALEXEY BRODOVITCH

➔ 1898–1971
➔ Graphic designer renowned for fine sense of arrangement of word and image
➔ Born in Russia and worked in Paris in 1920s
➔ Emigrated to United States and, at *Harper's Bazaar* from 1934, defined modern magazine art direction
➔ Introduced many leading modern artists, photographers and designers to America

Some of the most important figures in the development of the modern visual language worked as art directors for American magazines between the 1930s and 1950s, a golden period for modern graphic design. Among them was Alexey Brodovitch, who art-directed *Harper's Bazaar* for nearly 25 years.

Service in World War I prevented the Russian-born Brodovitch from receiving formal art training. In 1920 he moved to Paris, where he designed sets for Diaghilev's Ballets Russes and gained experience in layout for the magazines *Arts et Métiers Graphiques* and *Cahiers d'Art*. Working in several design areas, he received five medals at the Paris 1925 Exposition.

In 1930 Brodovitch moved to the United States, where he was invited to establish a department of advertising design at the Pennsylvania Museum School of Industrial Design in Philadelphia. After leaving the school in 1938 he continued to teach, organizing a peripatetic Design Laboratory, which he took to important cultural venues in New York and Washington DC.

When Carmel Snow, editor of *Harper's Bazaar*, appointed Brodovitch art director in 1934, she had already to begun to change the magazine from an elite publication which focused on Paris haute couture to a more broadly based cultural review with an emphasis on the modern lifestyle. Brodovitch helped to accomplish this aim by giving the magazine a fresh look. He introduced the European photographers Brassaï, Henri Cartier-Bresson, Lisette Model and André Kertesz to American audiences, as well as cultivating many American photographers, including Irving Penn and Richard Avedon.

Familiar with the visual strategies of the Surrealists André Breton and Man Ray, Brodovitch used shock and surprise to lead the reader through the magazine. His skills were in assigning illustrators and photographers and then selecting and arranging their work with an intuitive eye. The designs of the 1930s depended on many devices to enliven the page: silhouettes, torn-paper edges, hand-drawn headlines and photomontage. Brodovitch avoided grids and modular approaches, although he respected modernist designers who used them. Like other mid-century designers, he exploited the analogy between film and the magazine. Sometimes he arranged photographs as if in a film sequence, and often his understanding of the drama and pace of a single image came from cinematography.

By the 1950s Brodovitch was acknowledged for combining culture, fashion and celebrity in his spreads in a new way. His style changed to convey this integration in simplified, sophisticated designs. Other articles were in a more impressionistic style, with imaginative use of colour to capture the full atmosphere of textiles and fashion accessories.

Brodovitch resigned from *Harper's Bazaar* in 1958. He had always maintained freelance work, and among the most outstanding are his designs for books of photography. In 1982 he was the subject of a posthumous retrospective, "Homage à Alexey Brodovitch", at the Grand Palais in Paris.

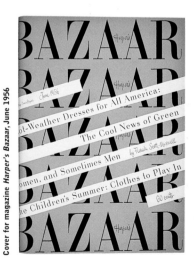

Cover for magazine *Harper's Bazaar*, June 1956

In his designs for magazine covers, Brodovitch recognized the power of immediate graphic language. In what would perhaps have been unthinkable at the end of the century for the cover of a mainstream women's magazine, here he simply used telegram-style lettering set against the repeated title masthead to announce the subject matter of the issue.

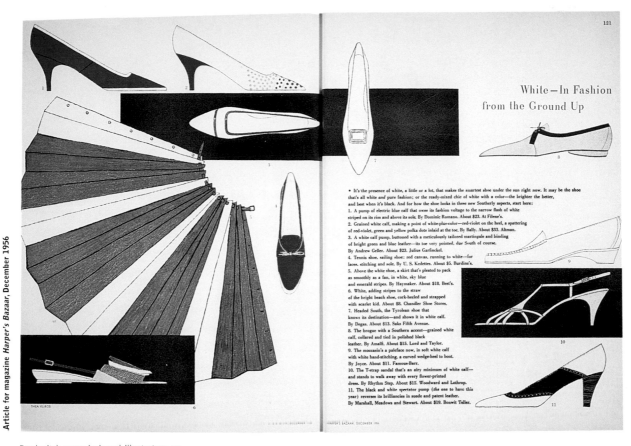

Brodovitch commissioned illustrators as well as photographers to supply detailed images of fashion garments. He arranged their work in striking ways that made full use of the page and a strong sense of positive and negative forms. The illustrator here was Thea Kliros.

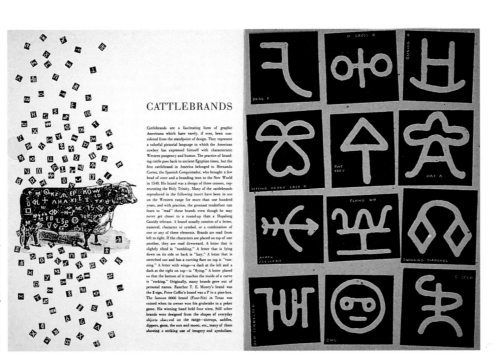

In 1949–50 Brodovitch was art director of *Portfolio*, a small-circulation cultural quarterly. Here, in features such as this one on the marks used to brand cattle, he adopted an exploratory approach to subjects that held interest for graphic designers.

ART DECO

The term "Art Deco" was invented to describe a style associated with the Exposition Internationale des Arts Décoratifs et Industriels Modernes held in Paris in 1925. Sometimes known as "Jazz Moderne" or simply "moderne", it was a popular style which spread quickly across the genres of design and architecture. Internationally successful, it was used in fashion, advertising and retail design, as a softened and more luxurious or popular version of modernism. In architecture, the style became associated with leisure, through its use in hotels, bars, cinemas and ocean liners, as well as in the more utilitarian context of banks, stores, apartment blocks, factories and filling stations.

Although the international Exposition in Paris of 1900 had drawn a huge number of visitors, it was not seen as having asserted France's pre-eminence in the decorative arts. As a result, already by 1905 French designers were indicating that the organic ornamentation of Art Nouveau needed to be superseded. Plans were taken up intermittently for another exhibition, solely dedicated to the arts of manufacture. The Société des Artistes-Décorateurs initially scheduled this for 1915, but because of World War I and the unsettled political and economic situation that followed in other parts of Europe, the exhibition did not take place until 1925.

The roots of Art Deco were in the traditions of the French decorative arts and crafts, and, characteristically for France, the "new" style incorporated much from the past. In terms of its forms the style is often interpreted as a reaction against the curvilinear tendencies of Art Nouveau, notably in its extensive use of rectilinear shapes and geometry in all genres of design.

After World War I France experienced what has been termed "a return to order" and the Deco style suited this politically conservative mood, which stressed continuity with national traditions as much as stylistic novelty. To this was added an exoticism in materials or iconography, and a conscious adoption of other sources: Egyptian, Mayan and Oceanic, as well as references drawn from the recent art movements of Cubism and Futurism. At the exhibition four of the major Parisian department stores, Au Printemps,

Bon Marché, Magasins du Louvre and Galeries Lafayette, established specialist pavilions where they promoted the work of contemporary designers. The elite traditions of Parisian haute couture had been among the first to define the new style, in particular the Atelier Martine, directed by Paul Poiret. The fashion houses offered ranges of perfumes and cosmetics, sold in luxury packaging which brought the Art Deco style to a much wider public. Fashionable designs sold in boutiques and luxury shops were very influential in broadening the appeal of Art Deco.

In graphic design, the Art Deco style was an eclectic mix. It was predominantly rectilinear and geometric, and zigzag lines were taken from both the visual style associated with the popular dance the Charleston and from the ziggurats of Egypt, which received considerable attention after the discovery of Tutankhamun's tomb in 1922.

Much of the graphic work associated with Art Deco was in fact produced in the years following 1925. The *livres d'artistes* and the exhibition catalogue were part of an elegant French typographic tradition. In the late 1920s there was a general move to broadened letterforms on magazine mastheads and to generous spacing, with chevrons and Egyptian motifs used as border decorations. Later newly designed typefaces became associated with

Art Deco reached the public through domestic accessories, most often luxurious French products like this elegant design, which carries no reference to the maker, Tokalon.

Powder compact by anonymous designer, France, c.1930

Jean Carlu, a contemporary of Cassandre, was one of the key poster designers to develop a simplified, elegant style, often using the mannequin head as a basis for his designs.

A new style of magazine cover emerged in the fashion magazine *Vogue*, established in New York in 1909. By the 1920s elegant models were illustrated in styles which combined neoclassical, Orientalist and Cubist elements. A formula was followed in which the representation of a model was accompanied by the magazine's title. The style of lettering was chosen to suit the overall design of the cover and modified for each issue.

81

ART DECO

Poster by Heinz Schulz-Neudamm for film *Metropolis*, 1926

Ritz cinema, Batley, United Kingdom, by F. Verity and S. Beverly, 1937

A poster for Fritz Lang's *Metropolis* captures the menacing mood of this film about a dystopian society. In Germany, Art Deco grew out of a combination of Expressionist and Futurist styles.

The popular expression of Art Deco in architecture was most evident in the cinematic "dream palaces" of the 1930s. Audiences experienced the style simply by entering these sumptuous buildings.

the style: for example, the typefaces Bifur of 1929 and Acier Noir of 1936, both of which were designed by A.M. Cassandre (see pp50–3)

Cassandre and his colleagues from the Alliance Graphique, Paul Colin, Jean Carlu and Charles Loupot, were some of the major exponents of the style in France in posters and magazine designs. In England some of the work of Edward McKnight Kauffer (see pp46–9) could be placed within Art Deco, while in other cases he remained distant from its influence.

In the United States the style was transformed from the late 1920s by the first generation of industrial designers, who took many of the visual motifs of Art Deco and applied them to product design as elements of streamlining. In Europe illustrations and photographs in fashion magazines offered a new visual style in which mannequin heads, often supported by neoclassical props,

were a familiar motif. Harlequins and pierrots were also abundant. This imagery appeared in the designs for accessories, perfumes, cosmetics and other small items produced by the haute-couture companies and department stores. Associated with feminine glamour, Art Deco was adopted as an appropriate idiom for the architecture of the new cinemas of the 1930s. The picture palaces, purveyors of dreams and fantasies through the new talkies, were defined in the street by the abundant use of neon lighting on their façades.

Art Deco was very often defined against the principles of modernism, which sought functional design through a minimum of materials and a stress on industrial production and standardization. In turn, the historicism, eclecticism and apparent superficiality of Art Deco were frowned upon by modernists for both aesthetic and political reasons.

A noted illustrator for French *Vogue*,
Georges Lepape was closely associated
with the moderne style. His compositions,
often inspired by Japanese prints, gave
great attention to overall harmony.

⊕ Antonio Boggeri,
1900–89
⊕ Xanti (Alexander)
Schawinsky, 1904–79
⊕ Pioneer graphic
design studio in Milan
⊕ Among first studios
to interpret modernism
for commercial clients
⊕ Advocates in 1930s
of "new typography"
and "new photography"

84

The situation of graphic design in Italy was distinct from that in other parts of Europe in the early decades of the twentieth century. Design and architecture flourished, but graphic design was less well developed and many traditionalists saw it as still a matter of either the typesetter, for books, or the painter, for posters. The exception was Italian Futurism (see pp42–3), which explored the possibilities of page layout of poetry and asymmetry for modern typographic design, although this remained confined to the area of avant-garde experimentation.

Antonio Boggeri was a pioneer of a new kind of industrial graphic design, more in tune with that of countries to the north of Italy. Born in Pavia, he attended the Technical Institute and Conservatory and then joined the printing company Alfieri & Lacroix before founding Studio Boggeri in Milan in 1933. He took the rigour he found in Italian rationalist architecture and applied it to an adjacent design practice. The studio became the centre of the new typography and graphic design in Italy, acting as an intermediary between printer and client. It was a caucus for designers from other countries, notably Switzerland and Germany. Among them in the first years were Xanti Schawinsky, fleeing Nazism, and Albe Steiner, while later came Max Huber, Enzo Mari, Carlo Vivarelli, Heinz Waibl, Theo Ballmer and Bruno Monguzzi (see pp194–5).

Boggeri was very interested in how the Neue Sachlichkeit (New Objectivity) photography, developed during the Weimar period in the Bauhaus (see pp60–3) and other art and design schools, could be incorporated in designs. The stress was on systems rather than individual designs, and commissions came from Olivetti, Pirelli, the food company Motta, the La Rinascente department store and the publisher Einaudi. Boggeri also worked for the emerging design press, which, together with the design Triennale, helped to establish Milan as one of the world's leading design capitals. Publications included the modernist graphic design magazine *Campo Grafico*, which first appeared in 1933, as well as the journals *Domus*, *Stile Industria*, and *Fotografia*.

Xanti Schawinsky was a member of Studio Boggeri in the initial years, from 1933 until 1936. After studying in his native Switzerland and Berlin he had joined the Bauhaus, where he taught stage design. He introduced many of the ideas developed by Herbert Bayer (see pp66–7) at the school. In his work for Olivetti typewriters, for example, he introduced a lower-case logotype and made an impact by using photomontage in advertisements.

The Swiss designer Max Huber joined Studio Boggeri in 1940 as an art director and later became a significant modernist designer, often working in Milan for clients established through the studio.

At the 1981 Milan Triennale a retrospective exhibition was dedicated to Studio Boggeri, with a catalogue to celebrate its continued existence prepared by Bruno Monguzzi.

Brochure by Marcello Nizzoli for Montecatini, 1933

For Montecatini, one of Studio Boggeri's first clients, Marcello Nizzoli incorporated a grid structure and photography, as in this cover and back page for a brochure. From 1938 he was art director at Olivetti, where he also designed typewriters.

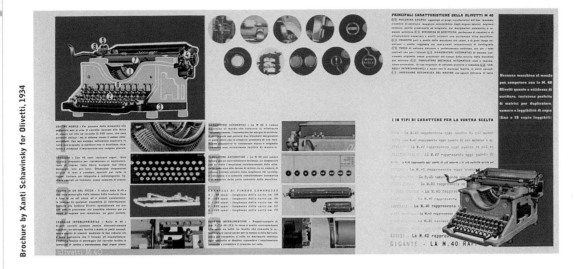

Having just arrived from Germany, Schawinsky was aware of the need to organize complex specifications for industrial goods, using close-ups of technical details and integrating a variety of visual systems. His approach is exemplified by this double page from the brochure for Olivetti's M40 typewriter.

85

Huber adapted the Constructivist principle of showing the tools of the designer's trade: tubes of gouache, dividers, paper clips and type itself. The "B" of the trademark for Studio Boggeri was first conceived by Bruno Munari.

This advertisement recalls Herbert Bayer's photomontages of elegant women for the covers of the magazine *die neue linie*. In 1936 Schawinsky left Europe to teach at Black Mountain College, North Carolina.

⊕ 1900–51
⊕ Czech modernist
architectural theorist
and graphic designer
⊕ Combined elements
of Constructivism and
Surrealism in his work
⊕ Wrote on new design
in 1920s and 1930s
⊕ Member of
advertising designers'
circle the Ring (Der Ring
Neuer Werbegestalter)

Karel Teige was the most important avant-garde architect and designer in Czechoslovakia in the interwar period. He worked internationally, and in his typographic designs he responded to the influence of Constructivism, Surrealism and the Bauhaus to create a sophisticated synthesis.

As a newly formed republic from 1918, Czechoslovakia experienced a period of social and cultural optimism, one characteristic of which was a growth in publishing and a strong commitment to modern architecture and design. In reaction to the previous generation, who had advocated the "book beautiful" and an Arts and Crafts-type return to vernacular styles, Teige announced a break with the past. As a committed communist he reacted against what he perceived as "the three stumbling blocks of decorativism, archaism and snobbism" of previous book designers.

In the early 1920s he visited the major centres of design, contributed to the Berlin magazine *Die Aktion*, met Le Corbusier and his cousin Pierre Jeanneret, who had an architectural practice together in Paris, and lectured at the Bauhaus (see pp60–3) in Weimar. Teige was a leading member of Devetsil, a group of Czech artists and poets formed in 1921. Taking inspiration from the modern worlds of advertising, tourism, sports and film, they formed a new "poetist" culture of everyday life, in which Teige's picture poems and photocollages played a major part. In his view poetism combined the visual and the literary, and the newly emergent graphic design became central to the movement.

Teige explained his design principles in two articles, "Modern Typography" (1927) and "Constructivist Typography, on the Way to New Book Design" (1930). In the former he outlined six principles of modern typography, which shared with other exponents of the new typography many ideas about the use of sans-serif typefaces, geometrical layouts and typophotos. Teige was a member of Der Ring Neuer Werbegestalter (see pp70–3), an international circle of new advertising designers formed in 1927 by Kurt Schwitters. However, unlike the more extreme functionalist designers who sought a set of universal principles in design, Teige suggested that a different approach to each typographic task was needed. "Advertising billboards, which should be visible from a distance, have different requirements than those of a scientific book, which are again different from those of poetry," he wrote.

Teige was commissioned by Jan Formek, who founded the Prague publishing house Odeon in 1925. He designed many poetry volumes in which a Surrealist collage of elements was combined with an orthogonal grid. As well as Constructivism, Teige drew on the analysis of syntax in the writings of the Czech linguist Roman Jakobson and on the arrangement of poetic text in the tradition of the French poets Mallarmé and Apollinaire. In his later graphic work he made remarkable collages based on the metamorphosis of the female body.

86

Design for Vitezslav Nezval's *Abceda*, 1926

An illustration for Vitezslav Nezval's book *Abceda* (Alphabet) shows the letter "G". The book consists of the letters of the alphabet as performed in dance by Milca Mayerova, with photography by J. Papsa. Teige's experimental book designs emphasized his theory of poetism, the triumph of optics over the literary in poetry.

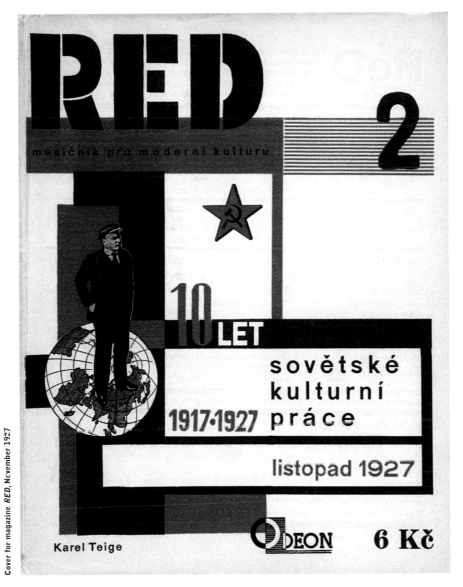

RED was a leading avant-garde review. For this issue, which celebrates the tenth anniversary of the Soviet Union and carries the legend "Soviet Cultural Work, 1917–1927", Teige provided a Constructivist-inspired design.

87

Teige wrote and designed the books *Stavba a Basen* (Building and Poem), 1927 (far left) and *Nejmensi Byt* (The Minimum Dwelling), 1932 (left). The covers of both illustrate the move from the new typography to the new photography in his work. As an architect Teige was strongly critical of much Western modern architecture, arguing for greater commitment to social housing.

LADISLAV SUTNAR

➔ 1897–1976
➔ Czech avant-garde graphic designer who explored ideas of Constructivism and abstraction in his work
➔ Worked in United States from 1939 as art director and designer of corporate identities
➔ Wrote important studies of design for visual information

Ladislav Sutnar made the transition from the early modernism of central Europe to the corporate design of the United States. The product of an analytical approach that stressed the importance of typographical elements and carefully chosen symbols, his designs are distinctive for their exactitude.

Sutnar trained at the Academy of Applied Arts and the Technical University in Prague. He was professor of design and then, from 1932 to 1939, director of the State School for Graphic Arts in Prague. In his own account of his design development he placed most significance on the impact of De Stijl (see pp54–5) and Constructivism, which broke from a superficial, decorative approach while benefiting from the international exchange between designers in the 1920s.

The rational application of visual communication greatly interested Sutnar, who, as his fellow Czech designer Karel Teige (see pp86–7) commented, hoped to achieve the progression of design from art to science. Sutnar's first major commissions came from the Prague publisher Druzsterni-Práce, a forward-looking company run on a cooperative basis. In 1939 Sutnar was the chief designer of the Czech pavilion of the New York World's Fair and stayed in the country, becoming a citizen of the United States. It was here that he fully realized the implications of his design theories.

Soon established in the American design world, he worked on cover designs for *Fortune* and *Scope* magazines. One of his most celebrated designs was for *Sweet's Catalogue*. Between 1941 and 1960 he developed for this supplier of architectural resources a coherent graphic system that covered a wide-ranging body of technical and industrial information.

In his later career Sutnar published several books on the organization of visual information. These included *Controlled Visual Flow: Shape, Line and Colour* (1943), *Package Design – The Force of Visual Selling* (1953) and *Visual Design in Action – Principles, Purposes* (1961).

Sutnar wanted to define how visual language could adapt to the demands of modern life. Arguing that functional information flow was necessary to enable fast perception, he reduced the essentials of communication design to "[creating] visual interest to start the eye moving"; "simplifying visual representation and organization for speed of reading" and "providing visual continuity for clarity in sequence".

Although he was analytical, Sutnar argued that the process of design should be based on thought and principles, not rules and formulae. Like Jan Tschichold (see pp68–9) before him, he analysed the whole sequence of visual information design, from corporate identity, consumer and business advertising, industrial catalogues and magazine design, to signs and symbols. What distinguished Sutnar's list from the earlier prescriptions of European designers was the addition of the new areas that corporate America had opened up for the graphic designer.

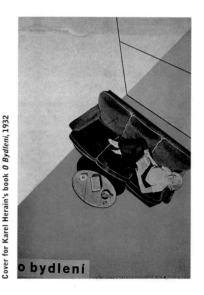

Cover for Karel Herain's book *O Bydleni*, 1932

Karel Herain's book, published in Prague in 1932, explored "the new living style" and the new home. Sutnar's cover depicts a "new woman" from a photographic bird's-eye viewpoint. The term "the new living style" was used by Czech modernists who aligned themselves to the new design ideas of Constructivism.

o bydlení

The magazine *Zijeme* (We Live) was published by the Union of Czechoslovak Industries and Design, the equivalent of the Deutsche Werkbund, which promoted functionalism and modernism in design. Sutnar based this design on an image of Charlie Chaplin, who was an admired figure among the artistic avant-garde throughout Europe at the time.

Sutnar's interest in symbols and direct visual language is apparent in this spiral-bound report, with its "HR" motif standing for the "Hudson River" of the title. The work described an ecological survey of the Hudson River area, near New York, carried out by the School of Architecture at the city's Columbia University.

⊖ 1882–1945
⊖ Artistic typographer and graphic designer
⊖ Ran small print workshop and studio, producing limited-edition books, prints and ephemera
⊖ Realized modern compositions with manual techniques

The contribution of Hendrik Werkman to the history of graphic design is as a maker of discreet and beautiful printed works. While many designers were stressing functionalism, and parallels between design and science were being drawn, he took pleasure in the chance expressiveness of printing. His designs were nonetheless modern and explored the combination of word and image in a way which was of great inspiration to later designers.

After working as a journalist and running a large printing office in Groningen, in the Netherlands, Werkman opened a small print workshop in 1923, where he produced all his subsequent work on a small scale and in limited print runs. He made pictures out of ready-made forms, whether type or other sources of mark. He called his works either *druksels* (from "to print") or *tiksels* (from "to tap") – words which stressed the physical, sometimes primitive, origins of his work. A later term he used for his whole output was "hot printing" – again to convey the sense of immediate contact with materials.

From 1923 to 1926 Werkman published *The Next Call*, a journal in which he explored many of his ideas. This he distributed internationally in order to maintain contact with like minds and exchange works by similar figures. Pages were devoted to abstract arrangements of woodblock typefaces or figures, turned on their side or arranged in repetitive sequences. This form of assemblage was similar to compositions by the Dadaists and Futurists, whose interest in type as a concrete form Werkman shared. The resultant visual poetry was at times like Lissitzky's experimental books (see pp56–7).

In his letterpress prints, such as this poster advertising the exhibition "The Plough at the Pictura Gallery", in Groningen, Werkman took pleasure in the effects of ink on paper and the accidental qualities of hand-setting woodblock letterforms. He shared an interest with De Stijl designers in the arrangement of poetry, but his abstraction was expressive rather than analytical.

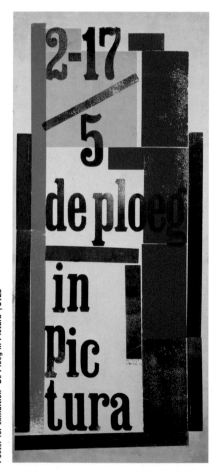

Poster for exhibition "De Ploeg in Pictura", 1925

90

Werkman was also a painter, a member of De Ploeg group. His colourist instincts were evident in his printed works, where he could pursue them less programmatically than more conventional design contexts allowed. He exploited the element of chance in printing: the irregularities of inking and the marks left where the press left the paper exposed. Many of the works were single prints – he used old woodblock type, pressed on to paper in an old hand press. In the 1930s he made extensive use of stencils, while other prints were a result of rolling ink directly on to the paper.

During World War II Werkman produced 40 issues of a subversive broadsheet, *De Blauwe Schuit* (The Blue Barge), which led to his being executed by the Nazis on the day before his country's liberation.

His work came to be recognized in the 1950s, when his aesthetic seemed to match the sensibility of many abstract artists. This was particularly apparent in the work of Willem Sandberg, whose informal approach to catalogue design in the 1940s and 1950s paid tribute to Werkman.

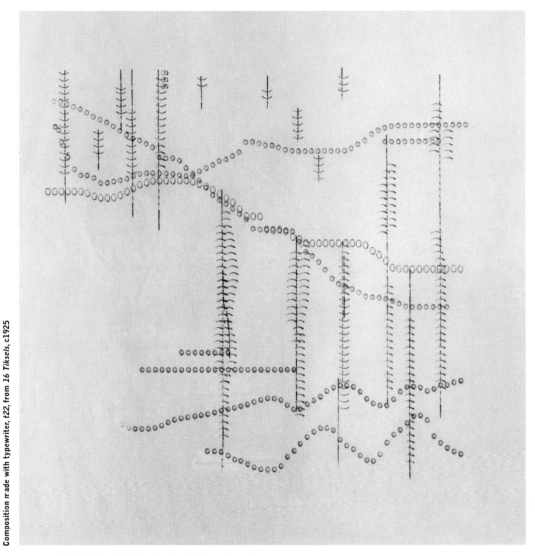

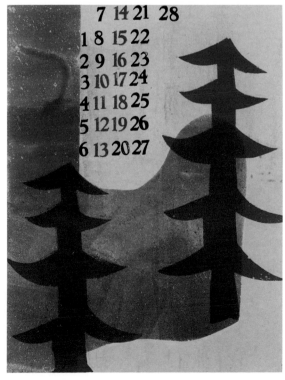

7 14 21 28
1 8 15 22
2 9 16 23
3 10 17 24
4 11 18 25
5 12 19 26
6 13 20 27

Page from calendar, 1943

Werkman's "*tiksels*" were arrangements of letters and words produced with a typewriter. They were reminiscent of the layout of poems by the French writer Stéphane Mallarmé and, in their way, prefigured concrete poetry.

During the Nazi occupation of the Netherlands in World War II, Werkman continued to work in secret. He produced his calendars, of which he published this example in 1943, by his "hot printing" method, applying inked rollers and stencils directly to paper and printing without a press.

91

NATIONAL IDENTITY

During the interwar years in Europe and North America graphic design was often used in printed propaganda material. Before the advent of television as a medium of mass communication, posters provided an immediate and accessible persuasive force, alongside radio, public speeches, rallies and processions. In their choice of designers to work on these poster campaigns, state organizations frequently revealed an underlying ideological attitude.

Europe experienced massive political turmoil as the polarization of parties on the Left and Right led to the assumption of power by several totalitarian regimes. For example, in the Soviet Union the experimental communist society pioneered by Lenin until his death in 1924 underwent transformation to a rigid totalitarian regime under Josef Stalin. Official aesthetic policies moved from supporting avant-garde artists and designers to advocating Socialist Realism. Accordingly, idealized heroic young workers, soldiers and citizens were portrayed in sculptures, paintings and films, as well as in posters and other forms of party propaganda. Through this shift in policy artistic innovation was reduced to a minimum and only state-approved artists were trained, and then commissioned to produce work that carried an unambiguous message.

In Italy, where Benito Mussolini became Prime Minister in 1922, the state continued to support modern art and design as a national style. Accepting that the world had changed irrevocably with mechanization, Mussolini interpreted Futurism (see pp42–3), with its references to technology, industrial progress and military power, as compatible with his modern, aggressive Fascist Party.

A further contrast was evident in Germany. On being elected to power in January 1933 Adolf Hitler was already aware of the important role propaganda could play in his conservative, reactive policy. Under Joseph Goebbels, the Reich Minister for People's Enlightenment, the National Socialists ridiculed modernism. Associated with the decadence of the Weimar Republic, it was dismissed as either "Jewish" or "Bolshevik". In its place they advocated art and design loyal to the German tradition. Some graphic designers adopted the Nazis' approved styles but many others were persecuted, banned or forced to flee the country. Photomontage (see pp74–7) and the latest film techniques were also selectively used, in part to satisfy the expectations of a consumer society as well as to show how Germany could compete with the entertainment industries of other nations.

In the United States the early interwar years were characterized by substantial industrial expansion, followed by the Wall Street Crash of 1929 and economic depression. President Roosevelt's New Deal, introduced to combat this national crisis, included federal arts projects to encourage the employment of artists, photographers and designers. A small group of American cultural activists, interested in embracing modern graphic design for such projects, welcomed many of the designers and architects who fled political oppression in Europe in the 1930s. Their message was that a direct, clear and popular form of modern design could help unify this relatively young country and affirm its democratic message, against the backdrop of the divided and politically unstable world across the Atlantic.

The figurative image of the heroic young man and woman apeared in Soviet posters and other visual media and was an attempt to find a generalized proletarian role model. Workers on a monumental scale were often used to represent agriculture and industry.

Poster by Klimaschin for USSR Agricultural Exhibition, 1939

Modernism became associated with American democracy in the series of posters Lester Beall designed between 1937 and the early 1940s for the Rural Electrification Administration, part of President Roosevelt's New Deal economic programme. The posters combined black-and-white photography and the colours of the national flag.

"The 16 Olympic Days" was the headline of the August 1936 edition of *Berliner Illustrirte Zeitung* (above). Hitler's propaganda department commissioned the leading German poster designer Ludwig Hohlwein to design publicity material for major events such as the Olympic Games of that year, held in Berlin. His idealized figurative style emphasized the mythical Aryan nature of the German people.

93

The "Exhibition of the Fascist Revolution", held in Rome in 1932 to mark the tenth anniversary of the coming to power of Italy's Fascist Party, contained installations designed by the Futurists Mario Sironi and Enrico Prampolini. Sironi also designed the catalogue (left).

MID-CENTURY MODERN

MID-CENTURY MODERN

Towards the middle of the twentieth century modern graphic design went through significant changes of scene, largely brought about by the migration of key designers. After 1933 it became increasingly difficult for graphic designers in Germany, until then a centre for the industry, to practise unless they conformed to National Socialist policy. With modernism officially banned, designers were dismissed or ridiculed as degenerate, Bolshevik or "Jewish". Like other citizens, many were forced to emigrate. Some were unable to work publicly at all and others were persecuted, imprisoned or murdered in the Holocaust.

Switzerland became an important focus for graphic designers from many countries, including its own and German émigrés. Many were based in Zurich and Basle, cities with important design schools and home to major publishers and printers. The trilingual nature of the country made it a significant base for graphic design in the years to follow; much graphic design journalism came from there, most notably *Graphis* (1944–) and *Neue Graphik* (1955–65). Milan, an Italian city looking north for its design inspiration, was also receptive to modernism and provides another link between the interwar and post-war years. Graphic design flourished there in conjunction with Italy's highly regarded architectural and furniture design traditions.

But the real fulfilment of "Mid-Century Modern" came in the United States. It was here that the characteristic combination of design professionalism, business pragmatism and aesthetic idealism emerged into a broadly distinctive style, often referred to as the New York style.

The success of the new graphic design was largely a result of its promotion through art direction. This provided a receptive context for graphic designers to contribute work for book and magazine covers, advertisements and large corporate identities. Designers arriving from Europe, such as Herbert Matter and Leo Lionni, adapted to these new circumstances, while Saul Bass, Paul Rand, Cipe Pineles, Lester Beall and Ivan Chermayeff, brought up during the experimental years of graphic design and now second-generation modernists, found themselves moving with ease into an established profession.

New York was home to concept-driven graphics, which came in particular from American advertising. A clean visual style, associated with Europe, was combined with the quick wit and humour of advertising copy. Acclaimed campaigns included those for the Container Corporation of America, the furniture companies Hermann Miller and Knoll Associates, and the Italian office equipment company Olivetti.

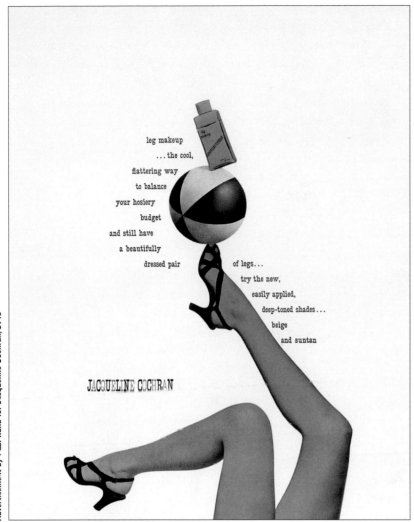

This characteristically witty and confident design marks the transfer in the mid-century of modern European graphic design to the United States. The style is epitomized in the work of Paul Rand. Hallmarks include the distinctive use of white space, clever copyline, coordination of type and image in a single idea and the incorporation of the trademark as an essential part of the design.

The most influential book from this time was Paul Rand's *Thoughts on Design* of 1947. Rand, already enjoying a prodigious career as a young graphic designer and art director, elevated the designer's role to that of "art". He stressed links between design and art, and suggested that they share a visual language, so that the colour theories and compositional ideas of, for example, Klee, Kandinsky, Arp, Picasso and Matisse could be taken into graphic design. Ironically, given that American graphic design was a specialized industry with a greater division of labour than its European counterpart at the time, Rand's argument depended on an individualistic interpretation of the designer as author. It attributed greater cultural meaning and status to graphic design.

In this transatlantic transfer the Museum of Modern Art, New York (MOMA) played an important role by recognizing European graphic design and increasing its cultural legitimacy. The first exhibition from its graphic design collections, in 1936, was the work of Cassandre, a supreme example of French poster design. This was followed in 1937 E. McKnight Kauffer, who, although originally American, had developed his mature style in France and then Britain. Other exhibitions at MOMA included "European Commercial Printing of Today" (1935), "The History of the Modern Poster" (1940) "Recent Acquisitions: Soviet Posters" (1943) and "Swiss Posters" (1951).

In Britain World War II created a space for a generation of designers who, informed by modernism, used the opportunity to reach a wider audience than peacetime would have provided. In Europe Mid-Century Modern was largely defined by Swiss typography. By contrast with the concentration on publication and advertising design in the United States, systems design, the grid and a rationalist approach prevailed, as in the work of Max Bill and Joseph Müller-Brockmann. Enthusiasm for sans-serif typefaces was at its height. Two of the most significant, both designed in 1957, were Helvetica, created by Max Miedinger and Edouard Hoffmann for Switzerland's Hass foundry, and Univers, a family of 21 faces by the Swiss typographer Adrien Frutiger.

As graphic design became a worldwide phenomenon and branches of international advertising agencies were set up in many cities, an increased exchange between the United States, Europe and Japan was made possible through the growth of international travel. Japan based its professional organizations on the Western model. The Alliance Graphique Internationale (AGI) was founded in 1951 by a group of Swiss and French designers in Paris, becoming a worldwide group who meet annually and organize exhibitions. A further fruit of internationalization, ICOGRADA (International Council of Graphic Design Associations), was formed in 1963 to represent over 50 design associations and promote international standardization.

The reputation of Hermann Zapf in twentieth-century graphic design is that of an enlightened traditionalist, interested in working with the historical foundations of typography but also ready to adapt designs for use with new technologies. He has proved to be one of typography's most lucid practitioners.

Born in Nuremberg, Zapf was self-taught as a designer. By studying the works of the German calligrapher and typographer Rudolf Koch, particularly the book *Das Schreiben als Kunstfertigkeit* (The Craft of Writing), and Edward Johnston's *Writing and Illuminating, and Lettering* (in German translation), he learned the principles of letter proportion and the discipline of attention to every detail required for harmonious composition.

In 1938 Zapf entered Paul Koch's printing house in Frankfurt and then became a freelance designer. His major work began in the late 1940s, when he started work for type foundries on new type designs. He is the designer of many typefaces, including Palatino (1950), Melior (1952), Optima (1958), ITC Zapf International (1977) and ITC Zapf Chancery (1979). One of his most acknowledged type designs is Palatino, named after the Italian writing master of the sixteenth century. A roman typeface, based on Renaissance forms, it has an open, graceful conception which was well received as being both contemporary and acknowledging tradition. By contrast, Optima, a sans-serif in thick and thin versions, has been called "one of the most original type designs of the second half of the twentieth century".

Zapf is also a book designer of considerable standing. Many of his projects are self-originated and extend his commitment to the understanding of the history of typography and calligraphy, which he believes are among the most expressive art forms of their time. For example, Zapf published *Manuale Typographicum* in two editions in 1954 and 1970, each consisting of 100 pages, designed with historical and contemporary quotations and printing in sixteen languages. To mark its sixtieth anniversary in 1987, the Society of Typographic Arts in Chicago published *Hermann Zapf and his Design Philosophy*. This elegant selection of Zapf's designs, accompanied by articles and lectures on calligraphy and type design, serves to indicate his great significance for the international world of typography.

In terms of smaller projects, Zapf has designed many colophons and trademarks which continue the tradition of Rudolf Koch's *The Book of Signs* and refer to medieval guild signs.

Other areas of Zapf's career are a long and impressive series of teaching positions in Germany and the United States, and work as an adviser to international type foundries. He was type director of the Stempel AG foundry in Frankfurt am Main (1947–56) and, in New York, of Mergenthaler Linotype (1957–74) and Design Processing International (1977–86), and is now chairman of Zapf, Burns and Co. in New York.

⊕ 1918–
⊕ Highly respected typographer, designer and art director
⊕ Adopted enlightened traditionalist approach, combining historical knowledge with grasp of new technology
⊕ Designed Palatino, Melior, Optima, Zapf and other typefaces

Palatino, originally worked up under the name Medici, was recognized as an elegant typeface and used widely. At a time when modernism was the dominant style, Zapf's work represented continuity with typographic tradition.

Drawing for Palatino typeface, 1935

Zapf executed these designs for German, British and American companies and institutions. A master of elegant compression, he met a client's need for an immediately identifiable symbol while giving nuanced, hand-drawn character to the design.

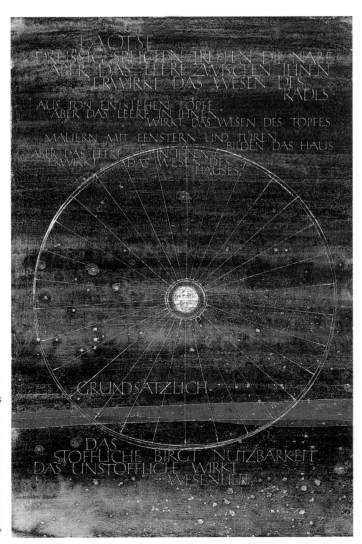

In the ambitious project to illustrate Lao-Tse's *Tao-Te Ching* (The Book of Changes), Zapf used the sgraffito technique, inscribing the lettering and images. This page from the book shows the influence of the British calligrapher and type designer Edward Johnston.

⮕ 1908–94
⮕ Swiss modernist graphic designer
⮕ Studied at Bauhaus
⮕ Pioneer of Swiss typography from 1930s
⮕ Believed in maximum expression with minimum means
⮕ Influential figure at Ulm Hochschule für Gestaltung 1951–6

Although he preferred to see himself as an architect rather than a graphic designer, Max Bill made a crucial contribution to graphic design at a time when his native Switzerland had become the centre for the continuation of experimental, avant-garde ideas. As the rest of Europe was at war, progressive design of German-, French- and Italian-speaking cultures came together in this neutral country, encouraged through patronage, exhibitions and publications, and developed the existing strengths of Swiss design education.

After training as a silversmith at Zurich's Arts and Crafts School, Bill studied at the Bauhaus (see pp60–3) in 1927–8 and, an admirer of Le Corbusier, he sympathized with its main aim to prepare all designers as architects. He also firmly believed that design could be used to enhance socially responsible life.

Bill's first notable designs were made on his return to Zurich in 1929, when he established bill reklame zurich, a graphic design agency. He took on work for the designs of publications for avant-garde architects associated with the Swiss Werkbund, catalogues for the furniture company Wohnbedarf, and cultural posters for various museums. Bill's approach was characterized by the use of single-case typefaces, which he saw as the "concrete element" in his designs. To posters he brought a refined sense of abstract proportion, often using organic sources shared with Swiss abstract artists, most notably Hans and Sophie Arp. In his work for publications he applied the more scientific approach of a modular system, which he derived from architecture, to create page layouts.

Along with Theo Ballmer, Karl Gerstner, Max Huber, Emil Ruder and Josef Müller-Brockmann (see pp124–5), Bill was a central figure in defining Swiss typography as the next development in modernist graphic design. Throughout his life he remained an advocate of new typography and he was to exert a strong influence on the following generation of designers.

In 1951 Bill returned to Germany as the first rector of Ulm's Hochschule für Gestaltung, founded by Inge Aicher-Scholl, and stayed until 1956. Ulm was committed to go beyond Bauhaus teaching, and its staff, Tomas Maldonado, Hans Gugelot, Otl Aicher and Herbert Lindinger, approached design as a purist, scientifically oriented discipline. It was here that the term "Visual Communication and Information" was used to replace graphic design, in the belief that contemporary film and televisual media opened up boundaries of definition. The school maintained that visual communication could also incorporate corporate identity and systematic approaches to environmental design, an important part of its interests.

From 1967 to 1974 Bill was professor of environmental design at the Hochschule für Bildende Künste in Hamburg.

Poster for exhibition "Zeitprobleme in der Schweizer Malerei und Plastik", 1936

Like the posters by Jan Tschichold for the Kunsthaus in Basle, this poster advertising the exhibition "Zeitprobleme in der Schweizer Malerei und Plastik" (Problems of Time in Swiss Painting and Sculpture) at Zurich's Kunsthaus shows Max Bill at his most modern and minimal. The design relies on striking contrasts between black and white and the immediacy of single-case type.

Poster for Wohnbedarf, Zurich, 1935

Wohnbedarf was one of the major retailers of modern furniture and lighting in Switzerland. In this poster for the company Bill used an organic shape to unify the various objects rather than the austere geometry previously associated with modernism. This approach heralded the route that graphic design would take, particularly in the United States.

Poster for exhibition "USA Baut", 1945

A few months after the end of World War II, a critical time for international politics and commerce, the Arts and Crafts Museum in Zurich staged an exhibition of modern American architecture, "USA Baut" (The USA Builds), organized by the architectural writer Siegfried Giedion. Using the colours of the American flag, Bill gave the design a dynamic emphasis with a diagonal arrangement of photographs of architecture.

⊕ 1907–84
⊕ Swiss-born designer and photographer
⊕ Used ideas from fine art in graphic design
⊕ Important for his softened modernism
⊕ Designed celebrated travel posters for Swiss National Tourist Office
⊕ Emigrated to United States 1936
⊕ Graphic design consultant for furniture manufacturer Knoll

An important figure in the transmission of ideas from fine art to graphic design, Herbert Matter realized the beneficial influence that photomontage could have on poster design and advertising design. He moved between circles of artists, architects and designers, contributing important designs, first in Europe and later in his adopted home of the United States.

Matter was born in the Swiss mountain resort of Engelberg. After training as a painter at the École des Beaux Arts in Geneva he moved to Paris to study at the Académie Moderne in 1928–9. Here the artists Fernand Léger and Amédée Ozenfant introduced Matter to the ideas of Purism. A variant of Cubism, this artistic movement revealed to him the abstract properties of everyday objects, something he applied when he assisted A.M. Cassandre (see pp50–53) with poster designs. For a short while Matter was also publicity manager for the Parisian type foundry Deberny Peignot, publishers of France's most important graphic design journal, *Arts et Métiers Graphiques*.

On returning to Switzerland in 1931 Matter continued his connection with printers, working on publicity material for Gebrüder Fretz of Zurich in which he combined Constructivist and Surrealist ideas. However, his most significant work there was a series of large-format posters for the national tourist office. These were printed by gravure, which gave them the same quality as that of illustrated magazines. Many of the posters depict large, smiling, positive faces, photomontaged against images of the contours of mountains and skiers. Others in the series stressed scale and space with their striking vanishing points.

In 1936 Matter moved to New York, becoming part of an international group of art directors and designers and working as a photographer for *Harper's Bazaar* and *Vogue* magazines. From 1946 he was graphic design consultant for Knoll, a leading manufacturer of modern furniture established by Hans and

Florence Knoll, a position he would hold for 20 years. Matter's appointment coincided with the flourishing of a second generation of American modernist designers, among them Charles and Ray Eames, George Nelson, Eliot Noyes, Harry Bertoia and Eliel Saarinen. Initially associated with the important exhibition "Organic Design in Home Furnishing" held at the Museum of Modern Art, New York in 1940, they developed designs with free-form lines, taking advantage of bent plywood, fibreglass and plastics. Matter's contribution was to find a graphic equivalent to this important shift in three-dimensional design. His solution stressed organic, biomorphic forms and employed sparse type and photography of objects.

Between 1958 and 1968 Matter was design consultant for the Guggenheim Museum in New York and the Museum of Fine Arts in Houston, Texas. He was also Professor of Photography at Yale University from 1952 to 1976.

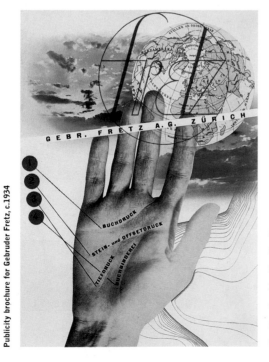

Publicity brochure for Gebruder Fretz, c.1934

Matter used the Constructivist graphic device of a self-reflexive hand in this design for the Zurich printer Gebrüder Fretz. He was interested in map contours, and here the lines extend into the palm of the hand.

In 1936 the Swiss National Tourist Office published a series of posters to promote international tourism. To each of the designs, which used his photographs, Matter added his hand-drawn lettering in English and the three main languages of Switzerland: French, German and Italian.

Poster, "All Roads Lead to Switzerland", 1936

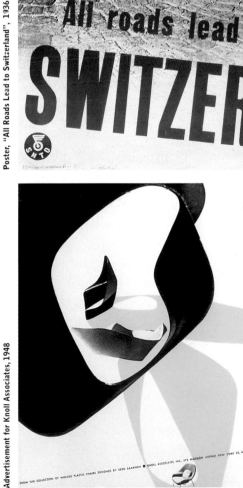

Advertisement for Knoll Associates, 1948

In this publicity material for the American furniture company Knoll, Matter interpreted three-dimensional organic form through a play on negative and positive two-dimensional forms. The design recalls the mobiles and stabiles of his friend the sculptor Alexander Calder, for whom he made a colour film in the same year that he designed this advertisement.

103

Poster for film *Anatomy of a Murder*, 1959

Simplified colour bands recall contemporary American abstract painting. Another innovative feature of this design was the silhouette of the corpse with the film's title cut into it.

Exodus told a version of the story of the birth of Israel. The striking motif shows the title engulfed in flames below arms struggling for a rifle.

Poster for film *Exodus*, 1960

➔ 1920–96
➔ Studied graphic design in New York
➔ Moved to Los Angeles 1950 and founded Saul Bass Associates
➔ Worked with Otto Preminger and Alfred Hitchcock on influential film title sequences

Saul Bass extended the boundaries of graphic design in the mid-twentieth century by devising a new approach to the packaging and marketing of films. In discovering parallels between the visual identity of film and other industrial products, he permanently changed the character of promotion, while also giving the films he worked on a strong and memorable form.

Born in New York, Bass studied at the Art Students League and then at Brooklyn College in 1944–5. Among his teachers was the Hungarian graphic designer Gyorgy Kepes, a colleague of Moholy-Nagy (see pp64–5) from the days of the New Bauhaus in Chicago (see pp60–3). Kepes was interested in filmic sequence in design, and investigated colour and light as a continuation of

Bauhaus ideas. His *The Language of Vision* (1944) was one of the most serious analyses of graphic design of its day and an important text for Bass's generation of students.

After graduating Bass became a freelance designer in New York, then in 1950 moved to Los Angeles, where he formed the design group Saul Bass Associates (Bass Yager Associates from 1981). An important part of his work was corporate-identity programmes, and among his clients were AT&T, Quaker Oats, United Airlines, Minolta and Warner Communications. His skill was in finding elegant, robust and immediate symbols, often distinctive pictographs, which distilled complex meaning – an approach he would later take to designing for film.

Los Angeles offered many opportunities to engage with Hollywood directors and Bass worked for Otto Preminger and Alfred Hitchcock, art-directing the

FRANK SINATRA · ELEANOR PARKER · KIM NOVAK

THE MAN WITH THE GOLDEN ARM

A FILM BY OTTO PREMINGER

With Arnold Stang, Darren McGavin, Robert Strauss, John Conte, Doro Merande, George E. Stone, George Mathews, Leonid Kinskey, Emile Meyer, Shorty Rogers, Shelly Manne. Screenplay by Walter Newman & Lewis Meltzer. From the novel by Nelson Algren. Music by Elmer Bernstein. Produced & Directed by Otto Preminger. Released by United Artists.

Poster for film *The Man with the Golden Arm*, 1955

This was Bass's earliest film poster to use torn paper, here mixed with action shots of the stars. The jagged arm, used on a range of posters and press advertisements, became a powerful visual symbol for the film.

notorious shower sequence in Hitchcock's *Psycho* (1960), for example. In the early 1950s film publicity was usually based around the celebrity of the actors. Bass instead developed a graphic language which brought together modern design, music and film. One distinctive feature was the reduction of graphic elements to a minimum, as with the simple paper cut-outs used in *The Man with the Golden Arm* (1955) and *Anatomy of a Murder* (1959).

The first of these, Preminger's film about a drug-addicted poker dealer, was marked by a strikingly new identity. The title sequence, an exercise in syncopation, gave the film a cool, modern and distinctly edgy feel. On its opening, slab-like white bars appear, accompanied by a shrill jazz score. Gradually the typography enters, giving the names of the cast and the film's title, before the white bars take the shape of a jagged arm with a

contorted hand and the director's credit appears. Bass's animated publicity graphics were drawn on for all other stages of the film's promotion.

For another Preminger film, *Exodus* (1960), a similarly striking motif was found. It worked like a trademark for the poster, newspaper advertisements and the stationery used in the film's production. A group of hands, reaching upwards for a rifle, symbolized the struggle of the new country of Israel. In the title sequence the word "Exodus" is dramatically engulfed by flames of burning paper.

Bass made his own films in the 1960s with his second wife, Elaine Bass (née Makatura), and their experimental documentary *Why Man Creates* won an Oscar in 1969. Inducted into the New York Art Directors Club Hall of Fame in 1977, he was also awarded a Gold Medal by the American Institute of Graphic Arts.

Poster for exhibition "The Graphic Art of Paul Rand", 1970

For the poster of an exhibition of his own work, Rand took the idea of a hand with the spinning top – a perceptive metaphor for the artful balance and harmony of his designs.

Magazine advertisement for Coronet brandy, 1945

In one of his first advertising campaigns Rand developed a set of variations on the theme of the waiter, whom he personified as the Coronet Brandy Man, with a head shaped like a brandy glass.

106

⊖ 1914–96
⊖ Master of modern American graphic design
⊖ Second-generation modernist who introduced modern art to corporate identity
⊖ Specialized in design of logos and trademarks

Paul Rand has been called a designer of lyrical beauty, and his work has been identified as possessing "an explicit straightness" – urbane, stylish and with a bright and witty humour. Of all American designers of the mid-twentieth century, it was Rand who epitomized the optimism of good design and believed that the world could be improved by what he called "the designer's art". He was a key figure in the reception of modernism in American design.

Rand studied at the Pratt Institute (1929–32), Parsons School of Design (1932–3) and Art Students League (1933–4), where his tutor was the former German Dadaist George Grosz. A gifted and talented young designer, Rand had been appointed art director of

Esquire and Apparel Arts magazines by the age of 23, and from 1938 to 1945 he held that post on Direction.

He was one of the first American graphic designers to publish his approach to graphic design, in the extremely influential Thoughts on Design, published in 1947. In this he established key concerns which would recur in his life and work, and he elaborated on these in the subsequent books A Designer's Art (1985) and Design, Form, and Chaos (1985). A guiding principle for Rand was that "The designer experiences, perceives, analyzes, organizes, symbolizes, and synthesizes".

Concerned to distance himself from the extremes of 1920s functionalist design, Rand suggested that "Visual communication of any kind ... should be seen as the embodiment of form and function: the integration of the beautiful and the useful."

Rapport Annuel
Westinghouse
1971

Devised in 1960, Rand's logo for the large American electrical company Westinghouse evoked electrical circuitry. Rand retained responsibility for the design of the cover of the annual report over the years.

Rand extended his work from art direction, designing many stunning posters and devising a remarkable series of corporate identities. Rather than looking to a strict lineage of graphic design, he was inspired by fine art, drawing on the ideas of colour, texture and collage in the work of modern painters such as Arp, Matisse, Klee and Kandinsky. To their influence was added a sure sense of the precise place of geometry and form. If all this was European in origin, the "American" element in Rand's design came in the crispness of his graphic conceit and his understanding of the importance of the word or copyline, learned from an association with Bill Bernbach of the Doyle, Dane and Bernbach agency.

This approach was evident in a series of remarkable trademarks that Rand designed for major corporations and organizations. He employed the rebus to powerful effect, as in the AIGA (American Institution of Graphic Arts) symbol, where the "I" doubled as the symbol of the eye. For the Westinghouse Corporation, he designed a logomark which dissected the letterform to resemble components of electric circuitry.

Rand also made use of graphic motifs as mnemonic devices. Stripes, originally taken from the horizontal lines used to prevent counterfeiting of legal documents, were applied to the corporate identity for IBM, which Rand worked on from 1956. Eventually stripes became a metaphor for computers through which the public could remember the company, to the extent that in some versions the letters "IBM" do not appear. Pop Art was another reference in the identity that Rand created for NeXT Company. This adapted a sculpture by Robert Indiana that broke the form of the word "LOVE".

Poster for Art Directors Club of New York, 1988

Modern art had taught Rand the power of negative and positive space and the arrangement of cut-out forms of colour. These elements are evident in his poster for the Third International Exhibition of the Art Directors Club.

The sign of
the NeXT generation
of computers...
for Education

Poster for NeXT computers, 1986

The logo for the new educational computer company NeXT resembled a child's building block while also making reference to the "black box" of computer technology.

Logo for Gentry Living Color, 1993

Rand commented that "a logo is more important than a painting in a certain sense because a zillion people see the logo and it affects what they do".

In 1960 Rand wrote one of the definitive summaries of how trademarks work:

"A trademark is a picture.

It is a symbol, a sign, an emblem, an escutcheon, an image.

A symbol of a corporation, a sign of the quality, blend form and content.

Trademarks are animate, inanimate, organic, geometric.

They are letters, ideograms, monograms, colours, things.

They indicate not represent but suggest and are stated with brevity and wit."

Reinforcing his role as a mentor for successive generations of students of graphic design, Rand taught at the Yale University School of Art from 1956, a position he did not relinquish until the age of 70. Even after leaving full-time teaching, however, he continued to participate in the summer programme offered by the school in Brissago, Switzerland.

Towards the end of his long career Rand continued to assert that the principal role of the designer remained the search for beauty. Increasingly he found himself at odds with the new generation of graphic designers who were interested in deconstructivist typography or in design as discourse. As a result he wrote in 1992: "Today the emphasis of style over content in much of what is alleged to be graphic design and communication is, at best, puzzling. Order out of chaos is not the order of the day."

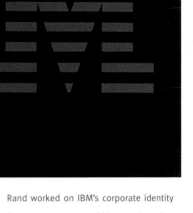

Rand worked on IBM's corporate identity for many years. One of his most ingenious logos for the business-machinery giant is based on visual representations of "eye" and "bee", combined with the "M" of the already familiar three-letter logo. IBM is said to have been initially reserved about the potential subversion of its identity through such graphic playfulness.

Paul

Rand

Art

Directors

Club

of

Cincinnati

Art

Museum

May

17

1994

7-8

pm

109

For this invitation, Rand adapted a design originally used in the book illustration "I Know a Lot of Things" (1956), in which the letters take the place of a human form.

Cover for magazine *Seventeen*, July 1949

Cover for magazine *Charm*, January 1954

The graphic rendition of the photograph for *Seventeen* (far left) stresses the visual equivalence between the striped umbrella and the typography of the magazine's masthead. Pineles also played with the idea of the reflected typography and subtle changes in the model's expression.

The theme of this issue of *Charm* (left) stemmed from the experience of Pineles and her fellow editors. The cover is based on the contrast between black and white and the use of running text as a backdrop.

110

⊕ 1908–91
⊕ Pioneer female art director in United States
⊕ Studied at Pratt Institute, New York
⊕ Specialized in modern women's magazines
⊕ Design consultant at Lincoln Center, New York

Cipe Pineles was the first independent American woman art director, and, thanks to recent feminist scholarship, she now occupies a much-deserved place in the history of twentieth-century graphic design.

Born of Jewish parents in Vienna, she spent her childhood at the family home in Gliniany, Poland. In 1923 the family emigrated to New York, where Cipe studied commercial art at the Pratt Institute from 1926 to 1929. Her first design job was for the association of European and American designers, Contempora Ltd, whose multi-disciplinary approach encouraged her to take on textile design, through which she became familiar with the field of women's fashion.

On joining the magazine publisher Condé Nast in 1932 Pineles found herself the only woman working in the design department led by the legendary art director Dr Mohamed F. Agha. Devoted to constant experimentation, Agha encouraged Pineles to apply this approach to the design of *Vogue*, *Vanity Fair* and *House and Garden*.

Her first full appointment as an art director was for *Glamour*, for five years from 1942. This was a fashion magazine which she regarded as miscast: an attempt to interpret Hollywood styles for a wider readership than the elite magazines of the time.

By the time she left *Glamour*, Pineles's career was thoroughly established and she was made art director at *Seventeen* by Helen Valentine, the magazine's influential editor. Valentine, Pineles and the production editor, Estelle Ellis, formed an influential team who recognized the importance of offering creative journalism in an unpatronizing manner to their young female readers.

smooth office
routine: the
jersey dress

Latest office décor: the jumper dress underlined
with a white linen shirt, banded below the waist,
and released in pleats. Coverage for the new silhouette, a matching hiplength cardigan jacket with
cropped ¾ sleeves. By Mr. Sidney for Re-Go. Heller's
Pride of Acrilan jersey. Red or black. 7 to 15.
About $60.
For pin, see listing on page 246.
THE TYPE FACE: IBM'S "MODERN"

Assembler etc. Waghin, New York
Henri Marin, Inc., Cincinnati
The Wm. H. Block Co., Indianapolis
Dunham's, Chicago
Gus Mayer, New Orleans
The Fashion, Beaumont
Battlestein's, Inc., Houston

The print's knitted in! A sequence of bold argyle
diamonds on a jewel-neck sheath, its relaxed line
nipped in with a leather and chain belt. By Westover,
Atlee Fabrics wool jersey. Blue and green, red and
purple, or brown and blue. 10 to 20. About $18.
THE KEYBOARD BY REMINGTON RAND*

Dress at, Arnold Constable, New York
L. S. Ayres, Inc., Buffalo
Stickelwig's, Providence
The Hecht Co., Baltimore and Washington, D.C.
L. S. Ayres & Company, Indianapolis
Carson Pirie Scott & Co., Chicago
Sakowitz, Houston
Bullock's Downtown, Los Angeles
Lipman Wolfe & Co., Portland, Ore.
The Bon Marche, Seattle

*For more information, see page 243.

Spread from magazine *Charm*, September 1957

This spread comes from the series
Pineles developed entitled "Women at
Work". The style of fashion photography
– this picture is by Carmen Schiavone –
emphasizes active women, while
Pineles's layouts made imaginative use
of references to the work environment.

111

Having introduced a visual style for a teenage
magazine, Pineles moved on to art-direct *Charm*, which
was aimed at working women. She drew on her personal
experience as a woman to interpret the subjects of many
of the articles she designed, and it was this that made
her work so distinctive. At *Charm* she devised new ways
of presenting well-established subjects – food, for
example – in a witty, light-hearted but stylish manner.

When designing illustrated fiction Pineles preferred a
traditional and quiet style, allowing well-defined space
for images. Through her considerable contacts she was
always keen to commission painters – including Ben
Shahn, Richard Lindner, Jan Balet and Lucille Corcos –
to contribute illustrations to her magazines, and she
sometimes encouraged them to cross the hierarchical
boundaries which separated fine art from commercial art.

In lead articles such as the "Women at Work" series,
where the lives of women working in 19 American cities
were reviewed, Pineles's approach to the dynamics of
the page and her combinations of photography, headline
and type interpreted what the cities offered women by
way of fashion, design, general culture and industry.

After her resignation from *Charm* and the death of
her husband, the art director William Golden, both in
1959, Pineles taught publication design at Parsons
School of Design, New York, where she worked on
several in-house publication projects. She also continued
to freelance as an illustrator and art editor.

In 1965 Pineles was appointed design consultant to
the city's Lincoln Center for the Arts – a prestigious role
in which her responsibilites included the design of
posters, programmes and an overall graphic identity.

Spread from brochure for Mite Corporation, 1964

The overlay of type and image, and the striking contrast of scale between titles and text, were hallmarks of Lester Beall's later design style. This brochure for a technological client, the Mite Corporation, shows skilled use of both elements.

Cover for magazine *Scope*, 1948

When Beall became art director of *Scope*, the house magazine of Upjohn Pharmaceutical, in 1944, he introduced a level of visual sophistication informed by the work of modern American and European artists and designers.

112

→ 1903–69
→ Important American modernist designer
→ Studied art history
→ Renowned for art direction of magazines, government posters and, later in career, design of corporate identities

Lester Beall was one of the first American graphic designers to incorporate European modernist ideas into his work. He moved seamlessly from posters to packaging to corporate identity, adapting avant-garde ideas to American corporate culture.

Having earlier taken classes at Chicago's Art Institute, Beall studied Art History at the University of Chicago from 1922 to 1926. In 1927 he set up a studio in the city and worked as a freelance designer and illustrator. Through publications such as the French journals *Arts et Métiers Graphiques* and *Cahiers d'Art*, he taught himself about graphic design, being drawn particularly to photomontage and montage in the works of El Lissitzky (see pp56–7), László Moholy-Nagy (see pp64–5), Jan Tschichold (see pp68–9), Piet Zwart and Man Ray. Beall

was struck by photographs taken from odd angles, photographic views from the air or below, close-ups, photograms and abstract images. His response was to equip himself with a lightweight Leica camera and to introduce photography as a serious part of his work.

In 1933 Beall designed a mural at the international exhibition "Chicago Century of Progress". About this time he also opened a design office with Fred Hauck, and among their commissions were a series of full-page press advertisements for the *Chicago Tribune* and work for the Lakeside Press and the Marshall Fields department store. He moved to New York in 1935 and became part of the modernist milieu of advertising and art direction around Agha (see p110) and Brodovitch (see pp78–9).

Some of Beall's most successful designs were the posters he produced for America's Rural Electrification

A Better Home

In three series of posters designed between 1937 and the early 1940s for the Rural Electrification Administration, Beall integrated photography and variations on the theme of the American flag. The client was a US federal project which aimed to improve the standard of living of the nation's rural population.

Poster for Rural Electrification Administration, "A Better Home", 1941

RURAL ELECTRIFICATION ADMINISTRATION
U. S. Department of Agriculture

113

Administration. Under President Roosevelt's New Deal a concerted effort was being made to introduce electricity to rural parts of the country not yet connected. The first of the three series of posters, dating from 1937, displayed a totally graphic treatment. The second series, of 1939, depicted montaged photographs of consumers, with slogans outlining the benefits as they saw them. The posters were intended to have immediate appeal and to be understood by people with limited reading skills. In this way they echoed the Soviet Constructivist posters of the 1920s by Klutsis and others (see pp74–7) in purpose as well as style.

Made from 1940, the third series consisted of photomontages with strong red, blue and white stripes and dots representing the labour force of the United States. By this time World War II had started and the posters conveyed the idea of ordinary citizens at work, using the benefits of electricity as a power source. The series' striking colour scheme inevitably contributed to its identity as popular, democratic images of a people collectively engaged in a national project.

Later in his career, working from a small studio at his home in Connecticut, Beall turned increasingly to overseeing work on the corporate identity of companies. At the time this was a relatively new application of graphic design and for most of his clients it involved no more than creating an apparently simple and coherent visual identity through trademark, choice of typography and colour. Beall saw creating a corporate identity as an extension of packaging design, and in his systematic approach to the task he continued to refine the visual language of modernism that emerged in the 1920s.

LEO LIONNI

➲ 1910–99
➲ European graphic
designer and illustrator
who emigrated to
United States 1939
➲ Early in career
worked in advertising
➲ Art director of
Fortune 1949–61
➲ Significant role in
development of "New
York style" in 1950s
➲ Wrote and designed
many children's books
➲ Returned to Italy
1961 to concentrate on
painting and sculpture

Leo Lionni's life reflects the uprootedness of many mid-twentieth century Europeans who settled in a number of places before establishing a professional or creative life. He was an important conduit at a time when an alliance was being forged between European graphic design, with its cultural and philosophical roots, and the progressive pragmatism of American business, which was seeking a sophisticated aesthetic identity.

Born in Amsterdam to a half-Jewish Italian family, Lionni studied economics in Genoa and Zurich before moving to his preferred field of art and design. He first became a commercial designer in Milan, working for the food company Motta as an art director between 1933 and 1935. Mussolini's threats to Jews made it necessary for Lionni to emigrate to the United States in 1939, and he settled in Philadelphia. After finding work with the advertising agency N.W. Ayer & Co. he was soon at the heart of American modernist design. One of his first commissions was to design press advertisements for the Container Corporation of America (CCA), which was already associated with modernism through employing designers such as Moholy-Nagy (see pp64–5), Bayer (see pp66–7) and Matter (see pp102–3). For this client Lionni made a series of photomontages which revealed his indebtedness to the Bauhaus (see pp60–3).

In 1949 Lionni succeeded Will Burtin as art director of *Fortune* magazine, and moved to New York. His 12-year stay saw the magazine change in line with a general softening of modernism in America. Often referred to as organic or biomorphic modernism, the style was less austere and avoided the pure geometry and primary colours of the 1920s. A self-confessed "anti-grid" man, Lionni recognized the importance of variety in arranging a magazine. Working with journalists, illustrators and photographers was one of his strengths and he applied the model of cinematography to magazine design, arriving at sequences of pages based on contrasts of scale, density and colour.

His familiarity with Italian design made Lionni an ideal choice as American art director for Olivetti. Between 1950 and 1957 he took on responsibility for the firm's corporate identity and design of showrooms with a sophisticated understatement and apparent informality.

Showroom by Lionni and architect Giorgio Cavaglieiri for Olivetti, 1956

In addition to producing posters for Olivetti's Lettera 22 portable typewriter, Lionni oversaw the interior design of showrooms for the company. Interiors such as this one in Chicago display the elegance that is associated with Italian design of the period.

Lionni's work is often characterized by its inspired sense of colour. He became a friend of Josef and Anni Albers, formerly teachers at the Bauhaus, and encountered their ideas on colour. Another friend was the sculptor Alexander Calder, whose work offered new ways of thinking about colour relations. The fruits of colour theory can be seen in Lionni's design for the poster and catalogue for "The Family of Man", a major exhibition of international photography held at the Museum of Modern Art, New York, in 1955. Other designs from this period included covers for *Print* magazine, which Lionni co-edited between 1955 and 1959.

After writing and illustrating his first children's book, *Little Blue and Little Yellow* (1959), Lionni went on to publish 30 more. In 1961 he settled in Italy, his "home", where he established a studio to pursue painting and sculpture.

Cover for book *Little Blue and Little Yellow*, 1959

An impromptu game Lionni devised for his grandchildren inspired the first of his 30 books for children. He wrote and illustrated this book, published by Ivan Obolensky Inc. of New York, to encourage exploration of colour.

Cover for magazine *Fortune*, February 1960

Lionni was art director of the prestigious American business magazine *Fortune* throughout the 1950s and into the 1960s. As well as commissioning graphic designers associated with the current "New York style" of graphic design, he created many covers himself. Here a black background makes the colours of the repeated words "New York" stand out in a way that is reminiscent of the city's grid-like structure.

115

Poster for Bally, 1974

The impact of this design is made through the striking use of white on a dark background and the semi-abstraction of the figure. The Swiss shoe company Bally had been acclaimed for its high-profile poster designs since the 1920s.

Poster for Orangina Light, 1970

To advertise a variant of the popular French drink Orangina, Villemot used his design to elaborate on the product's character. The word "light" and the play of form between the silhouette of the bottle and the line of the model's body enhance the message.

116

In the 1950s, while much of the Anglo-Saxon world turned to a form of graphic design in which word and image were coordinated by order and standardization, French graphic design took a different path. Its reputation depended on the tradition of the *affichiste* – the autonomous designer recognized by a signature style, mostly evident in poster designs. Likewise, Bernard Villemot, rather than stress the typographic roots of graphic design, continued to align the modern advertising poster firmly to painting, in which France had long claimed pre-eminence.

Villemot studied painting at the Académie Julian in Paris, and then was an assistant to Paul Colin, who introduced him to the principles of modernist poster design and the immediacy of working on a large scale. Like his contemporaries the well-known poster designers Raymond Savignac and André François, who had been assistants to A.M. Cassandre (see pp50–3), Villemot thus learned his profession from an older master.

The designer of more than 500 posters, Villemot believed that a perfect poster should be readable in a fraction of a second. He commented on this need for directness in an address to the Art Directors Club of New York in 1954, stating: "On the technical plane the poster must aim at the suggestive force and simplicity of the road sign. On the designing plane it must aim at Art, not forgetting Toulouse-Lautrec and Picasso."

In the immediate post-war years this approach was tested in works for charities and governmental bodies. Then, during the reconstruction of French industry and

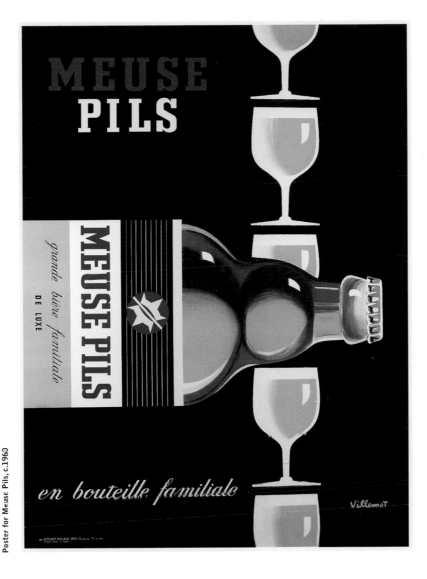

Poster for Meuse Pils, c.1960

At a time when photographic advertising had become the norm, Villemot was still being commissioned to produce posters for major clients, such as this producer of beer. The design is a well-planned exercise in repetition, controlled colour and simplification of form.

commerce in the 1950s, Villemot established corporate identities for clients such as Air France, Bally, Gillette, Perrier, Orangina and Bergasol.

The French poster tradition could be considered retrogressive in the context of a fully developing graphic design. Indeed one commentator, François Stahly, wrote in 1955: "As the metropolis of modern painting, Paris has an applied-art climate all of its own, and one in which the technical tendencies of present-day advertising design are not always given adequate scope. Yet whenever a poster artist of the Parisian vintage also has a feeling for effective graphic presentation, his works take on a quality that raises them above mere advertising to the rank of modern murals. This alliance of advertising technique and painting ability is happily exemplified in Villemot."

As well as advertising individual products, Villemot evoked "Frenchness" at home and abroad. At a time when the American model of multinational corporations was making an impact on western Europe, his work associated France and its products with the colours of the Mediterranean, modern art, *haute cuisine* and fashion. His style depended on a strong sense of colour, fluid outlines of the human form and stylized designs in which both the product and its packaging were often incorporated. In preferring painterly lettering to typefaces, he enhanced the informal character of his designs.

In his later life Villemot lamented the dominance of photographic advertising while continuing to produce posters. He was the recipient of several major awards and the subject of exhibitions, including a retrospective at the Bibliothèque Nationale in Paris in 1981.

ABRAM GAMES

● 1914–96
● First-generation British modernist, highly influential as graphic designer
● Largely self-taught
● Important design commissions for British government during World War II
● Posters and identity schemes for high-profile clients in 1950s and 1960s

In the history of graphic design in Britain since 1945, Abram Games holds a reputation for his graphic wit and deceptively simple designs. Many of his compositions reflect his design axiom of "maximum meaning, minimum means".

Games, the son of an artist-photographer, was largely self-taught, his only formal training being part-time evening classes at St Martin's School of Art in London in the early 1930s. After this, as an apprentice lettering artist, he gained a familiarity with the work of what was still called at that time "commercial art". Games later established himself as a freelance designer in London, where his first commissions were from those keen to improve the standard of English advertising and publicity, among them Frank Pick of London Transport, Sir Stephen Tallents at the Post Office and Jack Beddington of Shell. His signature and distinctive style on poster hoardings brought Games recognition throughout Britain.

The outbreak of World War II might have proved an unwelcome interruption to his design activities but for the fact that during wartime the best British designers were selected to work on government commissions. Called up in June 1940, Games became an official War Office poster artist, designing over 100 posters for the Army, the work for which he is best known nowadays. One of the most celebrated designs, "Your Talk May Kill Your Comrades", depicts three identical soldiers bayoneted by a spiral of "speech" which emanates from the central figure's mouth. Aware of the photomontages of contemporary modernist designers such as McKnight Kauffer (see pp46–7) and Moholy-Nagy (see pp64–5), Games adapted their more abstract properties in order to establish a clear narrative with a single message.

Games's career became firmly consolidated in the 1950s, when he worked for high-profile companies in the fields of newspapers, brewing, tourism and transport, including air travel. His output included a wide variety of posters.

He also devised identity schemes, which he called "emblems", including the logos for the Festival of Britain of 1951 and for the BBC in 1952. Many of the designs depict anthropomorphic objects, set on a plain colour field. Their impact is that of a gentle humour rather than more provocative shock of Surrealism. In this way Games's work joined a tendency among British designers to soften modernism in the years following the devastation of Europe by Nazism and the war.

Games was an articulate commentator on his approach to design and teaching. In his book *Over My Shoulder* (1960) he explained the key ideas of his visual language. Of Jewish background, Games regularly responded to invitations to work and teach in Israel, and this, along with retrospective exhibitions in many countries throughout the world, helped to place his distinctive modern style in an international context.

The deceptive simplicity of Games's mature style gave campaigns such as this, advertising the leading British daily newspaper *The Times*, a confident and direct authority.

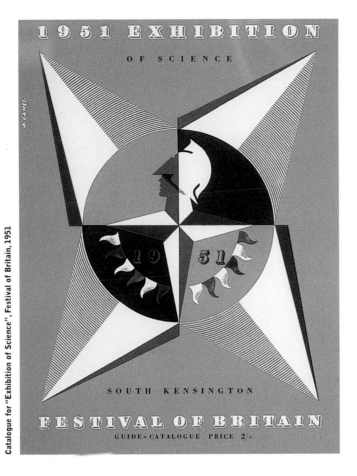

The "Exhibition of Science" was held in South Kensington, London, in 1951 as part of the Festival of Britain. Games had already designed in 1948 the graphic house style for the Festival. The curious blend of tradition and modernity in the cover of this catalogue predicted much of the contents of the exhibition.

119

In this poster for the British government, the face of the soldier appears to be a photograph, but Games created it with an airbrush, a technique in which he was highly proficient.

Poster, "You'll See Murphy Television", from 1948

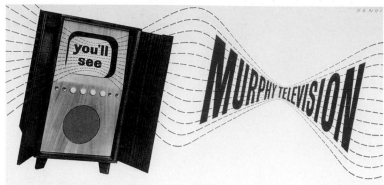

Produced in several variants from 1948, the poster shows a TV set designed by Dick Russell. A common theme was the use of expanding and diminishing type to suggest air waves.

Corpporate identity for KLM, from 1958

This corporate identity logo for KLM (Royal Dutch Airlines) was used on the company's aircraft, stationery and uniforms.

Poster for Philips, 1955

The schematized man in this advertisement for the Philishave electric shaver was developed into an international campaign.

120

➔ 1914–90
➔ Professionalized graphic design from 1940s
➔ Founded pioneering Studio H 1948 (later Henrion Design Associates)
➔ Important advertising commissions and corporate identities

F.H.K. Henrion was one of the pioneers of house style and corporate identity for industrial companies and services. His design practice, based around his consultancy, was a major influence on the professionalization of graphic design in Britain that took place after World War II.

Born in Nuremberg in 1914, Henrion studied textile design in Paris in 1933–4 and then trained as a poster and graphic designer in the studio of Paul Colin. As a freelance designer he worked on the Paris Exposition of 1937 and the New York World's Fair of 1939. This interest in exhibition design continued throughout his career, and he designed the Countryside and Agriculture pavilions at the Festival of Britain in 1951, and the British pavilion at Expo '67 in Montreal.

During World War II Henrion was one of a group of designers who introduced modernism to a wider public through poster campaigns. He worked as a consultant designer for Britain's Ministry of Information on health and rationing campaigns and also on cultural projects for the United States Office of War Information.

In 1948 Henrion established Studio H, which later became Henrion Design Associates. Along with the Design Research Unit run by Misha Black and Milner Gray, Studio H was one of the first design consultancies in Britain to be based on the American model of the industrial designer. While a large proportion of the commissions were for graphic projects, the practice also produced designs for a portable sewing machine, a coffee percolator and furniture, as well as designing many exhibitions.

This design was first shown at
Henrion's one-man exhibition at
the Institute of Contemporary Arts
in London, and donated to the
Campaign for Nuclear Disarmament
(CND), which added the caption.

Poster, "Stop Nuclear Suicide", 1960

Like his contemporary Abram Games (see pp118–19), Henrion had a graphic style that can be seen as part of the general softening of modernism in the 1950s. Aware of the potential of montage and simplification, he conveyed a gentle humour in his designs. His clients included many new electrical companies, keen to benefit from the improving post-war economy.

Henrion was Director of Visual Planning for the Erwin Wasey advertising agency from 1954 to 1958. In many cases his approach was to devise characters, reminiscent of animated cartoons, which appeared classless and international to their audience. Together these poster series encouraged the watching of television, the reading of magazines and the purchase of electrical goods.

The first house style developed by Henrion's team was for the paper manufacturer Bowater. Henrion himself devised a comprehensive range of designs that formed one of the first corporate identities in Britain. There followed the KLM Royal Dutch Airlines identity manual, which he oversaw as consulting designer between 1959 and 1984. The culmination of his interest in corporate design came with the publication in 1968 of the book *Design Coordination and Corporate Image*, which he wrote with the Cambridge mathematician Alan Parkin.

Henrion was an important figure in British graphic design. As well as teaching at the Royal College of Art (1950–9) and the London College of Printing (1976–9) he held several significant positions in the industry, including presidency of the Society of Industrial Artists and Designers (1960–2), of the Alliance Graphique Internationale (1963–6) and of the International Council of Graphic Design Associations (ICOGRADA) (1968–70).

DESIGN MAGAZINES

At the beginning of the twentieth century specialist magazines emerged to address the concerns of the main individual genres of graphic design: the poster, typography and lithography. Gradually, as the century progressed, publications with a broader scope were founded, and between them these embraced all aspects of the field.

One archetypal magazine helped to position Switzerland at the centre of post-World War II graphic design. This was *Graphis*, which began publication in Zurich in 1944. The format of the magazine was in many ways paradigmatic; laid out using a grid, it was published in three languages: French, German and English. As well as focusing on contemporary graphic design, it featured historical commentaries and reviewed printmaking and the graphic arts, which might be regarded as the crafts, as opposed to the industry, of graphic design.

A few years later the British typographer, teacher and editor Herbert Spencer founded the magazine *Typographica*. In 1967 he wrote: "I began to plan *Typographica*, in the autumn of 1948, because I believed that there was then an urgent need for a magazine devoted primarily to typography, that would be international in outlook and scope and critical and analytical in approach."

Typographica first appeared in a large format with a conventional, restrained and serious layout derived from book typography. It reviewed the literature on typography for printers and designers, covering business printing and technical changes in the industry. Gradually Spencer introduced readers to European designers of the interwar years, such as Werkman (see pp90–1), Bill (see pp100–1), El Lissitzky (see pp56–7), Rodchenko (see pp58–9), Bayer (see pp66–7), Sandberg, Berlewi, Zwart and Schuitema. As well as historical articles on what he would later call "pioneers of modern typography", Spencer featured contemporary artists, Concrete poets and typographers, including Edward Wright, Massin (see pp150–1), Diter Rot (later known as Dieter Roth) and Richard Hamilton, who regarded word and image as central to their activity.

The magazine's second series, begun in 1960, was more overtly modernist in outlook. Coloured papers, tipped in textured or transparent sheets and a slightly smaller format combined to give it a contemporary feel.

More eccentric elements in the magazine were articles on vernacular traditions of lettering. Over the years visual essays were published on subjects such as street signs, coal-hole covers, Dutch chocolate letters and the names painted on Breton fishing boats. This attention to the folk roots of lettering and ornament reflected a strain of English modernism that combined a Romantic sensibility and an attraction to European cosmopolitanism.

In 1958, when *Neue Grafik* was first published, Switzerland was widely acknowledged as the centre of modern functional graphic design. Through its designers and their contributions to design education, but most significantly through publications aimed at an international readership, the country's reputation was established.

Neue Grafik continued to appear until 1965, its own design consistently epitomizing its outlook. The co-editors were the graphic designers Josef Müller-Brockmann (see pp124–5) and Hans Neuburg, the Concrete painter Richard P. Lohse, and Carlo Vivarelli, an architect and artist who had worked at Studio Boggeri (see pp84–5). With a four-column grid and text in German, English and French, the magazine covered rational, constructive design, and attached special importance to design systems, signage and the public function of communication. It represented the climax of a certain faith in modernism before the social and cultural challenges of the late 1960s.

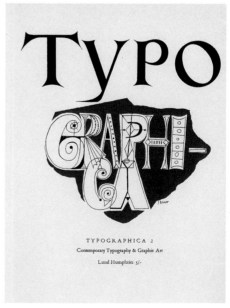

Cover by Imre Reiner for magazine *Typographica*, first series, no. 2, 1950

Spread by Edward Wright from magazine *Typographica*, second series, no. 12, December 1963

Arrows for pedestrians, cyclists, motorists – and flyers

The British graphic designer Edward Wright's photo-essay "Emphatic fist, informative arrow" examined incidental signage found in the urban environment, from official road signs to hand-made signs.

Cover by Herbert Spencer for magazine *Typographica*, second series, no. 7, May 1963

Typographica 7

Cover by Carlo Vivarelli for magazine *Neue Grafik*, no. 1, September 1958

Neue Grafik
New Graphic Design
Graphisme actuel

Internationale Zeitschrift für Grafik und verwandte Gebiete
Erscheint in deutscher, englischer und französischer Sprache

International Review of graphic design and related subjects
Issued in German, English and French language

Revue internationale pour le graphisme et domaines annexes
Parution en langue allemande, anglaise et française

1

Designed and edited by Herbert Spencer, *Typographica* (opposite), with its book-style layout, signalled a serious interest in typography and the graphic arts.

The second series of *Typographica* (above) had a distinctly European design, including imaginative use of coloured papers and experimental typography.

Neue Grafik, edited by Josef Müller-Brockmann, Hans Neuburg, Richard P. Lohse and Carlo Vivarelli, was published from 1958 to 1965. It appeared in three languages and was intended to be "an international platform for the discussion of modern graphic and applied art".

● 1914–96
● Central figure in Swiss modernist graphic design
● Studied and later taught at Zurich School of Arts and Crafts
● Advocated use of grid, sans-serif typography and objective photography
● Author of key books on graphic design

Swiss graphics became internationally known in the 1950s for its neutral, functional and objective approach. Josef Müller-Brockmann, a central figure in this movement, was a designer, teacher and author of several important studies of modern graphic design and visual communication.

Born in Rapperswil, Müller-Brockmann became an apprentice graphic designer immediately after leaving secondary school. Between 1932 and 1934 he studied in the classes of Alfred Willimann and Ernst Keller, two designers who were pioneering modern graphic design at Zurich School of Arts and Crafts. By the early 1930s a group of architects and designers interested in Constructivism, functionalism and abstraction had gathered in Switzerland. Among the graphic designers were Max Bill (see pp100–1), Anton Stankowski and Hans Erni, whose posters and exhibition designs were important in defining a possible path for Müller-Brockmann.

After Müller-Brockmann had worked for several years as a freelance illustrator and stage designer, his mature style emerged in a series of concert posters for the Zurich Tonhalle in 1952. In the first group, a combination of asymmetric typography, grids and abstract motifs evoked the works to be performed. Gradually the designs became more abstract and their fields of colour were registered in ways equivalent to contemporary abstract painting.

A second series of posters represented Müller-Brockmann's other major interest, in photomontage. Concerned at the increase in motor vehicles and other issues of road use in the post-war years, the Swiss Automobile Club commissioned a poster to address child safety in 1952. Although initially criticized by the public, the formula was followed in a series of road safety posters using objective photography, a sans-serif typeface – Akzidenz Grotesk – and minimal colour.

In 1960 Müller-Brockmann visited Tokyo to speak at the World Design Conference. The visit had a profound influence on him, and he later returned to Japan to study Zen Buddhism, inspired by the reduction to aesthetic fundamentals that characterizes the religion and philosophy.

In addition to designing, Müller-Brockmann was a commentator on design and design history. At the Aspen International Design Conference in 1956 he spoke on Swiss art, architecture and design. From 1956 to 1959 he taught graphic design at the Zurich School of Arts and Crafts, as successor to Ernst Keller, and later in Japan and at the Ulm Hochschule für Gestaltung in West Germany in 1963. He wrote *The Graphic Artist and His Design Problems* in 1960 and three other books on graphic design between then and 1981.

Having worked as a consultant designer for several companies, devising corporate identities, Müller-Brockmann co-founded the Müller-Brockmann & Co advertising agency in 1967. In the same year he became design consultant to IBM Europe, an appointment that confirmed his major stature in the field of graphic design.

124

Cover for book *Gestaltungsprobleme des Grafikers*, 1961

J. Müller-Brockmann

Gestaltungsprobleme des Grafikers
The Graphic Artist and his Design Problems
Les problèmes d'un artiste graphique

With his first book, published by Arthur Niggli of Switzerland, Josef Müller-Brockmann became one of the most influential commentators on the move of graphic design from print media to systems design in the form of corporate identity and environmental design.

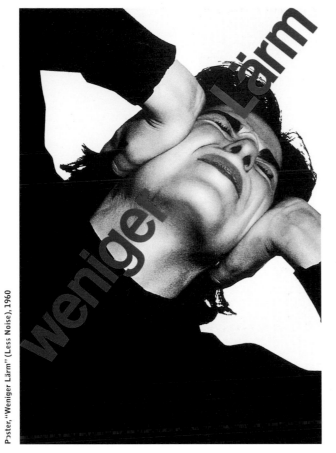

For a Swiss public-awareness campaign to prevent road accidents and encourage greater awareness of the risks of motor traffic, Müller-Brockmann developed a series of objective photographic posters overlaid with direct typographic messages.

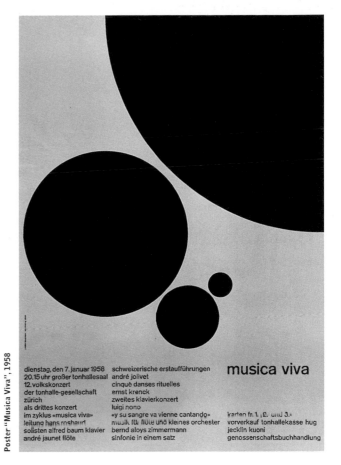

One of a series of posters designed for the Tonhalle in Zurich, this design uses abstract motifs to interpret the style of music it advertises. Like Max Bill before him, Müller-Brockmann chose minimum means to achieve maximum expression.

125

Under the trademark "L+C", Müller-Brockmann created a corporate identity for the packaging and printing company Lithographie und Cartonnage AG of Zurich. The design programme covered all the firm's products and services.

Poster for Campari, 1960

In this rare example of the use of collage in an advertisement, Munari reproduced the name of the manufacturer of the alcoholic drink Campari by colour photocopying. The various distortions were achieved by moving the sheet during this process.

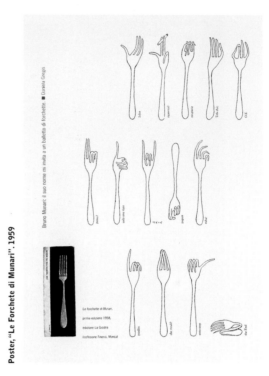

Poster, "Le Forchete di Munari", 1959

This ballet of "Munari's Forks" is a later development, in graphic and theatrical form, of the "Useless Machines" he began to develop in 1933. The poster recalls the pictographs made by Francis Picabia during his New York Dada period.

126

⊖ 1907–98
⊖ Italian graphic and industrial designer, artist, writer and teacher
⊖ Late member of Futurists in Milan
⊖ Developed "Useless Machines" from 1933
⊖ Founded Movimento d'Arte Concrete 1948

Bruno Munari was a maverick combination of artist, writer, teacher and graphic and industrial designer. During a full and varied life he worked for prestigious clients as a graphic designer. He also had a keen interest in the nature of creativity, working with children to explore the character of play at the same time as developing theories of avant-garde art. His approach was informed above all by the belief that art and design can be the same thing.

Munari's artistic life began as a member of the latter stage of Italian Futurism (see pp42–3) in his native land. He was largely self-taught and by the late 1920s was producing abstract paintings in homage to speed and flight. Encouraged by the older Filippo Marinetti,

Giacomo Balla and Enrico Prampolini, he became the leading exponent of the Futurist movement in Milan. Whereas most of Futurism had not been associated with humour, Munari introduced an element of associative play in his drawings, sculptures and paintings, more akin to the mood of Dada and Surrealism. From 1933 he developed a series of abstract constructions, *Macchine Inutili* (Useless Machines), which continued the Futurists' preoccupation with mechanization.

However, by contrast with the emphasis placed by other Futurists on pristine industrial engines and projections of the future, the *Macchine Inutili*, composed of woods, plastics and everyday materials, seemed self-contained. Like the contemporary mobiles of Alexander Calder, Munari's machines used movement to extend figurative art into another dimension.

Munari both designed and illustrated this book, seeking, like the Russian Constructivists and members of the Bauhaus, to create a dynamic interaction between work and image by breaking free of traditional layouts. One element of this approach was the creation of experimental images by superimposing transparent sheets containing designs.

127

Throughout his life Munari combined avant-garde experimental art with design, tending not to distinguish between these activities. In 1966 he wrote: "The designer is therefore the artist of today, not because he is a genius but because he works in such a way as to re-establish contact between art and the public."

In the 1930s Munari wrote for the modernist graphic design journal *Campo Grafico* and was art director of *Tempo*. His analytical and rational side forged links between abstraction in painting and inventive designs for trademarks, signs and symbols. For a number of years he worked with Studio Boggeri (see pp84–5) in Milan and subsequently retained some of the group's clients, including Cinzano, IBM, Olivetti and Pirelli. His style was a variation on Swiss modern design, informed by a profound knowledge of fine art.

In 1948 Munari founded the Movimento d'Arte Concreta (Concrete Art Movement) with Gillo Dorfles and Gianni Monnet, a further attempt to fuse art and design. In tune with the rise of industrial design, he also worked extensively in this field during the following decade.

Like Bauhaus masters before him, notably Paul Klee, Munari wrote about form and design, most significantly in *Arte come mestiere* (1966), published in English in 1971 as *Design as Art*. In this book he pursued a mode of visual enquiry, opening up ways of thinking about signs and symbols, variations on the human face, the shape of words and parallels between nature and design.

In his later career Munari spent a great deal of time teaching. He established a children's laboratory at the Brera art gallery in Milan and also taught Visual Communications at the city's Politecnico.

⊕ 1918–
⊕ Modern Swedish
graphic designer
⊕ Studied in Stockholm
and Los Angeles
⊕ Brought ideas of
international graphic
design to Sweden
⊕ Promoted graphic
design through books,
including important
Design = Ekonomi

Although Sweden is famous for its design traditions, graphic design has not reached the same level of international recognition as other genres. Olle Eksell is an exception in this: a pioneer who looked outwardly to develop a way of working that introduced Sweden to modern graphic design.

For much of the twentieth century, in political and economic terms Sweden offered a "third way" between the extremes of capitalism and communism. Design played a central part in this. A strong social-democratic tradition under interventionist governments placed the home at the centre of a national way of life. Architecture, design and the crafts were unified in a modern, humane way to produce a comfortable domestic setting with "beautiful everyday goods". This maxim was promoted by the the Swedish Association of Arts and Crafts, founded in 1845, and was brought to an international audience through a programme of design exhibitions and its magazine, *Form*. By contrast, graphic design, compromised by its associations with the false promises of advertising, was not easily received in a country with a strong Calvinist tradition and was relatively marginal to this positive national self-image.

Olle Eksell, determined to prevent his homeland's isolation in the field of graphic design, was part of a generation associated with modernism with a human face. In the late 1930s he studied in Stockholm under the German book designer and illustrator Hugo Steiner-Prag while working as a window-dresser, and from 1941 to 1945 was employed by the Ervaco advertising agency. The following year he studied at the Art Center in Los Angeles, and with this experience he returned to organize Sweden's first exhibition of American graphic design, held at the National Museum in Stockholm in 1947.

Eksell continued as a freelance designer during the 1950s, while also working as an illustrator for the daily newspaper *Aftonbladet*. In the field of book publishing, Swedish graphic design was divided between a strongly neoclassical typographic tradition and a more modern approach informed by Swiss typography. Distinct from both of these was the work of commercial artists who were responsible for generating advertisements for national companies aimed at the home market.

A versatile designer, Eksell synthesized these divergent approaches. At a crucial stage when strong resistance to American-style marketing was undermining the place of the graphic designer in Sweden, Eksell, influenced by the impact of Vance Packard's best-selling book *The Hidden Persuaders* (1957), published *Design = Ekonomi* (1964), his argument for design as an indispensable part of economic life. He worked fluently on book designs, advertisements and corporate identities, in some cases employing an abstract visual language and in others a figurative style that recognized the importance of Picasso or the Swedish ceramics designer Stig Lindberg.

Poster for SAFFT (Svenska Affischtecknare Utställer), 1954

SVENSKA AFFISCHTECKNARE UTSTÄLLER I

Nationalmuseum

2 NOV.–12 DEC. 1954

Olle Eksell has played an important role in promoting graphic design in his native country. He was commissioned to design the poster for the first exhibition of Swedish poster design, held in 1954 in Stockholm by SAFFT (Swedish Poster Design Association). The design reveals the lightness of touch that characterizes his work.

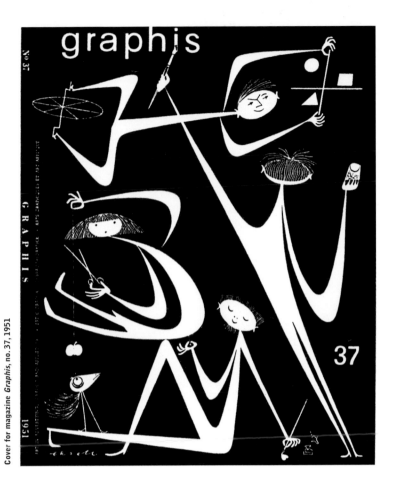

For Eksell it was a great honour to be commissioned early in his career to design a cover for the influential trilingual magazine *Graphis*. At this time his work referred to modern painting, particularly by artists of the School of Paris such as Picasso.

In *Design = Ekonomi* Eksell argued for the economic importance of design to modern society. First published in 1964 by Bonniers, the book inspired several generations of student designers and was reprinted in 1999

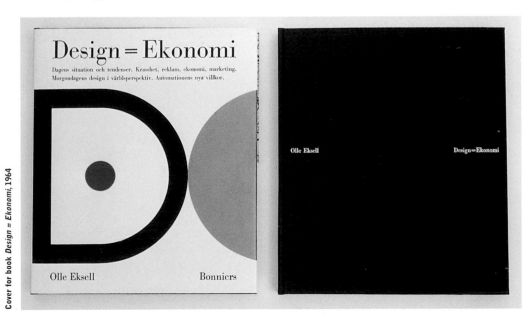

DESIGN FOR TRANSPORTATION

In the late nineteenth century the first graphic design for transportation systems arose out of posters and signwriting produced for companies competing to carry passengers. This work was criticized for lacking a visual system, but steps towards coherent design policies in transportation were made at the time of Germany's Deutsche Werkbund, formed in 1907, and its British equivalent, the Design and Industries Association, formed in 1915.

One of the most famous contributions was made by Frank Pick. Having joined the London Underground in 1906, he eventually became vice-chairman of the London Transport Passenger Board in 1933. At this time the company was newly unified, bringing together the Underground and buses. Pick conceived the entire architecture and design as a coordinated scheme, intending to represent it as a seamless and efficient system. He improved the infrastructure, commissioning new stations from architects who drew on contemporary European models, and employing industrial designers to make a modern travelling environment. In terms of graphic design, Railway Type, a new sign face, was introduced by Edward Johnston in 1916. This was an elementary sans-serif alphabet with a strong, open, geometric character. Eric Gill (see pp30–1) adapted it into Gill Sans, a series of typefaces for Monotype Corporation, from 1928. Combined with the memorable circle and bar symbol, Railway Type was used in all signage at station entrances and platforms, and on the fronts of both trains and buses, timetables, ticket machines and directional signs. Pick also developed an enlightened system of patronage for poster designers under which modernists, including McKnight Kauffer (see pp46–9) and Moholy-Nagy (see pp64–5), were commissioned alongside more traditional pictorial artists.

Most important for subsequent designs was Pick's commission of Henry Beck, an engineering draughtsman, to devise a plan of the entire Underground system in 1931. The solution became a paradigm for later maps in many other cities, including the subway plan for the New York Metropolitan Transit Authority designed by Massimo Vignelli and Bob Noorda (see pp136–7) from 1966 and the Berlin Transport Authority (BVG) plan of the early 1990s by Erik Spiekermann (see pp220–1).

In the expanding area of international travel the importance of corporate identity was fully realized in the 1950s. It was essential for transportation companies to use the more ambitious design consultancies, and for several of the most prominent of these graphic design for airlines became a major activity. Boosted by the falling cost of air travel and the growing number of airlines, mass tourism led to the building of international airports. It was usual for a corporate identity to be devised by a multidisciplinary team as the work embraced, in addition to graphic design, architecture, interiors and uniforms. Familiar solutions were to represent national airlines with symbols of flight, such as birds and arrows, or with national colours and symbols, for example a red maple leaf for Air Canada and a blue crown for KLM (Royal Dutch Airlines). PanAm, by contrast, stressed its internationalism with a globe.

It was also necessary to develop an international sign language for directing passengers through airports with

BRIGHTEST LONDON
IS BEST REACHED BY
[UNDERGROUND]

In Henry Beck's map, seen here in the 1959 version, each station on the London Underground system was identified on a colour-coded line. The lines were arranged as a grid of verticals, horizontals and 45-degree diagonals. Although in reality the distance between stations varied greatly, regular spacing gave the network the appearance of a unified structure. This may have encouraged passengers to undertake journeys that turned out to be longer than expected.

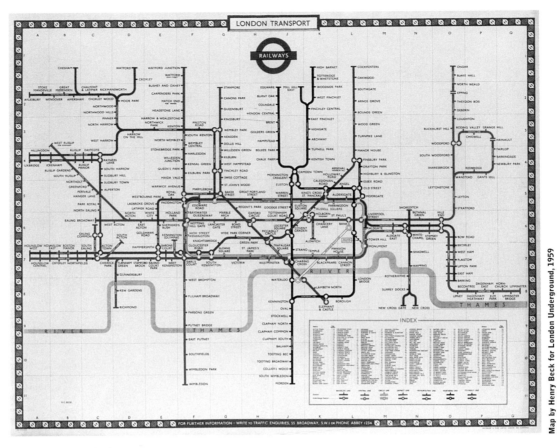

Map by Henry Beck for London Underground, 1959

Corporate identity by Raymond Loewy for Greyhound Bus, c1955

131

At London Underground stations spaces were allocated for advertisements such as this (opposite). The posters stressed the benefits of the various modes of travel, or depicted destinations in the city and the surrounding countryside.

The industrial and graphic designer Raymond Loewy's motif of a greyhound surging forward enhances the sense of speed that is also conveyed by the emphasis on horizontal lines and the shape of the windows.

Road signage by Margaret Calvert and Jock Kinneir, from 1964

Logos for Société des Chemins de Fer Français and British Rail, 1963

The system used colour-coded signs with town names in Transport sans-serif and unified directional arrows and symbols. The letter spacing allowed recognition of words when travelling at speed.

Two approaches to the task of creating a graphic identity for a national railway system. In France coherence was given through a symbol designed by Rémy Peignot and based on his single-case alphabet. In the UK the signage designed by Margaret Calvert and Jock Kinneir of the Design Research Unit combined a symbol and a new typeface.

ease. These busy and confusing environments lack many of the landmarks that help people to find their way. Therefore it was important to establish a hierarchy of information that helped passengers and made the buildings work efficiently. There was a tendency, regardless of geographical location, to introduce an international model for signage, based on sign language and standardized letterforms. International information graphics were also applied to road and motorway systems; to public spaces, including hospitals and educational institutions; and to international sporting events, such as the Olympic Games, often drawing on Swiss typography and the English language to form a universal system.

An example of such information design was the signage developed for Britain's new motorways in the early 1960s by Margaret Calvert and Jock Kinneir, associated at the time with the Design Research Unit. In response to the Geneva Protocol for the unification of road signage, Britain adopted European standards. The solution was not without controversy as it represented a very public assertion of modernist principles. Traditionalists offered alternative versions, but the project, using the upper- and lower-case alphabet Transport, went ahead in 1965.

Towards the end of the century thinking on corporate identity began to change. In the area of transportation design this was typified by the World Images scheme for British Airways introduced by Interbrand Newell and Sorrell in 1997. The aim was not to create a monolithic identity but to reflect the changing perception of Britain as a country of cultural diversity. In a scheme based on 33 different visual identities, most designs were abstract or semi-abstract, commissioned from painters, sculptors, ceramicists, weavers, quilters, calligraphers and paper artists. A softer typographic style was used, intended to establish British Airways as a world brand, like Coca-Cola and Microsoft, but with its roots in Britain.

Corporate identity by Karl Gerstner for Swissair, 1974

Karl Gerstner's design for Switzerland's national airline used lower-case type in the modern Swiss tradition, along with the national symbol and colours.

  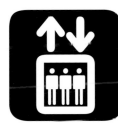  

Experiments with international sign language began with Otto and Marie Neurath, whose Isotype system (1928–) was a purely visual language. These principles were well suited to airport signage. The diagrammatic figures simplify and codify, in an attempt to avoid cultural inflection and ambiguity of message.

133

BRITISH AIRWAYS

A softer approach to the British Airways name, incorporating the red and blue swash, was introduced in 1997 as part of a major redesign of the company's corporate identity. Although this logo, designed by Newell & Sorrell, continued in use, the rest of the scheme broke convention and 33 different designs for the aircraft were introduced, helping to distinguish the British Airways brand in the international setting of airports.

Ivan Chermayeff has been a central figure in nurturing the principle that "design is the solution of problems rather than the arbitrary application of fashionable styles". A second-generation modernist, he is as much a maker of sculptures and co-author of children's books as a designer of company reports. For over 30 years he has been the principal of the design partnership Chermayeff & Geismar Inc.

The son of the Russian architect Serge Chermayeff, he was brought up in England in the 1930s. Chermayeff studied at Harvard University, the Chicago Institute of Design and Yale University. From his family he acquired a thorough grounding in European modernism, which his studies in Chicago reinforced. He wrote: "I came from a rigorous Bauhaus background of dogmatic insistence on a certain kind of vocabulary and sensibility, which is counterproductive to good communications." Aware that order and cleanliness in design can become cold and rigid, he has redefined his position in relation to modernism.

Chermayeff became an assistant to Alvin Lustig, designing record covers and book jackets, in 1955, at a time when American graphic design was becoming less formal. Two years later, with Robert Brownjohn (see pp138–9) and Thomas Geismar, he started the partnership Brownjohn, Chermayeff & Geismar, which became Chermayeff & Geismar Inc. in 1960 when Brownjohn left to work in London. Later John Grady and Stefan Geissbühler joined the practice as partners. By contrast to Push Pin Studio (see pp152–5), another major New York studio, which had its base in illustration, Chermayeff and Geismar emphasized the typographic roots of their work.

134

Mobil

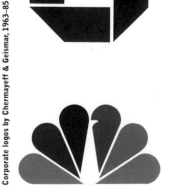

Corporate logos by Chermayeff & Geismar, 1963–85

These logos for Mobil, the Chase Manhattan Bank and NBC (National Broadcasting Company) were designed by Chermayeff and his partner Thomas Geismar in (from top to bottom) 1964, 1963 and 1985. The Chase Manhattan logo, which was used on the headquarters building, had to be legible from a distance and from below.

Taking on graphic, environmental and exhibition designs, the group counted among its major clients Pan-American World Airways, New York's Museum of Modern Art, New York University and the US Environmental Protection Agency. In 1963–4 it developed a corporate identity for the Mobil oil corporation. The logotype, a subtle and elegant solution, was composed of five vertical strokes, two circles and the angle of the "M". The distinctive red "o" retained a link with Mobil's former identity, a flying red horse, but otherwise the scheme was remarkable for its abstraction. To coincide with the launch a service station exhibition displayed the group's designs for station forecourts, based on cylindrical fixtures echoing the logotype.

Chermayeff later became a senior figure in the design profession. He was a trustee of the Museum of Modern Art, in New York, for over 20 years and Visiting Professor at the city's Cooper Union art school and the Kansas City Art Institute. With his wife Jane Chermayeff Clark he co-chaired the Aspen International Design Conference in 1980, when the theme was "Children".

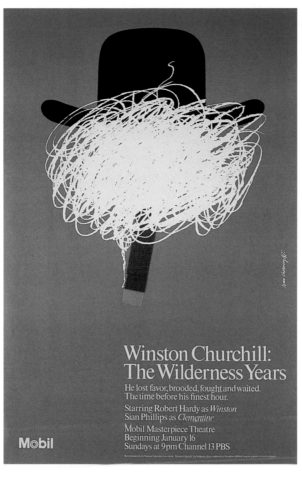

Reflecting his interest in identity, Chermayeff's poster for the play *Winston Churchill: The Wilderness Years* uses the conceit of people's familiarity with the face of a famous person. Churchill's iconic identity, revealed by his hat and cigar, is masked by the scribbled "smoke". America's Channel 13 televised the play in 1983 as part of the Mobil Masterpiece Theatre Season.

135

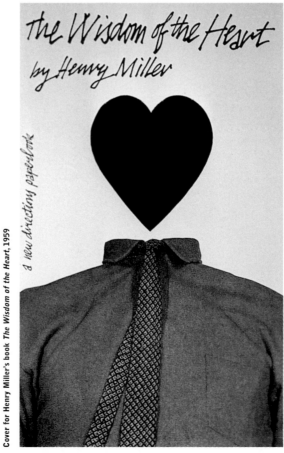

In reference to the verbal metaphor of the title of this collection of essays by Henry Miller, which was first published in 1941 and is seen here in an edition of 1959, Chermayeff used the black heart as a visual metaphor to connect heart and mind. He often incorporated handwriting in his designs, lending them freshness and informality.

MASSIMO VIGNELLI

- 1931–
- Studied architecture in Milan, Venice and at IIT, Illinois
- Formed partnership with wife, Lella Vignelli, first in Milan and later in New York
- Major designs for New York Metropolitan Transit Authority
- Vignelli Associates and Vignelli Designs founded 1971
- International clients in design, architecture and publishing

Vignelli has designed many books on architecture for the publisher Rizzoli, including this title, which was contributed by the United States to the Venice Biennale in 1993.

Cover for book *Peter Eisenman & Frank Gehry*, 1993

For more than 40 years Massimo Vignelli has been in a professional partnership with his wife, the architect and designer Lella Vignelli. They took Italian design to New York, fusing their understanding of the aesthetics of modernism with the professionalism of the American industrial design consultancy. Massimo directs the partnership's graphic design work, while Lella leads the furniture and architectural projects.

Vignelli studied architecture in Milan and Venice. He became a friend of Max Huber, who introduced to him the ideas of Swiss typography, an approach based on grids, sequencing and dynamic relationships of scale that would become important for Vignelli's subsequent designs. Between 1957 and 1960 Vignelli studied in the United States on a scholarship. In 1960, after his return to Milan, the initial version of the partnership was formed, the Vignelli Office of Design and Architecture. One of the first celebrated graphic designs was for the Piccolo Teatro in Milan.

In 1965 Vignelli co-founded Unimark International Corporation with Bob Noorda, the Dutch graphic designer and former art director at Pirelli in Milan. One of their first major commissions, on which they began work in 1966, was to redesign the graphic programme for the New York subway system. After analysing traffic flow, Vignelli and Noorda devised a modular system of units for the signage that could be put together to perform the role of informational sentences, with square panels to indicate line numbers and other directions. The system was standardized yet more flexible than the previous signs that had been made individually for each site. A commission for a map of the system followed in 1970. The result was a successful combination of a rational approach and research based on observation, but in 1979 it was replaced with a more conventional design.

In 1971 the offices of Vignelli Associates and Vignelli Designs opened in New York. As one commentator has said, Vignelli established Helvetica as "the default typeface for corporate America". Other hallmarks of his graphic style are a dominant use of red and black and of the classic typefaces Bodoni, Times, Garamond, Century and Futura.

In the introduction to the *Graphis* annual of 1983 Vignelli commented: "Historical information, introspection and interpretation are almost totally missing in our profession." His point of view prefigured the rise in the 1990s of critical writing on graphic design. Nevertheless, although Vignelli encouraged a debate which was central to postmodernism, his personal style remained thoroughly embedded in modernism. In his 1991 essay "Long Live Modernism" he reasserted the role of design to improve the visual environment: "Post-modernism should be regarded at best as a critical evaluation of the issues of Modernism."

This was the first Vignelli poster for the major furniture manufacturer Knoll International. The design partnership undertook the graphic programme for this client between 1966 and 1980.

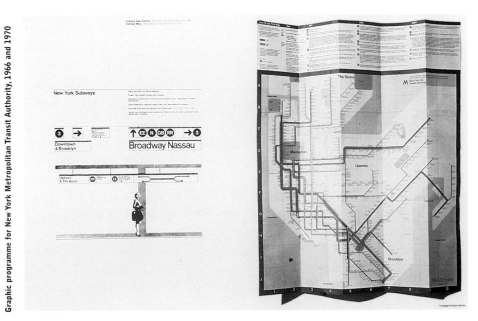

The map of the New York subway system designed by Vignelli and Noorda consisted of dots and lines, with each line given a strong primary colour. Like Henry Beck's diagram for the London Underground, it schematized the geographical relationship between stations, not indicating relative distances. Directions for travel were reduced to a simple system using only 45- and 90-degree angles.

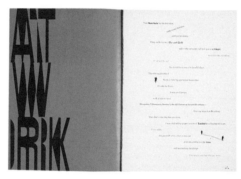

Cover for record *Si Si, No No*, 1959

In his cover for an album by Machito & His Orchestra (left) Brownjohn interpreted the rhythm of the Latin music by exploiting the repetition of the bright colours of the letterforms.

This design by Brownjohn, Geismar & Chermayeff (below) used a mixture of fonts to mirror Percy Seitlin's evocation of Manhattan in his book *That New York*.

Cover for book *That New York*, 1960

138

⊕ 1925–70
⊕ Studied painting, graphic design and architecture at Chicago Institute of Design
⊕ Member of Brownjohn, Chermayeff & Geismar
⊕ Designed title sequences for two James Bond films

Robert Brownjohn has been acknowledged as a key figure in the transformation of graphic design into conceptual art in the early 1960s. In a career that has been described as "explosively short", he was fuelled by a desire to eliminate the boundaries between experience and design.

Brownjohn was reputedly one of the brightest graduates from the Chicago Institute of Design, where he studied painting and graphic design with Moholy-Nagy (see pp64–5) and architecture with Serge Chermayeff. His career followed the route advocated by Moholy-Nagy in his books *Painting Photography Film* (1925) and *Vision in Motion* (1947). Moholy, always concerned to investigate the future of visual communication with the latest technology, had experimented with light and

abstraction in film. Brownjohn would likewise make the transition from graphic design to advertising to film.

As well as the "high" design of his education, he explored many other sources. He collected examples of lettering in a variety of contexts, often with surreal juxtapositions, accidents, broken or distorted forms.

Brownjohn was first active as a designer in New York, where he was a partner in Brownjohn, Chermayeff & Geismar (see pp134–5) between 1957 and 1960. For the Brussels World's Fair of 1958 the partnership designed "Streetscape", a graphic environment of a typical American street of mixed signage, revealing an interest in vernacular that predicted Robert Venturi's 1972 book *Learning from Las Vegas*.

Similarly, in 1961 Brownjohn contributed a photo-essay entitled "Street Level" to Herbert Spencer's

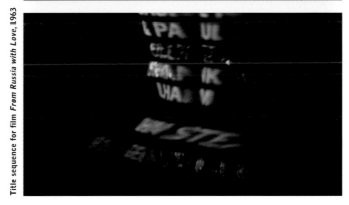

Title sequence for film *From Russia with Love*, 1963

Brownjohn's designs for the title sequences of two James Bond films, *From Russia with Love* and *Goldfinger*, were examples of the innovative technique of animated typography. He discussed them in the article "Sex and Typography", published in *Typographica* magazine in 1964.

magazine *Typographica*; in this piece he recorded the signs he encountered on a single day in London.

After moving to London Brownjohn worked as an art director for J. Walter Thompson and later McCann Erickson. Alan Fletcher and the American Bob Gill introduced him to the city's graphic design world. Between 1958 and 1963 the spheres of printing and design changed rapidly in London, and the American contribution was crucial. The protagonists, including Brownjohn, met at the Graphics Workshop, an informal forum for those interested in visual language. At this time the advertising agency Doyle Dane Bernbach, renowned for its clever copylines, opened a London office. New approaches to art direction, using wit and humour, along with opportunities offered by television and film, accelerated the pace and style of graphic design.

The designer's film work began with the opening frames of the James Bond film *From Russia with Love* in 1963. Inspired by seeing people walk across the projection of slides at a lecture, Brownjohn projected still typography on to a dancing model to create the title sequence. The result brought him great acclaim, and the following year he was commissioned to design the title sequence for the Bond sequel, *Goldfinger*.

Brownjohn's lifestyle was integral to his identity as a designer: he played the star in the "Swinging London" of the 1960s and enjoyed notoriety and contact with film actors and rock musicians. Among his last designs was the cover for the Rolling Stones' album *Let it Bleed*. His final years, before his premature death in 1970, were spent making films with the company Cammell, Hudson and Brownjohn.

YUSAKU KAMEKURA

→ 1915–97
→ Important member of first generation of modern Japanese graphic designers
→ Studied composition theory at Nippon University and Shin Kenchiku Kogei Gakuin
→ Co-founder of Japanese Advertising Artists' Club and Nippon Design Center
→ Specialist in design of symbols and trademarks
→ Designed corporate identity for 1964 Tokyo Olympic Games

Yusaku Kamekura was a leading figure in Japan's design movement after World War II. Like Ikko Tanaka (see pp196–7), he was one of the first generation of designers to understand and interpret Western notions of design, fusing them with Japanese characteristics. Based on strong geometric elements and an emblematic use of typography, Kamekura's designs reflected his interest in both contemporary trademarks and traditional Japanese signs.

In 1933 Kamekura graduated from Nippon University, Tokyo, and then studied composition theory at the Shin Kenchiku Kogei Gakuin. Its curriculum inspired by the Bauhaus (see pp60–3), this institute of new architecture and industrial arts was founded in 1931. Here Kamekura was introduced to the ideas of Bayer (see pp66–7), Moholy-Nagy (see pp64–5) and other exponents of the new typography. In 1938 he became editor of the English-language magazine *Nippon*, and then art director of the magazine *Commerce Japan*.

During the 1950s Kamekura continued to be one of the most active exponents of Western-style graphic design, advertising and art direction. In the interwar years Japanese printing had progressed from woodcut to lithography and the emergence of the graphic designer indicated a further separation between printer and client. Distinctively, Japanese designers used the country's highly developed photographic technologies in many of their designs.

Japanese graphic design underwent a rapid professionalization with the promotion of design by award-giving associations, exhibitions and journals. In 1951 Kamekura was a co-founder of the Japanese Advertising Artists' Club (JAAC), which was based on the Art Directors' Club of New York. He had a one-man exhibition in 1953. At this time he travelled in Europe and the United States, and on returning became a member of the Good Design Committee, a scheme similar to the Good Design programme of New York's Museum of Modern Art and the UK's Design Council. He was also a co-founder of the Nippon Design Center, a design group established with a consortium of companies, which offered graduate training in corporate identity and systems design.

Poster, 1973

Kamekura's interests in optical effects is seen in this poster for the Tokyo International Lighting Fixtures Design Corporation. The design appears to oscillate through the juxtaposition of green and blue concentric circles, evoking light, the poster's subject.

Increasing recognition came for Kamekura with the commission to design the interior of the Japanese pavilion at the 1964 New York World's Fair and, with Masuru Katsumi, the posters for the Tokyo Olympic Games of 1964. His many designs for international companies depend on their ability to communicate internationally through symbols. Like his contemporaries Paul Rand (see pp106–9) and Josef Müller-Brockmann (see pp124–5), he had an understanding of symbols that was in part informed by Constructivism. But to this was added the traditional source of the Katachi; these Japanese family crests are concentrated visual forms, often pictographic or ideographic in character. Kamekura analysed such connections in his book *Trademarks and Symbols of the World* (1965).

Poster for Olympic Games, Tokyo, 1964

The success of this poster depended on both the iconic treatment of the typography and the powerful graphic symbols of the Rising Sun and the Olympic Games. These drew extra strength from their association with Osamu Hayasaki's dramatic shot of runners starting a race against a stark, black background.

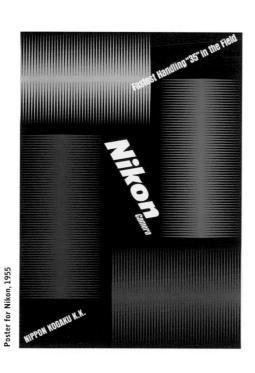

Poster for Nikon, 1955

Kamekura designed a series of press, poster and neon-lighting advertisements as well as packaging for the Japanese photographic company Nikon. The campaign explored variations on the theme of light refracted through a prism and so, by implication, colour photography.

- → 1914–
- → Master of Polish poster design
- → Studied at Warsaw Academy of Art, where he was later professor
- → Prolific designer of posters for theatre, films and exhibitions
- → Artistic identity kept pace with movements in modern art
- → Important figure in promoting international recognition for Polish graphic design

142

Poland was one of the few countries in the decades following World War II to contribute a national style in graphic design. This was largely a result of its strong poster tradition, in which one of the leading figures was Henryk Tomaszewski.

Tomaszewski studied at the Academy of Art in Warsaw from 1934 to 1939. In 1952 he was appointed Professor of Poster Design at the Warsaw Academy, where he was an influential figure in teaching and promoting his approach until his retirement in 1985.

For much of the twentieth century Poland experienced a difficult political history. After being allied to the Soviet Union in the fight against Nazism during World War II, it was incorporated, on the signing of the Warsaw Pact in 1948, into the Soviet bloc. The arts and culture came under centralized state control and in this way censorship was put in place. Responsible for overseeing graphic design was the State Publishing Agency, Wydawnictwo Artystyczno-Graficzne (WAG), under the direction of Josef Mroszczack, a colleague of Tomaszewski, and Henryk Szemberg. Polish artists and designers were determined to assert a relative autonomy from Soviet directives. Rejecting Socialist Realism, the Polish poster artists celebrated free artistic expression. In particular, they adopted a strong lithographic style which continued the *affichiste* tradition. Rather than look to Polish Constructivism, the radical Polish artistic experiment of the 1920s, Tomaszewski and his contemporaries, such as Mieczyslaw Berman, Jan Lenica, Waldemar Swierzy and Tadeusz Trepkowski, turned to the School of Paris of the 1930s and 1940s for their precedent.

Among its other activities, WAG published more than 200 film posters each year. No pre-film publicity material was provided and so the designers, free of the need to work with promotional photographs or copy-lines, could exploit their inventiveness. Similarly, designers of posters for the theatre, concerts and exhibitions extended the visual languages of Surrealism, Expressionism and abstraction. The notoriety of individual designers was recognized as the number of poster exhibitions and awards increased.

Poster for Peter Luke's play *Hadrian VII*, 1969

Many of Tomaszewski's designs for posters are based on striking images that work like paintings. Unburdened by the marketing information often necessary in Western posters of the time, they can remain vital combinations of hand-drawn words and image.

In the West during the 1950s and 1960s, the advertising agency replaced the older model of the poster designer, as visual communication grew international through the development of sophisticated television and press advertising and corporate-identity schemes. Despite this, international exhibitions continued to celebrate poster art.

Tomaszewski's work was awarded prizes in Vienna (1948), Warsaw (1953), São Paulo (1963), Leipzig (1965), Katowice (1971), Lahti (1979) and Toyama (1991). He became a leading figure in the foundation of the national Poster Museum in Wilanow, where the success of the international poster Biennale guaranteed recognition of the major contribution of the Polish poster school.

Poster for exhibition "Moore", 1959

In this poster advertising an exhibition
of work by Henry Moore, the blue colour-
field and the roughly cut letterforms
used for the sculptor's name recognize
the important influence of the cut-out
methods of Hans Arp and Henri Matisse.

Poster for Stanisław Tym's play *Pralnia* (The Laundry), 1981

In European painting of the late
1970s and early 1980s there
was a revival of interest in
loose figurative expressionism.
This finds resonance in the
gestural marks and directness
of the lettering in Tomaszewski's
theatre poster of 1981.

JAZZ COVERS

When 10-inch long-playing discs replaced 78s in the late 1940s, record covers developed as part of the larger field of graphic design for media. Their proliferation coincided with the wider development of book and magazine design and other forms of cultural packaging. Although its impact is hard to analyse, the album cover became an important element in consumers' awareness of modern design. Unlike much disposable packaging, records entered the home to be kept and could readily express a cultural attitude as an element in a room setting. The relationship between graphic style and musical content was crucial because the cover represented a permanent visual statement. Many celebrated design solutions were created for jazz and other genres of music.

In 1951 William Golden's celebrated symbol for CBS, the letters in Bodoni typeface with a symbol of an eye, signalled the recording company's need to establish brand identity through its covers. Alvin Lustig, a fellow member of the loosely affiliated New York School, designed covers for albums of classical music at this time, drawing on styles associated with modern European paintings.

The jazz record was a specialist sub-genre of music publishing. Jazz, the music of Black Americans, had its origins in the nineteenth century in the South of the United States, where it grew from a combination of Gospel, West African rhythms and European harmony. By the 1950s Black musicians in the Northern cities were in a position to explore music in ground-breaking ways. Improvisation and virtuosity were crucial. Jazz musicians such as Miles Davis, Charlie Mingus, John Coltrane, Freddie Hubbard, Thelonious Monk and Sonny Rollins developed a style to be performed in small ensembles of up to seven players. The music was known as "hard bop" and later modern or cool jazz. The increasing autonomy of Black musicians was shown by a number of independent record companies, including Atlantic, Blue Note, Debut, Prestige, Riverside and Contemporary. Of these, Blue Note became celebrated for its design policy.

The recording of jazz is important because its notation cannot be written down. From 1951, Blue Note's founder

and producer, Alfred Lion, made many performances available to a wider audience. For the covers, he called on the photographer Francis Wolff. They had been childhood friends and had both left Nazi Germany in the late 1930s. The team was complete when designer Reid Miles joined them and together the three men developed the formula.

Their approach incorporated Wolff's photographs, which were treated as one graphic ingredient in the design, counterbalanced by typography and bands of colour. Often the photographs were colour-toned and a second colour was added to highlight the performers' names or the title of the record. Illustrations were rarely used at Blue Note. On the reverse of the cover Lion established the company's reputation for authoritative liner notes and recording specifications, but there was no extra expenditure here.

Although the formula of Blue Note stands out for its consistency and has been celebrated by many historians of music and design, other record companies developed imaginative design policies, using Abstract Expressionist drawings, reportage illustrations and location shots to thematically interpret the music.

Blue Note's distinctive formula for record covers derived from the collaboration between photographer Francis Wolff and designer Reid Miles. Characteristic of their approach was the use of toned action photographs and bold type.

Cover for record *Blue Train*. 1957

A distinctive image of the leader of the quintet, trumpeter Freddie Hubbard, is created by tight cropping of an action photograph. The parallel black bands evoke the keys of a piano, while the dropped, off-centre band alludes to the rhythm of the recording, which has an incessantly repeating motif.

james spaulding/herbie hancock/reginald workman/clifford jarvis

STEREO
THE FINEST IN JAZZ SINCE 1939
84115 BLUE NOTE

hub-tones
freddie
hubbard

By the mid-1960s the art director at Atlantic Records was incorporating illustration, graphic symbols and photography in an eclectic mix of pop and historical, folk images.

Blue Note's designer Reid Miles gives this cover its impact by combining the large type size of the title with colours which resonate with the reflective mood of the music.

145

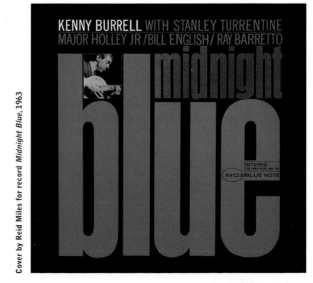

Even though they share the same historical period, the designers presented in the following pages are a less coherent group than those discussed in the previous chapter. They were not driven by a single or dominant aesthetic, but what many had in common was their view of the designer's role. Often this attitude was one of opposition to the model of the graphic designer in the service of industry or large corporations. Instead they saw graphic design as a vehicle for a critical, subversive or reflective language. Many of them resisted assumptions about the overriding significance of a universalizing aesthetic such as Swiss typography and questioned whether design should be used to promote the values of mass consumerism and political acquiescence.

In 1932 the critic and historian of typography Beatrice Warde had proposed the metaphor of the "crystal goblet" for a typography that could be a transparent container of its message, and in many ways this ideal had continued to prevail in modernism and Swiss typography. However, if by the 1950s modernism had been consolidated as the dominant approach for graphic design, by the 1960s it had become just one of several possibilities amid a loosening up of graphic styles and a stronger sense of emergent subcultures.

These changes were remarked on by the Canadian sociologist Marshall McLuhan, who formulated his influential concept "the medium is the message" from 1958 onwards. When considering the phenomenon of the new media industries, he stressed that important technological changes were leading the form of communication to be as important as its content. He was writing at a time when cycles of photographic and televisual imagery were accelerating in recognition of a greater emphasis on style and fashion change.

Pop art, which had its roots in Britain in the early 1950s, was the art and design movement most emblematic of such change and stood for a critique of the neutrality of the designer's position. It was interdisciplinary, and by no means led by graphic designers, being instead an amalgam of interests of painters, sculptors and architects. Perceiving British design to be too preoccupied with established values of good form or taste, the group broke away to formulate a more contemporary style. They generated a sophisticated range of references, drawing on Italian design, American car styling and, most importantly, the street as a source of what has been called the vernacular of everyday life. In place of longevity, Pop designers valued speed, ephemerality and the quick succession of styles. They were not

Page from magazine *Oz*, no. 8, January 1968

The underground magazine *Oz*, founded in 1963 and brought to London by Australian Richard Neville, was a leading force in the counter-culture of Britain in the late 1960s. Its free-style graphics, a combination of visual eclecticism, technical experiment and explicit content, provided an often subversive alternative to mainstream graphic design. The lettering of the *Oz* logo on this page is by Louise Ferrier.

anti-modern but wanted to retrieve a sense of Futurist modernity, which they considered to have been lost in a concern for design seriousness. In many respects the enthusiasm of Pop for the graphic nature of the environment as transitory predated the formulations of postmodernism.

By contrast, Massin was part of a quietist tradition in which the experimental French poets Stéphane Mallarmé and Guillaume Apollinaire had earlier played an important role. Like them, he saw poetry as an interpretative medium whose form and content are intimately combined. In the alternative European tradition of the designer-philosopher, Massin stood, during the 1960s in particular, as a cultural figure who eschewed the demands of marketing and was committed instead to forging links between design and poetry, literature, philosophy and aesthetics.

The early 1960s were years of dissent and outright revolt in Western society, marked by the Cuban missile crisis of 1962, civil rights and student movements and the war in Indo-China. Part of the clamour for change was a critique of the professionalization of design in the service of Americanization and global capitalism. This found visual expression in the underground presses and the psychedelic posters of London and San Francisco. Radicalization led to a wider critique of American cultural hegemony among the New Left. The German philosopher Herbert Marcuse, who taught at the University of California, characterized the loss of the aesthetic dimension in life and prescribed a critical revolt in *One Dimensional Man* (1964), which influenced students and dissidents all over the world. Marcuse saw the road to change as a fusion of psychoanalysis and Marxism: Freud's ideas of psychological repression and Marx's liberation through class struggle. Significantly, he identified the media's role in denying the full range of creative activities to people, causing alienation, and he suggested that the way forward depended on critique and finding alternatives.

In the field of graphic design this radical position was expressed through greater informality, the formation of collectives and small-scale, independent projects that addressed community interests and the politics of liberation. In the latter context Polish, Cuban and Chinese posters were admired by Western designers for the directness of their message and for the exotic alternative they offered. In New York the designers of Push Pin Studio showed how playful mannerisms, illustrated by their fascination with revivals and visual eclecticism, could in themselves be subversive. They stressed that imagery was as important as typography. Play and ornament could be explained as a return of the repressed within modernism, an assertion of history and the riches of graphic art that heralded the emergent sensibility of postmodernism in the late 1960s.

Design for text of Ionesco's play *La Cantatrice Chauve*, 1964

In this edition of Ionesco's play *La Cantatrice Chauve* (The Bald Prima Donna), published by Gallimard in 1964, Massin distinguished the different voices by setting the female parts in italics. Words and phrases are arranged at angles or change size for emphasis, forming stark contrast with the images of the actors.

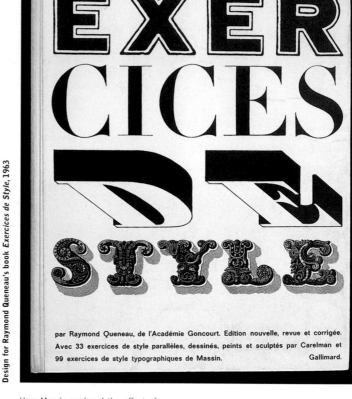

Design for Raymond Queneau's book *Exercices de Style*, 1963

Here Massin explored the effect of typographic arrangement on narrative by rendering Queneau's story in 99 type styles.

150

⊕ 1925–
⊕ French experimental typographer, book designer and art director
⊕ Interested in relationship between expressive typography and literary content
⊕ Art director for Galliamard, Paris
⊕ Designer of Ionesco's *La Cantatrice Chauve*

In the early 1960s American art direction stressed the visual origin of effective communication, and the clever concept dominated advertising. By contrast, Massin, as he is known professionally, is a writer as well as an art director, whose design work is informed by a great love of literature.

A Frenchman born near Paris, Massin did not attend art school, but instead gained much of his early design experience working, from 1946, with Pierre Faucheux, the book designer and art director of the Club Français du Livre. He went on to work for eight years as an art director at the Club du Meilleur Livre and then as art director for the publisher Gallimard for 20 years.

Massin is quoted as saying that his aim is to "try to penetrate beyond mere 'layout' and to use paper, type and ink as flexible means towards a cultivated and flexible interpretation in print of the author's written text". The advantage of his early work with the book clubs was that it offered more opportunity to experiment than other publishers. Working on the principle of subscription, the book clubs did not need to compete on the shelf – this was a period when the potential to market books like any other industrial product was realized. Instead, with books sent direct to readers, attention could be given to binding, paper and the commissioning of illustrations and photographer, and more individual solutions for each work could be found.

The *tour de force* in Massin's career is his interpretation of the stage version of Eugène Ionesco's play *La Cantatrice Chauve* (The Bald Prima Donna), published by Gallimard in 1964. The book consists of a

In this interpretation of a play by
Ionesco, published by Gallimard in 1966,
Massin mixed calligraphy, ink blobs and
typography to show how graphic layout
can mimic vocal expression.

151

typographic arrangement which transcribes the lines of
the actors in contrasting typefaces. The severe blackness
of the type is complemented by high-contrast
photographs of the characters in the play, taken from
photographs by Henry Cohen. An example of the
"Theatre of the Absurd", the play reveals the petit-
bourgeois conflicts of two couples in Victorian England.

In Massin's design each character speaks in a
different typeface, often in speech bubbles. The women
"speak" in italics and no punctuation is used apart from
question and exclamation marks. Massin varied the type
sizes, setting them at extreme angles and overlaying one
sentence on another as the exchanges become more
heated towards the end of the play.

Massin has said that he wanted most to convey the
sense of the passage of time and of space in book form,
through the gradual change in typographic treatment.
The process of designing the book coincided with
significant changes in technology. Typesetting was
moving from hot metal to photosetting, and printing was
changing from letterpress to lithography. Massin could
therefore take advantage of the new opportunity to
arrange the whole work as a paste-up, combining type
and image, often distorted photographically, at the stage
of artwork before sending it to the printer.

Such remarkable works were carried out alongside
Massin's other responsibilities at Gallimard. When he
joined the company in 1960 he took on a catalogue of
10,000 titles and was expected to guarantee, at a time
when publishers' house styles were deemed extremely
important, that Gallimard's distinctive covers, with their
red and black titling, retained their refined elegance.

PUSH PIN STUDIO

- ⊕ Milton Glaser, 1929–
- ⊕ Seymour Chwast, 1931–
- ⊕ Studied at Cooper Union, New York
- ⊕ Formed Push Pin Studio 1954
- ⊕ Use of eclectic sources, satire and wit
- ⊕ Represent revival of interest in illustration
- ⊕ Important teachers of graphic arts

Push Pin Studio was established in 1954 by Milton Glaser and Seymour Chwast, students at the Cooper Union art school in New York. They were later joined by Reynold Ruffins, Edward Sorel, George Leavitt, Tim Lewis, James McMullan and Vincent Ceci, but by 1958 they were left as sole partners. At the time of its formation and throughout the 1960s Push Pin Studio provided an alternative to the high modernism of contemporary American design. Many of its strategies, references to other styles, interest in vernacular printing and use of self-aware pastiche predicted the later full emergence of postmodernism.

The studio made decoration respectable in mainstream graphic design. Perhaps for the first time since Art Deco, revivalism and reference to other periods and cultures were as important in the search for a contemporary form of expression as was clear typographic communication. Push Pin's reaction against modernism was prompted by a wish to be more inclusive than it had been. Modern functional design of the Swiss and American schools had embraced the machine and standardization as ideals and the studio's principles of composition were derived from a Neoplatonic sense of order and harmony in geometry and the grid. In turn photography was preferred to the hand-drawn illustration. Push Pin's designers and illustrators sought to reunite drawing and typography at a time when abstraction and conceptualism had led many fine-art departments to abandon the teaching of drawing. They also wanted to connect with both American vernacular printing and contemporary commercial illustration.

Glaser studied etching with the Italian artist Giorgio Morandi, an experience which confirmed his interest in Italian Renaissance painting. By contrast, many of Chwast's references came from vernacular sources. He was fascinated by nineteenth-century display typefaces used in American print advertising. Other sources of inspiration were Mayan architecture, Victoriana, Art Nouveau, Art Deco, 1920s and 1930s film posters, comics and cartoons – all well suited to editorial and book design, record covers and packaging.

Poster by Seymour Chwast, "The Sensational Houdini", 1973

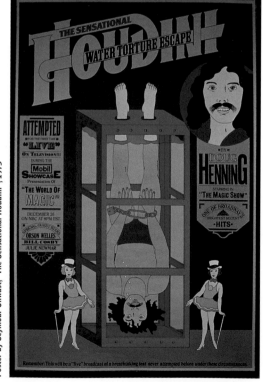

Elektra moves.

Elektra Film Productions moves to 501 Madison Avenue, New York 10022, PL 8-4830.

Chwast designed this poster in the mid-1960s to announce the relocation of the Elektra record company. Eclectic letterforms in motion take the name across the sheet to the new address.

153

Chwast's imitation letterpress posters, such as "The Sensational Houdini" (opposite), show his use of pastiche and vernacular design style. Familiar references in his work included Art Deco and historical forms of popular American printing.

In 1976 Push Pin Studio published a special issue of *Push Pin Graphic* on "Mothers" (left). The monthly *Push Pin Almanac* had become the *Monthly Graphic* and later the *Push Pin Graphic*. Glaser devised the title using a variant of German Fraktur type.

Chwast's anti-Vietnam poster recalls the "Uncle Sam" recruitment poster of World War I and combines its rhetoric with the directness of children's art.

Poster by Seymour Chwast, "End Bad Breath", 1968

End Bad Breath.

For this poster advertising the birth of a new independent record label, Glaser used the symbol of a poppy blooming from a block of concrete.

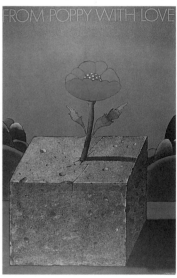

Poster by Milton Glaser, "From Poppy With Love", 1968

154

American mainstream commercial illustration based on realism was challenged by photography in the 1950s. Push Pin offered an alternative style that interpreted the narrative content, often through graphic wit and surrealist devices. Rather than realism, its styles drew on the modern movement in art, including the Metaphysical paintings of De Chirico, the cut-outs of Matisse and Marcel Duchamp's Dadaist ready-mades, to achieve personal and original visual statements which valued interpretation.

Glaser combined painting, drawing, typography and film, and many of his designs collapsed the conventional distinction between design and illustration. He used thin black contour lines and added adhesive colour films to provide plain, light-infused tones. He made use of silhouettes and suggested letterforms, geometry and numbers in illusionistic dimensions that cast shadows.

Chwast wrote, designed, illustrated and printed his own books and made pop papier-mâché sculpture. His style, by contrast with Glaser's, was flat and decorative and he devised many novelty typefaces. The freshness of his approach often evoked children's or primitive art.

Leaving Chwast, Glaser established Milton Glaser, Inc. in 1974. He maintained a broad involvement in print graphics while expanding his work in environmental and interior design. In 1976 he devised the "I [heart] NY" logo for New York State and graphic and decorative programmes for the World Trade Center. He also designed house styles for the magazines *Paris-Match*, *L'Express*, *Esquire* and *Village Voice*. With Walter Bernard he formed WBMG in 1983. At this time he also taught at New York's School of Visual Arts.

Chwast maintained the Push Pin name, first as director of the group Push Pin Lubalin Peckolick and then, from 1985, of the Push Pin Group. He taught at the Cooper Union while continuing to publish the magazine *Push Pin Graphic*. The last version of this was a standard-format, full-colour publication and its final issue appeared in 1980.

Glaser's silhouette of Bob Dylan recalls a self-portrait by the French-born artist Marcel Duchamp. Like the poster artists of the Art Nouveau period, Glaser separated colours by thin black lines. Six million copies of the poster were produced, to be given free with the album, a compilation for the American market.

Poster by Milton Glaser for Columbia Records, "Dylan", 1966

155

Masthead for magazine *U&lc*, 1973; proposed logo for *Mother and Child*, 1966

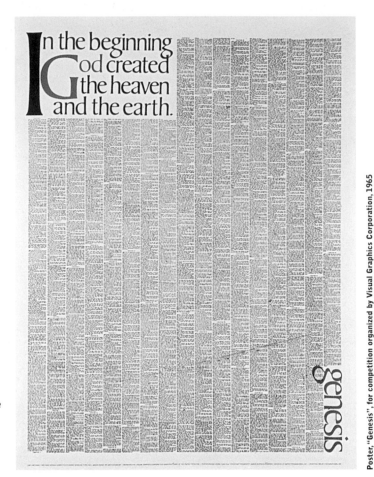

Poster, "Genesis", for competition organized by Visual Graphics Corporation, 1965

The journal *U&lc* (above top) was published by Lubalin, Burns and Rondthaler, initially to promote International Typeface Corporation fonts. The encircled ampersand in the proposed logo for *Mother and Child* (above) evokes a foetus in a womb.

Laid out as a single broadsheet, the Book of Genesis, the first book of the Old Testament of the Bible, functioned as a specimen sheet for Arthur Baker's typeface Baker Signet, sponsored by the Visual Graphics Corporation. The company organized the competition for which Lubalin's design was an entry.

⊕ 1918–81
⊕ Typographer, editorial designer and art director
⊕ Studied design at Cooper Union, New York
⊕ Founded Herb Lubalin Inc 1964
⊕ Expressive and conceptual typography

Herb Lubalin was one of America's most celebrated typographers and art directors. He opened up modern magazines to new opportunities of layout, responding to a looser and more eclectic set of inspirations than modernism had previously encouraged. His work sought to do away with the distinction between type and image.

Lubalin studied design at the Cooper Union art school in New York. After graduating he worked on the city's World's Fair of 1939. His first major appointment came in 1946, as art director at Sudler and Hennessey, a company specializing in design for pharmaceutical products. The position offered an opportunity to become versed in quick decision making in layout, working up sketches and selecting illustrators and photographers.

Among Lubalin's colleagues were the renowned designers Aaron Burns, Seymour Chwast and George Lois. He left in 1964 to form the design partnership Herb Lubalin Inc.

Lubalin's style was witty and exuberant, sharing many features with the work of his contemporaries Seymour Chwast and Milton Glaser at their Push Pin Studio (see pp152–5). He emerged as a highly innovative typographer who rejected functionalism in favour of expressive typography. The introduction of photocomposition in typesetting in the 1960s offered designers great flexibility in selecting and arranging type. Replacing the physical restrictions of hand-set metal type, which had existed since Gutenberg, phototype systems increased the range of available type sizes. Lubalin used technical changes to enhance meaning. By manipulating letterforms with distorting lenses, he developed contrasts of striking

The *No More War!* competition attracted over 2000 entrants. *Avant-Garde*'s logo was later developed by Tom Carnase into the typeface Avant-Garde.

scale. Large headlines, accompanied by tight blocks of type, became one of his hallmarks. Familiar with the work of the Doyle Dane Bernbach agency, which developed conceptual advertising, he was part of the American movement which sought to give visual form to an idea. This was most evident in his typograms – images made of type that symbolize their meaning.

As an experienced editorial designer, Lubalin was asked to redesign the *Saturday Evening Post* in 1961. For the high-profile weekly he introduced a new logo and restyled the interior, making dramatic use of picture editing. In recognition the National Society of Art Directors made him Art Director of the Year.

In the 1960s, when a younger critical and anti-establishment press was growing, Lubalin also designed small-circulation magazines published by Ralph Ginzburg,

including *Eros*, *Fact* and *Avant-garde*. Editorially, these titles reflected, in their progressive coverage of current affairs, the increasing political engagement of the anti-Vietnam generation. Visually, their pioneering exposure of erotic subjects opened up challenging imagery, which was rendered photographically or by illustration. For *Avant-garde* Lubalin devised a logo which was then developed by Tom Carnase as a full typeface, with upper and lower cases, for commercial distribution in 1970.

In that year Lubalin formed the International Typeface Corporation with Aaron Burns and Edward Rondthaler, and over the following years they produced 34 type families and 60 display faces. The Herb Lubalin Study Center of Design and Typography, founded in New York in 1985 to promote research into typographic design, commemorates the designer's achievements.

POP IN THE HIGH STREET

The emergence of Pop art and design was symptomatic of a fundamental change in the character of society in postwar Britain. Not just a style, Pop reflected a change in people's spending patterns and their expectations as consumers, and, in some cases, a changed attitude towards modernity. Unlike other design movements, Pop depended less on a tight network of individual designers than on a broad change in cultural sensibility that affected social attitudes and lifestyles.

The ideas behind Pop art were formulated in the 1950s, but the full flourishing on a mass level of "High Pop" took place between 1958 and 1965. It began in 1952 with the formation of the Independent Group, which met at London's Institute of Contemporary Arts (ICA). Among the members were the artists Richard Hamilton, John McHale and Eduardo Paolozzi, the architects Alison and Peter Smithson, the photographer Nigel Henderson and the critics Lawrence Alloway and Reyner Banham. They held lectures on Detroit car styling, the relationship between art and science, the design of consumer goods, fashion, advertising, comics books and other aspects of American popular culture, all rich in an overlooked iconography. Their exhibitions included "Parallel of Life and Art" (1953), "Man, Machine and Motion" (1955) and "This is Tomorrow" (1956).

The Independent Group reacted in particular against the official taste of the Council of Industrial Design, with its preference for Arts and Crafts principles and stress on functionalism. In 1957 Richard Hamilton listed the characteristics of American popular culture as "popular, transient, expendable, low cost, mass-produced, young, witty, sexy, gimmicky, glamorous and big business", a list that proved prophetic in Britain in the years to follow.

The discussions at the ICA coincided with the founding of Bazaar, a small clothes shop in King's Road, Chelsea, opened by the dress designer Mary Quant in 1957. Quant's own designs emphasized simplicity, geometry and plain colours and were determinedly modern, being identified by the use of a simple daisy device as a graphic trademark.

At the same time the menswear retailer John Stephen started to sell "Italian-look" suits in Carnaby Street. This initiative rapidly expanded until the whole street was dedicated to shops for young people. To give the shops distinctive identities, fascias became more adventurous, with a stress on individuality through choice of scale and colour in lettering. Painted interiors displaying blown-up photographs, striking point-of-sale material, posters and carrier bags all contributed to the increasingly graphic nature of the environment. Pop aimed to be classless and non-hierarchical. At street level this was apparent in the proliferation of Union Jack flags and target symbols on posters, T-shirts, waste-paper bins, spectacles and mugs.

The mixture of fashion, graphics and pop music was most apparent in magazines and record covers. The woman's magazine *Queen* was remodelled in 1957 and *Man about Town* was relaunched as *Town* in 1960. From 1962 the colour supplements that came with the Sunday editions of various prestigious national newspapers helped to disseminate the Pop design style with their high-contrast photography and bold headlines. Nevertheless, the quick succession of styles led to the eclipse of Pop's geometric, modern period by Psychedelia (see pp158–9).

The Union Jack and large, stylized female heads reminiscent of fashion magazines helped to make Carnaby Street, once a traditional shopping street, into a lively and fashionable graphic environment, here decorated also for Christmas.

Photograph by unknown photographer of Carnaby Street, London, December 1967

Cover for Tom Salter's book *Carnaby Street*, 1970

This style of Pop illustration, featuring "soft" figures, bright folk colours and the Union Jack, was also used on record covers and posters. Tom Salter's book on the street at the heart of the Pop scene was designed by Peter Windett and illustrated by Malcolm English.

Paper bags for habitat, c1966

The exuberant design of the Pop emporium's fascia (below), and the reference to the Union Jack in the poster on the window, underline the intimate connection between graphic design, youth, fashion and music.

The use of lower-case Baskerville for the name "habitat" signalled Englishness. A variety of typefaces, stencilled lettering and Art Deco and other revivals reflected the modern eclecticism of the domestic accessories sold by the London shop.

159

Photograph by unknown photographer of Carnaby Street, London, April 1968

PSYCHEDELIC GRAPHICS

By the early 1960s modernist graphic design, once linked mainly with socially progressive ideals, had become the official language of the corporate world. At the same time the reaction to America's role in the Vietnam War, the Civil Rights movement and the increasing pressure for a more liberal attitude towards sex and drugs amounted to a counter-culture among the young. In many ways fashion, graphics and music became the popular media through which their challenge to the status quo was expressed on both sides of the Atlantic.

In California much progressive or underground music involved improvisation through the use of hallucinogenic drugs such as LSD. The flowering of the hippie lifestyle led to a revival of interest in decoration, in part inspired by the organic shapes of Art Nouveau and the Romantic and Symbolist poets and painters.

The most celebrated manifestation of American psychedelia was a series of posters advertising concert performances by West Coast bands at the Avalon Ballroom, Fillmore West and Matrix. They were created by the San Francisco-based designers Rick Griffin, Alton Kelley, Victor Moscoso, Stanley Mouse and Wes Wilson: known collectively as "The Big Five". The members exhibited together in "The Joint Show" at the Moore Gallery in 1967.

Moscoso, born in Spain in 1936, had studied at the Cooper Union art school in New York before a period under the former Bauhaus teacher Josef Albers at Yale University in New Haven. Albers's teaching introduced him to advanced colour theory, which he implemented to extraordinary effect. His characteristic style involved intricate, highly coloured and illusionistic designs. Word and image were printed in complementary colours of equal register to produce an oscillating effect on the retina. Barely legible, names became disguised in the overall scheme, and the implication was that only those who were "turned on" or in tune with the wider cultural scene would appreciate the designs.

With an emphasis on workshops or informal, collective activity, psychedelia and pop graphics collapsed the conventional distinctions between public and private or amateur and professional. This was certainly the case in London, where the style sprang from similar roots in music culture but quickly spread to the retail context of the high street in fashion boutiques and shop design.

For just a few months in 1966 and 1967 a few designers became the leaders of the new style in London. They included the Australian Martin Sharp, who designed the iconic "Mister Tambourine Man" poster and the underground magazine *Oz*. More on the American model, Hapshash and the Coloured Coat was a short-lived association between Nigel Waymouth and Michael English, who produced posters for concert venues, most notably U.F.O. (Unlimited Freak Out). Their designs employed new Day-Glo and metallic inks. The silk-screen print technique allowed the use of large areas of flat colour reminiscent of contemporary Pop art and abstract painting.

The short-term impact of psychedelic graphics was felt in the spread of shops selling posters to hang in the home, whether reproductions of Art Nouveau or more recent designs. The more significant challenge of psychedelia was to open the door to the expressive potential of decoration, preparing the ground for postmodernism.

The cult women's clothes shop Biba was founded in London in 1963 by the fashion illustrator Barbara Hulanicki and her husband, Stephen Fitz-Simon. John McConnell's logo reveals the influence of Art Nouveau on psychedelic graphics.

Logo by John McConnell for Biba, early 1960s

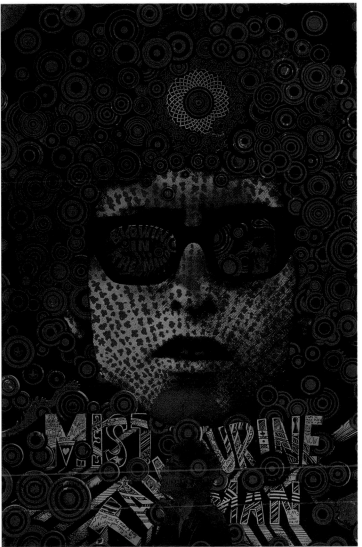

Poster by Martin Sharp, "Mister Tambourine Man", 1967

This best-selling poster by Martin Sharp is based on the imaginative lyrics of one of Bob Dylan's most popular songs. It was reprinted about 40 times and sold over 100,000 copies. The image was used on the cover of issue seven of *Oz* magazine in the same year.

Poster by Moscoso for concert, 1967

161

In this concert poster Moscoso combines a figurative and a typographic approach. Both elements were aspects of his posters for the San Francisco music promoters Family Dog. This example interprets the painting *Jupiter and Thetis* (1811) by the French nineteenth-century neoclassical artist Ingres, but in the place of the drapery in the earlier work, Moscoso inserts a large fish.

THE UNDERGROUND PRESS

Amid a tide of social and cultural change in the second half of the 1960s, the underground, or alternative, press was part of a move towards freedom from constraints. The new magazines and newspapers were a reaction against the over-professionalization of the "adult" press, particularly its reliance on publicity and advertising, and they devised radical design styles to present their call for the overthrow of society.

The American academic Theodore Roszak, in *The Making of a Counter Culture* of 1970, saw the counter-culture as a reaction specifically against technocracy. Youth in many Western societies experienced a simultaneous wave of dissatisfaction with the existing order. Disillusioned by conventional politics and aware of the earlier Civil and Black Rights campaigns, they brought conflict to a head in 1968 in anti-Vietnam War demonstrations, the student and workers' revolts in France and the Prague uprising against Soviet rule.

The underground press subsumed political issues within a wider cultural programme. Political outlooks varied from the activism of the Trotskyite *Black Dwarf* to the mysticism of *Gandalf's Garden*. Two of the longest-running British titles were *Oz* (1967–73) and *International Times* (1966–72), renamed *it* after a successful lawsuit initiated by the establishment newspaper *The Times*.

Richard Neville, who founded *Oz* in his native Australia in 1963, wrote retrospectively about the design of the magazine: "Black inks were drained from rotary presses, and replaced by gold, turquoise, cyan blue, sienna, saffron, heliotrope, and even white. A photographic process enables sweeping visual versatility, so the whole world can be plundered for decoration – from food labels, oriental comic books, Tibetan scrolls and *Encyclopaedia Britannica*. Copyright is ignored."

As art director of *Oz*, Jonathan Goodchild was largely responsible for the layout, which changed from each issue, along with the masthead. Illustrators included fellow Australian émigré Martin Sharp, Michael English, Nigel Waymouth, Michael McInnerney and David Vaughan. Imaginative use was made of the IBM "golfball" typewriter for the arrangement of text, while the assembled artwork was printed by web-offset lithography. This easy transfer encouraged eclecticism as to imagery, which included Far Eastern motifs, Victoriana and sexually explicit photographs.

An indication of the subject matter of *Oz* comes from the titles of various issues: "Psychedelia" (3 and 4), "Magic Theatre" (16) "Beautiful Freaks" (24) "Yippies" (31) and "Angry *Oz*" (37). Like other alternative magazines, it embraced mystic and oriental philosophy, experimentation with drugs, sexual liberation and psychiatry, as well as avant-garde music, art and literature.

In many respects the graphic style adopted by the underground was a return of the repressed. All that had been disallowed by modernism's search for order reappeared, along with a stress on the playful, pleasurable, sensuous and erotic. The underground press found more sophisticated parallels in the work of Milton Glaser and Seymour Chwast of Push Pin Studio (see pp152–5) and Herb Lubalin (pp156–7) in the United States. Always sensitive to the pressures of censorship, and in a changed social climate, the presses ceased in the early 1970s, *Oz* closing in 1973 as a result of the high-profile court case over the notorious "School Kids" issue.

This cover design for a New York underground magazine incorporated a found image that had been used in April 1966 by Wes Wilson in a Family Dog poster for a concert at Fillmore West.

Cover by "Fosso" for magazine *The East Village Other*, vol. 3, no. 6, 1967

Cover by Graham Keen for magazine *it*, no. 43, 1968

A cover for the magazine *it*, published in London, shows a mix of found images – a design style commonly used by underground publications of the time. References to the East and the hippie lifestyle are combined with decorative type to reflect *it*'s eclectic outlook.

The fourth number of UK *Oz* – known as the "psychedelic issue" – featured a cover in the form of a three-section poster. The design incorporated whiplash lines, reminiscent of Art Nouveau, together with Eastern mystical figures in stylized, flat graphic form.

Poster-form cover by Michael English and Nigel Waymouth for magazine *Oz*, no. 4, 1967

CHINESE GRAPHIC DESIGN

Graphic design in China in the twentieth century has reflected the country's extreme political circumstances. For most of the period China pursued isolationism, separated from both its Asian neighbours and the West. State control of imagery under communism after 1948 led to a form of mass propaganda in which posters played a significant part.

China has long been of great interest to historians of graphic design because of its traditions of innovation and invention in papermaking, printing and typography. The ancient religious philosophy of Confucianism accorded great respect to the artist-scholar figure. In the pursuit of the harmonious life and the principles of Yin and Yang as defined in *I Ching* (*The Book of Changes*), the graphic arts played an important role, and they were often at a more developed stage than in the West. Movable type, for example, was introduced between 1041 and 1048 by Bi Sheng, over 400 years before an equivalent technique was invented by Gutenberg. By contrast, Western-style graphic design was not known in China until the early twentieth century, when foreign manufacturers introduced advertising for cosmetics, tobacco and pharmaceutical goods.

In the 1920s and 1930s, with the metropolis of Shanghai acting as a clearing-house for Western imports, a thoroughly modern approach to graphic design evolved, known as the "Shanghai style". This was in large part an adaptation of Art Deco (see pp80–3) and combined Chinese letterforms with stylized figures encouraging Western lifestyles. An avant-garde also developed at this time. Chinese typography can be set to read vertically and horizontally or from right and left, but some Chinese designers, aware of modernism and the Bauhaus (see pp60–3), applied the principles of the new design with greater flexibility to extend the picture plane.

By 1948, on the foundation of the People's Republic of China, Mao Tse-tung established a revolutionary programme for all areas of life. In design Soviet Socialist Realism was one model, offering a way to depict the heroicized worker, political leaders or the masses. However, the Chinese variant of communism added a romanticism to this, often drawing on folk traditions of poetry and printmaking. Rules for the official styles were established at the Beijing National Congress of Artists and Writers of 1949.

In graphic design these rules were implemented through the increasing number of poster collectives and censorship of stylistic individuality. Foreign influences and commercial graphic design were discouraged. The increasing cult of personality of Chairman Mao meant that the majority of posters featured him as a symbol of the transformation of China. This process culminated in the Cultural Revolution of 1966–76, when quotations from Mao's speeches were compiled in the *Little Red Book*.

Mao's death in 1976 led to a reaction against China's isolation, and under Teng Hsiao-p'ing an Open Door Policy was gradually introduced. Once again graphic designers were allowed to refer to external influences and a new generation addressed the threat of environmental destruction, religious freedom and other social issues, often using a symbolic or conceptual approach that shared ideas with Japanese and Western design.

Originally a family-interest magazine, *The Ark* underwent a stylistic change in the mid-1930s, reflecting interests in the photomontage of Soviet designers such as Alexander Rodchenko. The technique was used here to depict young pioneers.

Cover for magazine *The Ark*, January 1937

千年古樹開了花
十年古國成了新國家
三大敵人都打倒

慶祝中華人民共和國成立

五星紅旗呼啦啦飄
毛主席帶著我們跑
跑遍了五湖跟四海
一統呀江山樂陶陶

老百姓自己當了家

Anonymous poster, "Tiananmen Square", 1950

Celebrating the founding of the People's Republic of China, this poster depicts crowds hailing communist leaders in the huge Tiananmen Square in the capital, Beijing. Posters of this kind took elements such as bright colours, a highly illustrative technique and decorative repetition from folk art. The text is based on folk poetry and likens China to a 1000-year-old tree in bloom.

没有核恐吓 没有核战争!

Poster by Liu Yi-bing, "No Nuclear Threat, No Nuclear War", 1989

This design combines the international poster language of Swiss–style modern and modern Japanese styles. Working on a conceptual level, the symbols representing nuclear missiles and the mushroom cloud of a nuclear explosion are incorporated in the Chinese character for "No".

Roman Cieslewicz was an important figure in bringing together the ideas of Expressionism and Constructivism of the 1920s from central Europe and reviving them for the next generation of artists and designers, especially in his adopted France.

Born in Lwow, Poland, Cieslewicz graduated from the Cracow Academy of Fine Arts in 1955. In the midst of doctrinaire Socialist Realism, the official artistic style of the Soviet bloc countries, Cracow Academy was the fulcrum of the Polish poster school. Instead of the official pictorial system of idealized representation, which aimed to explain correct political ideas as transparently as possible, the Polish poster school engaged with symbolic and psychological ideas, using a visual vocabulary which developed from pre-1945 European modernism and the School of Paris as well as from Poland's own visual history.

Under masters such as Tomaszewski (see pp142–3), Cieslewicz interpreted ideas in symbolic ways in his early posters. Often for film and theatrical performances, they included expressive and experimental lettering which formed an integral part of the design. As a young professional, Cieslewicz worked for the national organization of graphic designers, WAG, which produced nationally approved designs for all cultural and political initiatives. He then moved to art-direct the independent *Ty I Ja* (You and I), a Polish women's magazine, which opened up the international magazine scene to him.

Cieslewicz was of a second generation of film-makers and graphic designers who reinterpreted the experimental ideas of collage and photomontage originally devised by Constructivism. While interested in the Polish group Blok, formed in 1924, he was aware that the subject matter of contemporary graphic design must embrace modern style and fashion if it was to appeal to young people. In this way he transformed the principles of Constructivism for the 1960s.

After leaving Poland to work in Paris in 1963, Cieslewicz became a French citizen in 1971. He first worked as art director for *Elle* magazine. Many of his designs, in page layouts or posters, depend on a strong central focus using the circle; other designs use the symbols of hands, eyes, jaws or legs. Aware of the ambiguities of political radicalism, Cieslewicz participated in the protests of May 1968 in Paris, particularly the attack on the media and the perceived banality of much mass-produced, consumer-oriented, American-influenced popular culture.

Cieslewicz intentionally crossed boundaries between "serious" and "popular" graphic design. He was drawn to work on magazines just as much as prestigious cultural events. In the late 1970s he devised the house style for publications at the Centre de Création Industrielle and the Musée National d'Art Moderne in Paris. His designs appeared in exhibitions exploring the history of avant-garde cultural exchange between architecture, film, photography and painting, such as "Paris–Berlin 1900–1933" (1978), "Paris–Moscow 1900–1930" (1979) and "Paris–Paris 1937–1957" (1981).

⊖ 1930–96
⊖ Polish-born graphic designer who worked in Paris
⊖ Studied graphic art at Cracow Academy of Fine Arts
⊖ Early designs posters in Polish tradition
⊖ Brought Expressionism and Constructivism to design and art direction
⊖ Politically active in Paris in May 1968
⊖ Commissions for Centre Georges Pompidou and Musée Nationale d'Art Moderne in Paris
⊖ Designs shown in international exhibitions in 1970s and 1980s

166

Poster, "Zoom contre la pollution de l'oeil", 1971

Zoom, a magazine which looked critically at the impact on society of photography and visual culture under capitalism, was a product of the New Left and arose from the events of 1968 in France. Cieslewicz's design, with its attack on "the pollution of the eye", comments frankly on the limitations of mediated cutlure.

Poster for Witold Gombrowicz's play *Yvonne, Princesse de Bourgogne*, 1982

Cieslewicz introduced the Polish tradition of strongly individual posters to Parisian cultural life, as in this design for a 1982 production at the Théâtre de l'Odéon in Paris. Often dominated by a single element, his posters were marked by their graphic energy and immediacy.

167

Cover for catalogue for exhibition "Paris–Moscow 1900–1930", 1979

From 1975 Cieslewicz worked closely with the Centre Georges Pompidou in Paris on posters and catalogues for many exhibitions. For the catalogue for "Paris–Moscow 1900–1930" he designed the cover and the interior contents. His interest in art movements of the early twentieth century allowed his designs to evoke the work shown in the exhibitions without lapsing into pastiche.

CUBAN POSTERS

In Cuba, a revolutionary communist society since 1959, the poster remains an important form of public address. At a time of visual overload in international communication, Cuban posters are remarkable for their visual vibrancy and the energy of their messages.

Unlike the Soviet revolutionary graphic design of the early 1920s, when Constructivism was the preferred avant-garde style, in Cuba there was no dominant style. Instead, by avoiding the heroism of socialist realism and the more overt strategies of capitalist advertising alike, designers produced cultural and political posters in an eclectic variety of artistic styles.

On 26 July 1953 Fidel Castro and a group of young radicals attacked the Moncada barracks in revolt against the right-wing regime led by President Fulgencio Batista, which had come to power in Cuba after a coup d'état in March the previous year. This event was subsequently commemorated as the origin of a resistance movement that led to the successful revolution. This began on 1 January 1959, when Batista left Cuba and Fidel Castro became the first and only successful communist leader in the Americas. Cuba's location as a large island to the south of the United States gave it a high-profile strategic position. All eyes were turned towards its future, especially during the Cuban missile crisis of 1962, when war between the United States and USSR-supported Cuba briefly seemed inevitable.

The artistic question faced by Cuban communists was whether revolutionary culture could be different or, alternatively, whether it was sufficient to democratize existing bourgeois culture. Cuban politicians and leading cultural figures were especially concerned to define themselves against the cultural hegemony of their powerful neighbours in the United States. Much use was made of less hierarchical forms, in particular film and theatre, posters and leaflets, songs and poetry. The works produced displayed a greater concern for liberation and class struggle than did the culture of escapism and luxury associated with capitalism.

At that time among the leading poster designers in Cuba were Raúl Martínez, Alfredo Rostgaard and Félix Beltrán. They received commissions to advertise official events, the anniversaries of political struggle and the screening of films, often political in nature, by ICAIC, the Institute of Cuban Film Arts and Industries.

The visual styles of Cuban posters were varied and ideas were borrowed from Pop art, psychedelia and folklore, as well from as the modern graphic design of members of the New York School, such as Herb Lubalin (see pp156–7). Amid this wealth of imagery, Che (Ernesto) Guevara became an icon of the revolutionary movement for the younger generation. Guevara had left Cuba to lead a group of guerrillas in Bolivia, where he was assassinated in 1967. At a time of widespread protest against the Vietnam War, his face was used in many posters to symbolize the oppression of the Third World, and in this way he became a mythic hero. The legendary image of Guevara was based on a photograph by Alberto Korda which showed the communist star on his beret, his long hair and his bearded, slightly upturned and resolute face. It suited the anti-establishment culture of the time, and from the late 1960s the image spread throughout the world as part of the visual language of student politics and wider political protest.

Poster by Raúl Martínez, "26 Fidel", 1968

In a design that unites Latin-American folkloristic, bright, dense colours and a drawn image, the number refers to the 26 July Movement.

DIA DEL GUERRILLERO HEROICO 8 DE OCTUBRE
JOURNEE DU GUERILLERO HEROIQUE 8 OCTOBRE
DAY OF THE HEROIC GUERRILLA OCTOBER 8

يوم المقاوم الباسل ٨ اكتوبر

Che Guevara's image, with beret and revolutionary star, is framed by pulsating lines of radiation, indicating strength. The poster was published by the Havana-based OPSAAAL (Organization of Solidarity with the Peoples of Asia, Africa, and Latin America) to indicate the spread of revolutionary struggle across South America.

Poster by Elena Serrano, "Day of the Heroic Guerrilla", 1968

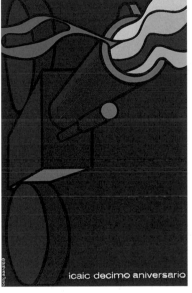

icaic decimo aniversario

Poster by Alfredo Rostgaard, "icaic decimo aniversario", 1969

169

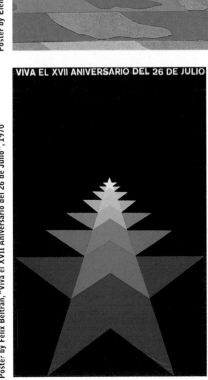

VIVA EL XVII ANIVERSARIO DEL 26 DE JULIO

Poster by Felix Beltran, "Viva el XVII Aniversario del 26 de Julio", 1970

Cuban posters were designed in various styles that acknowledged international modern visual languages. Here the graphic emblem of the revolution, the red star, is the basis of a poster that commemorates the seventeenth anniversary of an attack, led by Castro, on an army barracks in Santiago de Cuba on 26 July 1953.

ICAIC was the main promoter of the modern poster in Cuba through its publicity campaigns for the popular film movement. In this poster celebrating the tenth anniversary of the revolution the film camera is seen as a weapon in the revolutionary struggle.

⊖ Pierre Bernard, 1942–
⊖ François Miehe, 1942–
⊖ Gérard Paris-Clavel, 1943–
⊖ Radical collective of French poster designers committed, following events of May 1968, to political, social and cultural intervention through graphic design
⊖ Links with Polish poster tradition
⊖ Later work included identity for Louvre museum and signage

170

Members of the French poster collective Grapus have been described as the guerrillas of graphic design. Formed in the aftermath of the student worker uprising in Paris, May 1968, the group continued for over 20 years to work only for political or cultural concerns to which it was sympathetic. The original members were Pierre Bernard, François Miehe and Gérard Paris-Clavel. In 1974 Jean-Paul Bachollet joined them, and a year later Alexander Jordan.

In spring 1968 10 million workers and students demonstrated on the streets of Paris against the government of General De Gaulle, demanding political and cultural change. Central to the student movement was the perception that a cultural hegemony was being imposed by the United States and supported by conservative Western governments. The writings of New Left philosophers informed the movement's views, and struggles in Cuba and Vietnam and the independence of African nations gave it an international perspective. Culture became radicalized and alternative artistic activities were adopted.

The three founder members of Grapus met at the Atelier Populaire at the École Nationale Supérieure des Arts Décoratifs in Paris, while Miehe was still a student. The emergency Atelier was producing silk-screen images for fly-posting in the streets. A slogan would be agreed and a forceful image produced in one day. In the 1960s French graphic design was largely preoccupied with advertising. In response, Bernard and Paris-Clavel had studied with Henryk Tomaszewski (see pp142–3) in Warsaw to find an alternative. Bernard later said: "We wanted to speak on the walls about cinema, theatre, poetry, history as had been done in Poland, and about politics as we had seen in the Cuban magazines."

Grapus, the name adopted in 1970, has been explained as a nonsense word for graphics but it also refers to "crapules staliniennes" (Stalinist scum), a label given to the members because of their extreme politics. The group maintained a strong allegiance to the French Communist Party, which they tried to persuade to take on a more experimental approach to campaign posters.

Their approach was collective and it is not possible to attribute individual designs to members of the group. They preferred handwriting to typography, as it gave their designs an immediacy and energy. Collage was favoured for the same reason, and many posters used an iconography of heads, globes or hands, in what has been called a "graphic slang".

By 1991, when it disbanded, Grapus had grown into a substantial graphic design agency, designing signage and corporate identities, including one for the reopening of the Louvre in 1989. Bernard formed Atelier de Création Graphique to continue major public graphic design projects. Paris-Clavel pursued his belief in creative conflict by working in the group Ne Pas Plier (Do Not Bend).

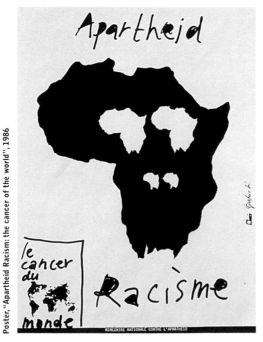

Poster, "Apartheid Racism: the cancer of the world", 1986

In a graphic attack on South African racism a haunting skeleton emerges from the repeated outline of Black Africa, from which the southern tip of South Africa is omitted. The preference for the handwritten is clear, and Pierre Bernard has been quoted as saying: "You cannot lie when you write with your hand."

This poster was unusual in the work of Grapus for its incorporation of photography. The spectral background image of Paris recalls Hiroshima.

An exhibition of the work of Grapus, including this poster, was held at the Musée de l'Affiche (Museum of the Poster) in Paris in 1982. In a reference to American popular culture the face evokes Mickey Mouse, even though the eyes are a hammer and sickle and a military target, and Hitler's forelock is unmistakable. The graffiti-like mark-making and lettering are characteristic of the group's style.

171

LATE MODERN AND POSTMODERNISM

The last 30 years of the twentieth century were marked by important changes in the cultural and philosophical premises of Western society, and these strongly influenced the way in which graphic design developed. The terms "late modern" and "postmodernism" are used to describe the two major design tendencies of the late twentieth century, although they are by no means all-inclusive. These two styles co-existed throughout this period rather than occurring sequentially. While the late modernists continued with accepted values, the postmodernists defined new ground that challenged fundamental assumptions about the meaning and purpose of design.

Late modern is easier to understand than postmodernism as it is less theoretically complex. The label refers to designers who were interested in extending or adapting principles of modernism in the changed situation in which they found themselves towards the end of the century. In the Netherlands, for example, graphic design represented a late flowering of modern design. The belief that visual communication could enhance life through corporate identity schemes and well-planned signage systems, or that the graphic designer could contribute to the richness of cultural life, was in direct continuity with the vision of the experimental designers of the 1920s. Heavily subsidized public programmes allowed design to play a central role in the creation of a national identity in which social welfare and culture were linked with social democracy rather than with the market economy.

Philosophers and historians were divided in their diagnosis of the degree of change that occurred in the change from a technological to an information society or, as it is sometimes described, from an industrial to post-industrial society. Postmodernists argued that a category shift had occurred in the economic and technological base of society, from high to late capitalism. Modernism had been inspired by the machine and a production-oriented view of design based on the principles of Fordism – industrially organized labour based on standardization and named after the car manufacturer Henry Ford. By contrast, postmodernism became associated with a consumer-oriented view of society, in which emphasis was placed on design for pleasure and to establish identity. The postmodern graphic designer no longer searched for a single dominant message or visual form but instead used hybrid imagery, mixed typographic styles and delighted in complex composition.

On one level postmodernism represented the return of ornament, symbolism and wit, qualities already present in much Pop-oriented graphics. However, it was in architecture rather

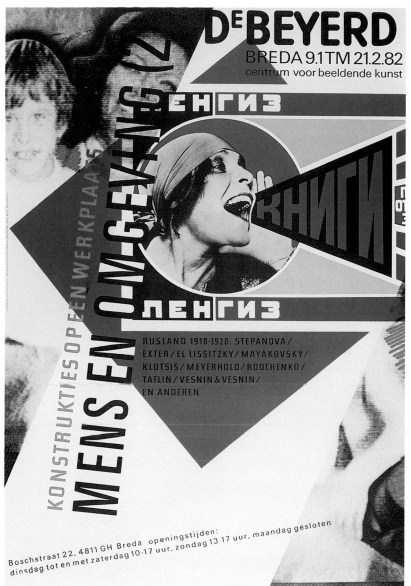

In this poster for an exhibition held in Breda, in the Netherlands, Jan van Toorn incorporates a poster by the Russian Constructivist Alexander Rodchenko. The earlier work's initial graphic energy is extended by the use of additional photomontage. Such layering of design languages, which has a parallel in intertextuality in recent literature, became a central part of postmodernism.

than graphic design that the first definitions of the postmodern were articulated. In 1972 the architects Robert Venturi, Denise Scott Brown and Steven Izenour published *Learning from Las Vegas*. This extremely influential book explained how the commercial strip of American cities is replete with signs that act as symbolic systems. Rather than disparaging or dismissing these as kitsch, the authors advocated their use as a way of enriching architecture and design. Architecture was perceived as a language and this analogy also offered many possibilities for the graphic designer. In turn the architectural critic Charles Jencks, in *The Language of Postmodern Architecture* (1984), also took the linguistic and symbolic character of architecture as central to his definition of the postmodern. He considered the style to be a play on artistic languages, exploiting elements such as parody, pastiche and quotation from previous historical styles and deliberate eclecticism. Jencks identified the symbolic end of modernism as the destruction in 1972 of the Pruitt-Igoe housing development in St Louis, a large-scale heroic modernist project that had proved uninhabitable. For him, postmodernism replaced the modernists' entrenched faith in the "master codes" of such functionalism.

By the early 1980s postmodernism was evident in all fields of design. In furniture and product design, for example, the Milan-based Studio Alchymia and Memphis engaged with the cultural meaning of objects, enriching their designs semantically through allusions that were reflected in the titles. In graphic design a serious critique of the Bauhaus premise "form follows function" was sustained by Wolfgang Weingart, who, at Basle in the 1970s, flouted many of the conventions of Swiss typography in order to re-examine the nature of typographic design. An influential teacher, Weingart provided a link between the new wave in Switzerland and the United States through students such as April Greiman and Daniel Friedman, who became important polemical designers on returning to America.

In France, the philosophical tradition of structuralism defined an openness of meaning that inspired graphic designers. In particular, Roland Barthes, in his book *Mythologies* (published in French in 1959 and in English in 1972) and the later essay *The Death of the Author* (1968), suggested that elements of popular culture could be understood as multi-layered processes of signification. By contrast with what modernist graphic design had proposed, it was no longer the designer's role to try to control meaning or to solve the problem of communication. Instead typography could be a discursive practice, not concerned with the delivery of a certain message but inviting a multiplicity of readings. As the recipient "deconstructed" the visual message, communication became a self-reflexive process.

⊖ Theo Crosby, 1925–94 writer and architect
⊖ Alan Fletcher, 1931–
⊖ Colin Forbes, 1931–
⊖ Kenneth Grange, 1929–
⊖ Mervyn Kurlansky, 1936–
⊖ International design partnership formed in 1972 by Crosby, Fletcher, Forbes, Grange and Kurlansky
⊖ Interdisciplinary approach to graphic, product, interior and architectural design
⊖ Offices in London, New York, Los Angeles, Austin, Texas and San Francisco, and major clients in Europe, America and Far East

Pentagram is a multi-disciplinary partnership specializing in graphic design, product design, and architecture. Its name was inspired by the fact that there were five founding partners: the graphic designers Alan Fletcher, Colin Forbes and Mervyn Kurlansky, the architect Theo Crosby, and the product designer Kenneth Grange. In 1969 Kurlansky joined the partnership Crosby/Fletcher/Forbes and in 1972 the four, together with Grange, formed Pentagram. The company represents the high end of professional design, and in a survey published in 1987 by the British newspaper the *Financial Times* it was rated by its peers as the "Rolls-Royce of Design".

In 2000 there were, in addition to the original headquarters in London, offices in New York, San Francisco, and Austin, Texas, and a total in England and the United States of 19 partners. The partnership model on which the organization is based allows it to be flexible in handling changes in the world of design. New partners, appointed on the strength of their existing design reputations, join the company and bring fresh perspectives, many of them representing the ideas of a younger generation. Nevertheless, the group's philosophy remains strongly informed by the co-founders. It can be summed up as tackling the management of design identity through whichever means is appropriate. In Pentagram's graphic design there is no dominant style but rather a confident, easily recognized approach. The main components are a clean, crisp visual appearance and a sense of humour, often expressed through graphic wit and visual puns. These characteristics are accompanied by exacting professional standards in photography, illustration, and typography, as well as in print and film processes at the post-design stage.

Each partner acts as the creative head of a team that consists of senior designers, who are sometimes given associate status, and two or three junior designers. The layout of the London office reflects this working pattern.

The company originated in the design group Fletcher Forbes and Gill, which was founded in London in 1962. Alan Fletcher had studied at the Central School of Art and the Royal College of Art, both in London, in the early 1950s before going on to complete his education in the United States, at Yale University. Fletcher's period in America coincided with the high point of the New York school of design and while there he worked at the Container Corporation of America and *Fortune* magazine before returning to England to introduce the new ideas of concept-driven graphics and art direction to the London design world.

Colin Forbes also studied at the Central School of Art, where he later became head of Graphic Design. At this time the school was an important focus for the teaching of Swiss modernism in

Alan Fletcher's corporate identity for Reuters (below) evoked the punched tape used at one time by news agencies. David Hillman's masthead for the *Guardian* newspaper (bottom) was unusual at the time in combining two typefaces.

Logo for Reuters, 1968; masthead for *Guardian*, 1988

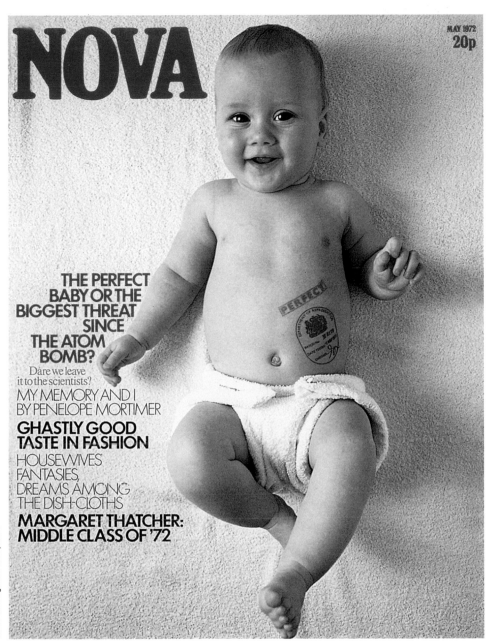

Cover for magazine *Nova*, 1972

Nova was a British monthly magazine that gained a reputation for tackling socially challenging subjects previously considered taboo. The art direction of David Hillman stressed the equal importance of the visual impact and the editorial content.

Poster by Alan Fletcher for Pirelli, 1965

Created by Alan Fletcher in 1965, when he was a member of the Crosby/Fletcher/Forbes partnership, this poster makes the passengers part of the design. Seated in the top deck of the bus, they supplied heads and shoulders for the figures wearing Pirelli slippers.

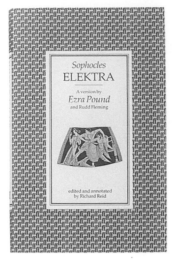

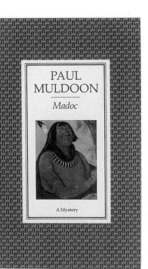

Faber & Faber, a literary publisher with a strong reputation for its earlier design policy, turned to Pentagram to revive this pre-eminence. The solution relied on a combination of patterned papers and a panel carrying an illustration. The scheme won the Design and Art Direction gold award.

Pentagram was commissioned to carry out a comprehensive branding campaign for an alliance of multinational airlines formed in 1997. The Star Alliance logo, made up from the crowns of five pyramids, was carefully incorporated to sit alongside individual existing identities.

Book covers by John McConnell for Faber & Faber, 1981–

Identity for Star Alliance by Justus Oehler, 1997

178

London. Before the formation of Pentagram, Forbes worked as an assistant to Herbert Spencer, the editor of the magazine *Typographica*.

Bob Gill, an American, was the third partner. He had studied at the Philadelphia Museum of Art School and worked on record covers for CBS before moving to London in 1960. The three designers were well placed to combine the best of European and American approaches and realized that by joining forces they could take on big clients at a time when the character and technologies of graphic design were rapidly changing.

In 1972 various changes in staff led to a reformulation of their original concept. Kenneth Grange, the designer of the Kodak Instamatic camera and the Kenwood food mixer, joined the graphic specialists, bringing expertise in product design. The architect Theo Crosby, who had recently curated the exhibition "How to Play the Environment

Game" at the Hayward Gallery in London, also joined the group, and Pentagram was established.

Over the years Pentagram's clients have included Olivetti, Rank Xerox, IBM, Reuters, the *Guardian* newspaper, the Victoria and Albert Museum, Swatch, the shoe retailers Clarks, the Crafts Council, the Pet Shop Boys, the publishers Penguin Books and Faber & Faber, and many others. The group's work covers all aspects of design for publication, packaging and advertising, and there is a strong emphasis on exhibition, environmental and retail design.

The subsequent roll-call of Pentagram partners and associates reads like a who's who of graphic design. Aware of its pre-eminent position in the profession, the group has sponsored a design prize and the Pentagram Lecture at the Design Museum in London. Five volumes illustrating the designs of the partners and explaining their underlying philosophies have been published.

日経 デザイン 9
NIKKEI DESIGN   1999

特集／カラーデザイン
●色は力, 色は財産
特別リポート／スターバックスのデザイン

Cover by Angus Hyland for magazine *Nikkei Design*, 1998

Angus Hyland joined Pentagram as a partner in 1998. On the strength of three trial designs he took on the styling of *Nikkei Design*, Japan's leading design magazine, aimed at in-house designers, design managers and executives. The brief required that each cover should depict the general theme of an issue. In this case Sumo wrestlers are used to interpret the impact of the iMac computer on Japanese product design.

Packaging for CDs by Daniel Weil, 1993

London-based Pentagram partner, Daniel Weil created a hard plastic case for the Pet Shop Boys' CD *Very* and a soft plastic version for the limited-edition CD *Very Relentless*. These pieces of work show how the boundaries between graphic design and industrial design are blurred.

⊕ 1928–
⊕ Leading figure in modern Dutch design
⊕ Studied at Minerva Academy of Arts and Crafts in Groningen and Institute of Industrial Arts in Amsterdam
⊕ Creator of "new alphabet" intended for computer reading
⊕ Designer of identities for art galleries and corporate identities
⊕ Director of Boymans-van Beuningen Museum in Rotterdam 1985–93

In Dutch graphic design of the second half of the twentieth century Wim Crouwel represents the continuation of the belief in form and function working together to increase the possibilities of typographic communication. An experimental designer, he has been quoted as saying: "Typography must be visually orderly for the purpose of good readability."

Crouwel trained as a painter at the Minerva Academy of Arts and Crafts in Groningen from 1947 to 1949 and then in design at the Institute of Industrial Arts in Amsterdam in 1951–2. On graduating he opened his own studio in Amsterdam and, inspired by Swiss typography, interpreted design as a matter of problem-solving. Crouwel felt attuned to the contemporary interest in Minimalism in the visual arts and became the designer for a series of exhibitions at the Stedelijk van Abbemuseum in Eindhoven, where he applied a cool, systematic approach. In 1964 he followed the director, De Wilde, to the Stedelijk Museum in Amsterdam, where he introduced a rigorous house style for standardized catalogue sizes, using grids and standard typefaces.

A keen supporter of international debate, Crouwel became, in 1963, the first general secretary of ICOGRADA (International Council of Graphic Design Associations). In the same year he was a founding member of Total Design with the graphic designer Benno Wissing and the industrial designer Friso Kramer. The broad model was that of Henrion Associates in London (see pp120–1). Through their name the three signalled a preparedness to take on graphic and environmental corporate design as the first multi-disciplinary design group in the Netherlands. Early commissions came from the oil company PAM, to design petrol stations and a complete visual identity. Total Design made a significant impact on the design infrastructure of the modern Netherlands. For example, from 1968 the company took on the corporate identity for the PTT (Postal, Telegraph and Telephone Authority) and Crouwel designed the basic set of denominational stamps, using the design to signal a modern, democratic country. In a similar way visitors entering the country via Schiphol international airport were greeted by a signage system designed by Wissing and Crouwel in 1965–7. This formed one of the first rigorously consistent design systems and became a model for many of the world's transport systems.

Crouwel developed his "new alphabet" in 1967. Extending the idea of the grid as used in Swiss typography, he applied rectangular units as a basic matrix for letterforms. The typeface was intended for computer reading: because the alphabet is composed of units on a grid, letters could be translated to the screen without distortion.

In his later career Crouwel held several important teaching positions and has been an influential force in Dutch graphic design. From 1985 to 1993 he was also director of the Boymans-van Beuningen Museum in Rotterdam, where he oversaw a major extension of the design collections.

Poster for exhibition "Jean Dubuffet Grafiek", 1960

jean
dubuffet
stedelijk van abbemuseum eindhoven
24 september tot 30 oktober 1960

dagelijks geopend van 10-17 uur
zondag van 14-18 uur
dinsdag-en donderdagavond van 20-22 uur

grafiek

In this poster for an exhibition of graphic work by Jean Dubuffet, and in subsequent designs, Crouwel tested how much of the letterform was needed to achieve visual recognition and understanding. The design characteristically asserted an identity for the institution rather than the individual artist.

While "new alphabet" was an exercise in rational design, the resultant typeface, as seen in this catalogue, was perhaps too esoteric for general legibility, requiring considerable concentration to be understood.

A poster for an exhibition held at the Stedelijk Museum in Amsterdam in 1968 illustrates one of the more extreme applications of Crouwel's typographic design. The letters are defined by the squares they occupy in a grid.

Stamp for PTT (Postal, Telegraph and Telephone Authority), 1980

This stamp commemorates the hundredth birthday of Willem Drees, a former Social Democrat prime minister. The lettering, composition and colours, which include those of his coalition government, were chosen to signify aspects of his career.

Covers for magazine *DA+AT (Dutch Art + Architecture Today)*, 1985–8

This magazine was published between 1977 and 1988 by the Netherlands Ministry of Welfare, Health and Cultural Affairs. Van Toorn's design for the cover acted as packaging and included a removable seal. The illustration, which differed with every issue, was an adhesive address label.

182

⊕ 1932–
⊕ Polemical designer who challenges social role of designer
⊕ Studied at Institute of Industrial Arts, Amsterdam
⊕ Designs for art galleries and self-directed projects
⊕ Director of Jan van Eyck Academy, Maastricht

In the Netherlands, a country renowned for both its three-dimensional and graphic design traditions, Jan van Toorn has a reputation as a polemical, critical voice who pursues an independent path in his work. He challenges what he sees as the repressive tolerance of a culture of consensus, a determined stance which has led to his being called "the Brecht of graphic design".

Van Toorn studied at the Institute of Industrial Arts (later the Rietveld Academy) in Amsterdam at a time when its director, the architect Mart Stam, introduced many ideas inspired by the Bauhaus (see pp60–3) for a functionalist and socially responsible design. Among van Toorn's first jobs was to work as in-house designer, from 1965 to 1973, for the Stedelijk van Abbemuseum in

Eindhoven. Under the direction of Jean Leering the art gallery had been pursuing a programme of challenging exhibitions which questioned the relationship between art and society. Instead of following a consistent house style, van Toorn flouted design taboos by incorporating handwritten and typed texts and responding to each catalogue or exhibition in an individual manner. In one instance the design of a catalogue required the reader to destroy the binding to gain access to the information. However, one of his most memorable designs was the white fake-fur cover he used on a catalogue for the artist Piero Manzoni in 1969. In many ways van Toorn's approach has contrasted with that of his contemporary Wim Crouwel (see pp180–1), a supporter of systematic design. In 1972 this marked difference led the two designers to engage in a public debate.

zondag   maandag   dinsdag   woensdag   donderdag   vrijdag   zaterdag

30 1 2 3 4 5 6

kalender negentientweeënzeventig-drieënzeventig

APRIL   MEI

Calendar for Mart. Spruijt, 1972

Van Toorn produced weekly calendars for the Amsterdam printer Mart. Spruijt from 1966 to 1977, making the designs increasingly provocative. This example combines portraits of "everyday people", with the discredited President of the United States, Richard Nixon, highlighted in the crowd.

183

As art editor of the Ministry of Culture's influential publication *Dutch Art + Architecture Today*, van Toorn extended his technique of using papers distinguished by a variety of textures and tones. A novelty of this series was that the cover doubled as the packaging for postage. Van Toorn also designed calendars in the 1960s and 1970s for the Amsterdam printer Mart. Spruijt. Using satirical photographic juxtaposition, he stimulated frank discussion of the issues of sexual exploitation, corruption, consumerism and citizens' rights.

Van Toorn further developed his use of photomontage when working for the Netherlands' PTT (Postal, Telegraph and Telephone Authority). For this client, a consistent patron of modern graphic design, he applied bold, energetic typography to postage stamps, posters and reports. On being appointed director of the Jan van Eyck Academy in Maastricht in 1991, van Toorn began to concentrate on publishing, lecturing and organizing events. In 1997 he set up "design beyond Design", a forum in which international speakers addressed issues raised by commissioned visual practice.

Over the past 30 years the Netherlands has championed modern design in graphics, industry and architecture alike. In addition, many state structures exist to encourage a literate, liberal and cultured tradition among its people. Nevertheless, Jan van Toorn has retained a critical standpoint since the 1960s, believing that graphic design inevitably supports the status quo. He has always maintained that he is primarily interested in graphic design which displays a clear social commitment, and his credo is "subjective, open and flexible" design.

Poster by Martin Venezky for Zeebelt Theatre, 1994

Corporate identity manual for PTT, 1989

Studio Dumbar retained the distinctive red, blue and green identities for the Postal, Telegraph and Telephone Authority's services while introducing a single-case logo and postmodern elements (above).

In a poster for a theatre company that Dumbar co-founded, two visual systems work together and against each other (left). An area of floor covered by smashed plates, a rolling pin, and other organized débris was photographed by Lex van Pieterson as the setting for the typography.

184

⊕ 1940–
⊕ Dutch postmodernist renowned for improvised installations and dynamic typography
⊕ Studied at Royal Academy of Fine Arts, The Hague, and Royal College of Art, London
⊕ Founded Studio Dumbar 1977

Gert Dumbar, head of Studio Dumbar, based in The Hague in the Netherlands, has held a prominent place in Dutch design of the past 30 years. In his work on corporate identity schemes and many cultural projects he has developed a free and experimental style.

Dumbar's teaching has had considerable influence on young designers passing through his studio, including Why Not Associates (see pp224–7) and several alumni of Cranbrook (see pp214–15). He wrote in the journal *Kunstschrift* in 1986: "My colleagues sometimes scold me for being an artist among designers but that is exactly what I want. I have always taken the fine arts to be a sort of breeding ground for all sorts of applied design."

Dumbar studied painting and visual communication at the Royal Academy of Fine Arts in The Hague from

1959 to 1964 and typography at the Royal College of Art, London, from 1964 to 1967. The contemporary Fluxus art movement, which combined installations, happenings and multi-media art works, removing the distinction between product and process, had a profound impact on him. Initially he was a co-founder of the group Tel Graphic Designs in 1967, working on corporate identity projects, most notably for the Dutch railways. Finding the approach too restricted towards commercial clients, he established Studio Dumbar in 1977, retaining contact with many clients while also developing an artistically oriented set of projects.

Studio Dumbar became renowned for its flexible environment, or what has been called a version of "controlled chaos". It was based on a group of about 12 designers, with many visiting students from America's

Poster for "Holland Festival", 1987

Experimental dimensional typography, giving the illusion of three dimensions. was used by Studio Dumbar's designers for a series of posters for the "Holland Festival", which took place at the Teatro Comunale in Bologna, Italy, in 1987. The most striking characteristics of the style are the layered and intertwined graphic material.

Cranbrook Academy and the Royal College of Art, London, where Dumbar held a Professorship in Graphic Design in 1987–8 and again from 2000.

In the 1994 article "Room for Chance" Dumbar wrote about serendipity and the need to find the unanticipated in design. He placed emotion, sensitivity and expression above the rational or functional outlook that had been central to Dutch graphic design since World War II.

This outlook provoked a degree of controversy, particularly when Studio Dumbar won commissions for major designs in the public sector. The PTT (Dutch Postal, Telegraph and Telephone Authority) commissioned the practice to devise a new corporate identity to accompany its privatization in 1989. This job was especially sensitive as the PTT was associated in the minds of many design critics with the enlightened public

patronage of J.F. Royen which started in the 1920s, when he commissioned De Stijl (see pp54–5) designers. Subsequently Studio Dumbar received commissions from Nike, Apple, Philips and the Rijksmuseum in Amsterdam.

The practice combined work for major industrial and government clients with private cultural projects for which there was a much less definite brief. Many designs originated as a constructed studio environment, in the form of an arrangement of models and installations photographed by Lex van Pieterson. Complex typographic designs were then added to the resulting images.

Dutch graphic design of the 1980s and 1990s was profoundly affected by the debate about postmodernism. When a postmodern approach was applied as a design strategy, the viewer was required to deconstruct the design in order to comprehend its message.

⊕ Willem Kars
⊕ Tom van den Haspel
⊕ Rick Vermeulen
⊕ Gerard Hadders
⊕ Dutch design group founded in Rotterdam, led by Rick Vermeulen
⊕ Part of postmodern reaction in early 1980s
⊕ Favour reference to design of previous times

The partnership Hard Werken – the name means "working hard" – was part of a postmodern reaction against uniformity of style in graphic design in the Netherlands. Formed as a result of contact made at the Graphic Workshop of the Rotterdam Art Foundation, the group first published the magazine *Hard Werken* in 1979 and set up a studio the following year.

Hard Werken was a loose affiliation of designers, and those associated with the group included Rick Vermeulen, Henk Elenga, Gerard Hadders, Ton van den Haspel, Willem Kars and Jan Willem de Kok. Working either individually or collectively, the group originally embraced an "everything is possible" aesthetic. Reacting against much graphic design of the period because it applied a tasteful homogeneity to design solutions, the members celebrated eclecticism. Vermeulen justified this position when he stated: "You can't smother such diverse clients as the Stedelijk Museum, the Netherlands Opera and a fringe theatre in one uniform style as if it were a sauce."

Initially calling themselves the "*jong wilden*" (young wild ones), Hard Werken were the contemporary equivalent of the generation of German artists of the early 1980s who, after a long period of conceptualism and abstraction, had turned to agitational expressionist subject matter to reactivate painting. The group's early works were sometimes dismissed as brash, tasteless and decadent by an audience unfamiliar with their eclectic sets of imagery and apparently discordant combinations of styles in graphic design. Many of the first commissions were for cultural projects. In the early 1980s Rotterdam was emerging as a lively city with strong municipal support for the arts and culture, and was building new museums, promoting a very active dance and music scene and holding its own film festival. Posters, book and magazine designs figured importantly in the early years, but Hard Werken also took on furniture and lighting design as well as exhibition and audiovisual presentations.

Vermeulen's personal interests included American popular culture and subcultures. Typographical elements reinstated letters from the 1950s that had been deformed and weakened through photosetting. The designs themselves included found images, staged photographs and unusual formats in many typefaces.

However, by the end of the 1980s, in a recessionary financial climate, the group came close to bankruptcy. Changes in the following decade saw Henk Elenga open Hard Werken Los Angeles Desk, with Warner Brothers and ESPRIT as clients. Vermeulen, also familiar with the United States from teaching at Cranbrook (see pp214–15) and North Carolina State University, replaced Elenga as head of the LA group in 1993. In that year Hard Werken merged with the packaging design company Ten Cate Bergmans. The merger marked a change in the scale of corporate clients as well as an engagement with multimedia design. By 1994 the new name Inizio was adopted.

The exhibition "From Hard Werken to Inizio" was held in Frankfurt am Main and Rotterdam in 1995.

Cover by Rick Vermeulen for magazine *Hard Werken*, 1980

Eleven issues of the cultural broadsheet *Hard Werken* were published between 1979 and 1982. The all-capitals title and jagged border are characteristic of the group's design approach.

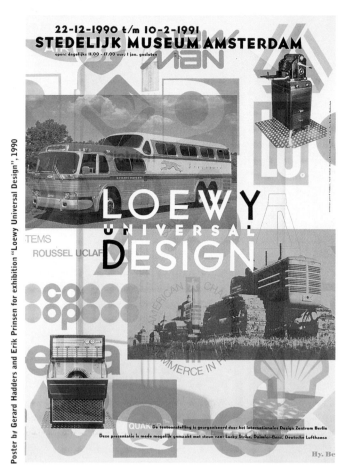

An exhibition poster by Gerard Hadders and Erik Prinsen is an appropriate marriage between the retrospective nature of the design and the subject matter: the French-born industrial designer Raymond Loewy, who emigrated to the United States in 1919.

Poster by Gerard Hadders and Erik Prinsen for exhibition "Loewy Universal Design", 1990

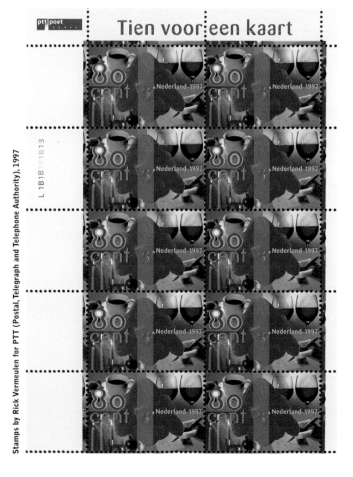

These stamps were designed by Rick Vermeulen under his own name after Hard Werken had ceased to exist. The theme for the series was picture postcards and Vermeulen developed the idea of gift-giving and exchange.

Stamps by Rick Vermeulen for PTT (Postal, Telegraph and Telephone Authority), 1997

187

Cover for book *Bauhaus*, 1969

In designing this book, published by MIT
Press, Cooper used Helvetica typeface
and a grid to marshal complex archival
visual evidence, diagrams, drawings and
records of documents as well as
photographic reproductions of works.

Cover for book *Learning from Las Vegas*, 1972

A Significance for A&P Parking Lots,
or Learning from Las Vegas. Commercial Values and Commercial
Methods. Billboards Are Almost All
Right. Architecture as Space. Architecture as Symbol. Symbol in Space
before Form in Space: Las Vegas as
a Communication System. The Architecture of Persuasion. Vast Space
in the Historical Tradition and at the
A&P. From Rome to Las Vegas.
Maps of Las Vegas: Las Vegas as a
Pattern of Activities. Main Street and
the Strip. System and Order on the
Strip, and "Twin Phenomena."
Change and Permanence on the

Cooper organized this seminal book on
architecture, full of content-laden images,
around interdependent rhythms. The text
was typeset by IBM typewriter in Univers
and the book was published by her
long-term client MIT Press.

➔ 1925–94
➔ Renowned pioneer of
computer typography and
design for digital media
➔ Head of publications
at Massachusetts
Institute of Technology
(MIT) from 1952
➔ Co-founded Visible
Language Workshop at
MIT Media Laboratory

Muriel Cooper was a pioneer of digital
media. A teacher and researcher as well as a
book and graphic designer, she made the
transition from conventional print design to
computer design in the late 1970s, at an
advanced stage of her career. In doing so
she left static typography for dynamic media.

In 1952 the American designer was appointed
director of the Massachusetts Institute of Technology's
new Office of Publications (Design Services) in
Cambridge. MIT was the first university in the United
States to take seriously the design of its publications
and subsequently grew into a major publisher of studies
on architecture, design and popular culture. In 1958
Cooper visited Milan on a Fullbright Scholarship. On her
return to the United States she established the Muriel

Cooper Designer Studio, while her links with MIT Press
continued as the publisher remained a major client. She
designed the MIT Press logo, a minimalist series of grey
or white vertical stripes. In 1967 Cooper became Design
and Media Director at MIT Press, for which she designed
more than 500 books.

An articulate designer who wrote and lectured a
great deal, Cooper positioned herself as part of a
response to the information revolution, much as the
Bauhaus (see pp60–3) was a response to the industrial
revolution. She was well aware of the legacy of the
Bauhaus that had been played out in American university
architectural faculties. It was therefore appropriate that
she should be entrusted by MIT Press with the design of
Bauhaus (1969), Hans Maria Wingler's definitive study of
the German art and design school.

Screen captures from TED5 three-dimensional information programmes, 1994

Muriel Cooper, David Small and Suguru Ishizaki developed the TED5 information programmes from which these images were taken. The programmes were used in a project in three-dimensional narrative undertaken by the Visible Language Workshop to explore layered information, simultaneity and typographic texture. Information could be approached from any angle, and in some cases the type is reversed or upside down.

In the early 1970s Cooper co-founded Visible Language Workshop, one of the 12 research groups at MIT's Media Laboratory, and held the position of Professor of Interactive Media Design. Under its director Nicholas Negroponte, the Media Laboratory developed interdisciplinary research in the fields of architectural design, the social sciences, electronic music, artificial intelligence and visible language. Cooper ran the Visible Language Workshop as an international experiment based on the open studio principle of art and design education. In many ways its investigations predated the full impact of the computer revolution of the 1980s.

Cooper has explained her wish to present the arguments of texts in non-linear ways: "creating virtual time and space in 2 dimensions has always intrigued me". This was the case with *Learning from Las Vegas* (1972), by Robert Venturi, Denise Scott Brown and Steven Izenour, and *Is Anyone Taking Any Notice?* (1973). The latter is a study of war atrocities by the photographer Don McCullin interspersed with extracts from Alexander Solzhenitsyn's Nobel Prize acceptance speech.

In an interview in 1989 Cooper remarked: "I was convinced that the line between reproduction tools and design would blur when information became electronic and that the lines between designer and artist, author and designer, professional and amateur would also dissolve." While her designs remained consistent with the aesthetic of late modernism, adhering to the grid for a rational organization of a body of text, for example, many of the conceptual insights she encouraged through teaching and publication led to the full emergence of postmodern typography in the late twentieth century.

WOLFGANG WEINGART

↳ 1941–
↳ Influential Swiss
graphic designer who
led reaction against
Swiss typography
↳ Taught Advanced
Course for Graphic
Design at Allgemeine
Gewerbeschule, Basle
↳ Significant figure in
1980s in deconstructive
typography in Europe
and United States

The change from modern to postmodern typography and graphic design occurred during the last quarter of the twentieth century. Epitomizing this transition, Wolfgang Weingart is a designer whose career crossed both stages and who has been a notable participant in the discourse on the future of design.

Born in Constance, Germany, Weingart studied design and the applied arts at the Merz Academy in Stuttgart, before apprenticing himself to a printer, Wilhelm Ruwe, in that city, and then to a typesetter in Switzerland. Determined to study at the Allgemeine Kunstgewerbeschule in Basle, where the leading exponents of Swiss typography were teaching, he established himself as an independent student there in 1964, studying with Emil Ruder and Armin Hofmann.

To his surprise, Weingart found that the teaching at Basle was leading to a point of stagnation, international typographic style was in his view sterile and anonymous. In tune with the climate of social unrest of the student generation of the late 1960s, he decided to break the rules; but to do this he first had to understand them. In 1968 the Advanced Course for Graphic Design was established, a Master's course and parallel to the programme offered at Yale University. On the unexpected death of Emil Ruder, Weingart was asked to teach and this offered him the opportunity to contribute to the future direction of the School and to breathe new life into Swiss typography.

Weingart examined all the principles taught by the Swiss school: rules forbidding the indentation of paragraphs and wide spacing of letters were tested and broken, consistency of weights of typeface were upset, the "rule of the right angle" and the integrity of single images were challenged. Most symbolic of all, the grid was established and then violated in his works. Weingart used rules and bars for emphasis and typographic space as an active field of tension, recalling much of the "new typography" of the 1920s. What were to become identifiable characteristics of postmodernism emerged in his move to find a more interpretative and less objective approach.

From 1968 to 1974 Weingart experimented with the syntax and semantics of designs, using traditional typographic composition and often hand-setting, drawing on his experience of ten years earlier. He has always believed that designers should be aware of the technologies they use. From 1975 a second phase of designs depended on the layering of film, using offset printing and film setting. In these Weingart devised a way of enlarging the half-tone dots of the printing technique to assert the character of the poster as a printed entity.

Weingart's teaching had a great impact on the next generation of graphic designers, among them his students April Greiman (see pp204–5) and Dan Friedman (see pp192–3). He also lectured extensively in Germany and the United States.

In the 1990s Weingart ceased to design. He had not intended his approaches to become a style, yet they became mannerisms in the hands of others, unaware of his original purpose and context. In recent years he has focused on teaching and writing, publishing in 2000 *Wege zur Typographie, Ein Rückblick in zehn Teilen* (My Way to Typography, Retrospective in Ten Sections).

Cover for book *Wege zur Typographie*, 2000

Weingart's substantial autobiography, issued by Lars Müller Publishers, explains the designer's cultural context through personal photographs and passages of writing interspersed with examples of his designs.

Poster for exhibition "Kunstkredit" (Art Credit), 1976–7

Weingart's posters of the 1970s, like this one for an exhibition at the Kunsthalle in Basle, were important forerunners of postmodern and deconstructive typography. They layered information, introduced different visual systems in one design and, initially, seemed to break all the rules.

Poster for exhibition "Das Schweizer Plakat 1900–1984" (The Swiss Poster 1900–1984), 1984

This poster for a major historical exhibition of posters at the Gewerbermuseum in Basle is characteristic of the period. Weingart, who also designed the catalogue, pushes the type to the edges of the poster, allowing space for symbols to register on an ambiguous colour field.

191

→ 1945–95
→ Studied graphic design in Pittsburgh, Ulm and Basle
→ Influenced in Basle by Wolfgang Weingart
→ Designed many corporate identities and later engaged in artistic projects
→ Taught at Yale University and State University of New York
→ Evaluated legacy of modernism in 1994 book *Radical Modernism*

Dan Friedman was a polemical designer whose work ranged from the strictly functional area of graphic design to self-generated projects, exhibitions and books. He condemned what he saw as premature and reactionary proclamations about the death of modernism. Instead he developed his own design beliefs in the book *Radical Modernism*, published in 1994.

In the mid and late 1960s Friedman studied at the Carnegie Institute of Technology in Pittsburgh, then at the Ulm Hochschule für Gestaltung, where science-based rationalism prevailed, and the Allgemeine Gewerbeschule in Basle, which promoted an art-based intuitive logic. In Basle he was taught by Armin Hofmann, whose basic design and principles of visual form influenced Friedman when he went on to teach, first as Senior Critic at Yale University and then at the School of Visual Arts of the State University of New York.

In his early work Friedman countered what he saw as the rigidity, boredom and exclusiveness associated with modernism. His graphic designs included posters, packaging, visual identities and more than 40 logos and symbols for a variety of mainstream and progressive companies. For him, interpreting identity was no longer a matter of imposing a monolithic, static system, but rather a question of managing visual diversity. Playing with the idea of anti-functionalism, Friedman also made installations that incorporated his own designs for furniture and lighting. He witnessed and participated in the shift from function to semantics in design, or as he put it, concentrating on the way things look rather than what they mean.

Like the contemporary Milan-based design movement Memphis, Friedman interpreted the role of design as a form of cultural critique. Using references drawn from popular culture, Italian designers had reformulated a theory of decoration for industrial application in their patterns for plastic laminates. An important part of Friedman's work was the interior design of his own New York apartment. This he used as a test bed for an industrial and folk-inspired approach to decoration. He suggested that appropriation, simulation, reuse and eclecticism change our notions of originality, beauty and authenticity.

Increasingly Friedman took on issue-related design, addressing AIDS, nuclear war, terrorism and ethnic cleansing in experimental formats for books, posters and magazine layouts. In the early 1980s he worked with the New York graffiti artist Keith Haring on catalogues and exhibitions. While these strategies could be interpreted as part of a postmodern critique, Friedman believed that they did not necessarily contradict modernism but could actually reinvigorate and broaden it. In 1994 he wrote: "Radical modernism is therefore presented here as a reaffirmation of the idealistic roots of our modernity, adjusted to include more of our diverse culture, history, research and fantasy."

This screen, made for the Milan company Driade, was one of a series of folding screens constructed from painted medium-density fibreboard, feathers and drink cans. Friedman interpreted these as an intermediate form between furniture, sculpture, painting and architecture.

Screen for Driade, c.1985

Book and exhibition project, "Artificial Nature", 1990

Taking the theme of nature, science and globalism, the picture-text narrative is set out to highlight keywords in white Franklin Gothic on a black ground which functions to deconstruct the text. This was one of a series of book and exhibition projects undertaken by Friedman for the Deste Foundation for Contemporary Art, Athens; the others were "Cultural Geometry" (1988) and "Post HUMAN" (1992).

193

Logo for CITIBANK, from 1975

A new logo and symbol introduced by Friedman in association with Anspach Grossman Portugal, Inc. marked the change of name from First National City Bank to CITIBANK. In this instance Friedman's design continued the mainstream modern tradition of more established designers such as Rand, Chermayeff and Geismar.

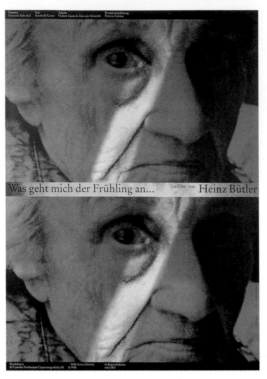

Poster for Heinz Bütler's film *Was Geht Mich Der Frühling An...*, 1987

A poster for a film by the Swiss director
Heinz Bütler about a Jewish home for the
elderly near Vienna took a small part of
a negative of one of the residents and
constructed a narrative from the light
cast across the face.

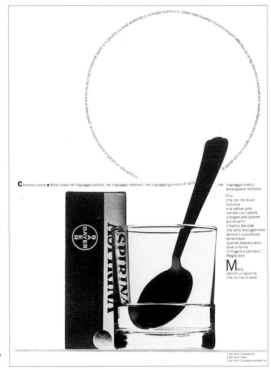

Page from book *Arti Grafiche Nidasio*, 1981

Published in Milan, this book was
designed as a gift for clients of the Art
Grafiche Nidasio company. It took the
form of an amusing spelling book on the
theme of communication. This page
explores the idea of circumlocution.

194

⊖ 1941–
⊖ Later Swiss modernist
interested in editorial
content of design
⊖ Studied in Geneva
and London
⊖ Worked at Studio
Boggeri in Milan 1961–3
⊖ Corporate identities
for cultural clients such
as Musée d'Orsay, Paris

Bruno Monguzzi represents the second
generation of modernist designers in Europe.
Swiss by birth, he has worked in the UK,
Italy, France, Switzerland and the United
States, specializing in publication design and
graphics for exhibitions and museums. The
designer has justified his stand against the
more overt expressions of postmodernism by
saying: "I find our society a bit noisy. I just
would like to contribute a little silence."

Monguzzi studied at the School of Decorative Arts in
Geneva and then in London. A native of the Ticino, the
Italian-speaking part of Switzerland, he developed a
sphere of activity between his homeland, Milan and
France. Inspired by the second issue of the journal *Neue
Grafik*, which focused on Italian graphic design, he

settled in Milan, where he worked at Studio Boggeri (see
pp84–5) from 1961 to 1963. Monguzzi has explained how
Antonio Boggeri introduced him to the idea of the
spider's web. As a newly arrived Swiss designer, he was
warned by Boggeri against over-perfection in design. The
tradition of Swiss "new typography" had been associated
with a concern for neutral, functional but perfect
communication. Just as the spider's web is harmed but
enlivened by its entrapment of the fly, so Monguzzi
turned to Italian design to give his work a new twist.

This broadening of approach continued when
Monguzzi grew interested in contemporary American
design, particularly the designers of the New York School
in the early 1960s. The works of Lou Danziger, Gene
Federico, Herb Lubalin (see pp.156–7) and Lou Dorfsman
combined word and image with a deep understanding of

9 décembre 1986

Poster for the opening of the Musée d'Orsay, Paris, 1986

This design, 4m (13ft) wide, used the museum's logotype in Walbaum typeface, radically cropped. Monguzzi originally planned a typographic poster, but then used a reference to a photograph by Lartigue as a metaphor for the launch.

content, which gave many of their designs more impact than those of their Swiss counterparts.

In London in 1960–1 Monguzzi studied Gestalt psychology and perception to find a more analytical, objective way of understanding his design which went beyond personal taste or style. The United States has always held an attraction for him. He has worked and taught intermittently there and in Canada, contributing designs for nine pavilions at Expo '67 in Montreal.

Monguzzi's book *Note per una tipografia informativa* (Notes for a Typography of Information), published in 1965, was a summary of his lectures at the Cini Foundation in Venice. He then taught these theories at the School of Applied Arts in Lugano, on the Italian-Swiss border, where in 1971 he was appointed Professor of Typographic Design and the Psychology of Perception.

Increasingly Monguzzi turned to design in the context of museums, first in association with the Brera art gallery in Milan. In 1983 he joined Jean Widmer and the Visual Design Studio in Paris to develop the signage systems and corporate identity for the newly opening Musée d'Orsay. Housed in the Gare d'Orsay, refurbished to a design by the Italian architect Gae Aulenti, the museum holds the French national collections of nineteenth-century painting. The logotype, in Didot, was designed by hand and based around the letters "M" and "O", separated by a fine line and the distinctive apostrophe; it was applied to stationery, gallery guides and posters. The project was characteristic of Monguzzi's approach to design, with its calm control of visual elements, elegant contrast of type and clear understanding of the integration of photography.

➔ 1930–
➔ Studied ancient Japanese art at City College of Arts and textile design at University of Fine Arts, both in Kyoto
➔ Co-founder of Nippon Design Center
➔ Promoted professional graphic design in Japan
➔ Fuses East and West in graphic design
➔ Posters for 1964 Olympic Games and 1972 Winter Olympics and exhibition design for Expo '70.

To achieve effective communication, the work of the Japanese graphic designer Ikko Tanaka incorporates what might initially be seen as contradictory impulses. His designs combine a respect for tradition and spirituality, both of which are customarily accorded great value in his homeland, with a fascination with excellence in materials and techniques.

Tanaka was born in the ancient city of Nara and studied in Kyoto: ancient Japanese art at the City College of Arts and textile design at the University of Fine Arts. Kyoto is the centre of traditional Buddhism and its arts and traditions remained significant for his professional life. Tanaka has been a key figure in the encouragement of modern Japanese graphic design. With Yusaku Kamekura (see pp140–1), Hiromu Hara and Ryuichi Yamashiro, he was a founder member of the Nippon Design Centre in 1959. This group looked towards contemporary American design and art direction and offered training for newly qualified graduates to prepare them as designers for large companies.

The World Design Conference held in Tokyo in 1959 attracted an international range of designers, including Herbert Bayer (see pp66–7), Saul Bass (see pp104–5), Otl Aicher, Josef Müller-Brockmann (see pp124–5) and Bruno Munari (see pp126–7). In 1960 Tanaka visited New York, meeting further American designers. The Tanaka Ikko Design studio followed these encounters (founded in 1963, it became the Tanaka Design Atelier in 1976). Tanaka continued to participate in important stages in Japan's increasingly international profile as a poster designer for the 1964 Tokyo Olympic Games, exhibition designer of Expo '70 in Osaka, and another poster for the Winter Olympics in Sapporo of 1972.

Tanaka's designs reveal a concern for traditional Japanese style, but also modern art and design. His inspiration is partly from the graphic art of the Edo period, particularly the *ukiyoe* prints of Kitagawa Utamaro and Ando Hiroshige. An expert in No theatre, Tanaka also promoted among artists and designers the revival of the traditional Japanese tea ceremony. Underlying his designs is an enquiry into the nature of abstraction. He suggests that abstraction changed radically during the twentieth century from a simplicity which signified spirituality to the contemporary view that simplicity can mean that there is "nothing there".

In Europe during the 1970s exhibitions of Japanese posters and the interest these generated led to global exposure for Japanese design. The 1980s opened with the important exhibition "Japan Style" at the Victoria and Albert Museum in London, for which Tanaka designed the poster and catalogue. Tanaka has also interpreted the work of contemporary textile and fashion designers Issey Miyake, Hiroshi and Hanae Morey, as well as the performing arts of Japanese dance and theatre.

This poster was designed in 1968 for a competition relating to publicity material for the 1972 Winter Olympics, which took place in Sapporo. It depends on abstract motifs of waves of snow, the rising sun of the Japanese national flag and a symbol of a snowflake.

Poster, "Sapporo 72", 1968

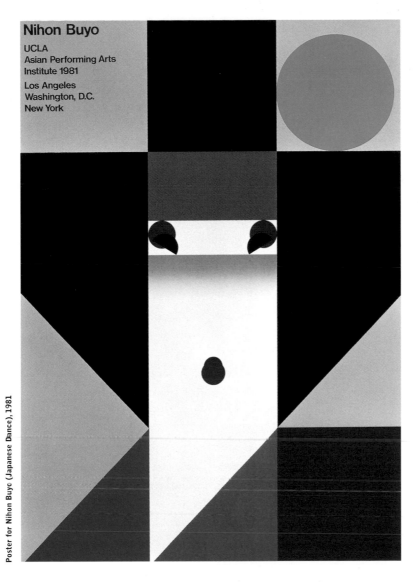

Nihon Buyo

UCLA
Asian Performing Arts
Institute 1981

Los Angeles
Washington, D.C.
New York

Poster for Nihon Buyo (Japanese Dance), 1981

In this poster advertising a display of Japanese dance that toured the United States in 1981, Tanaka adapted the traditional portrait style of *ukiyoe* prints to simple colour fields and geometry.

Poster for exhibition "World Graphic Design", 1959

1959年 7月14日—7月19日 池袋 三越 6階ホール 主催 共同通信社

世界商業デザイン展

季刊誌 グラフィック・デザイン 9月創刊 発行所 芸美出版社

Japanese graphic designers have the potential to work with four different sets of characters – the pictograms and ideograms (Kanji), phonetic characters (Kate kana), cursive forms of Kanji (Hiragana) and the Western or Roman alphabet. All four have played a part in Tanaka's designs and the overall design of this poster is constructed with symbols.

JAMIE REID

◉ 1940–
◉ Graphic designer
most closely associated
with British Punk scene
◉ Studied painting at
Croydon School of Art
◉ Designed Sex
Pistols' album covers
and posters
◉ Designs referred to
as "the art of plunder"

Cover for record and CD Shamanarchy in the UK, 1992

Reid called this design, for a vinyl album
and CD released by Evolution Records,
"Boudicca Arising". Boudicca, Reid's
astrological clock and his OVA symbol
are motifs which occur frequently in the
designer's work.

Punk is a potent example of design meshing politics with graphic form. Jamie Reid is recognized as the art director of British Punk at its most extreme, in the late 1970s and early 1980s. Punk occurred immediately before the rise of digital typography and so is not a result of computer-aided design. Instead it asserted the hand-made. Nevertheless, its energy and assault on conventional meaning recharged graphic design and, more broadly, marked a generational shift in sensibility. It was an important seedbed for design of the next 20 years.

From 1964 to 1968 Reid trained as a painter at Croydon School of Art, in south London, where he became interested in left-wing politics. On graduating he co-founded the Suburban Press and ran a radical community newspaper of the same name from 1970 to 1975. He developed slogans in the form of stickers such as "This Store Welcomes Shoplifters", "Never Trust a Hippie", "A Brick will do the Trick" and "Save Petrol, Burn Cars".

British Punk developed in the mid-1970s, at a time of high unemployment and general disillusionment with conventional party politics among the young. Its roots were often suburban and stemmed from boredom and a sense of no hope and no future. This was coded as frustration and rebellion through sarcasm, cynicism and rupture. Malcolm McLaren, manager of the Sex Pistols, orchestrated some of Punk's crucial stages. With the fashion designer Vivienne Westwood he opened in King's Road, Chelsea, the clothing store Sex and later Seditionaries, where punk clothing and accessories were available. McLaren approached Reid, an old college contemporary, to design the record sleeves, advertisements, posters and T-shirts for the Sex Pistols, the band he managed, which was led by John Lydon, alias Johnny Rotten.

Reid developed a do-it-yourself aesthetic that mirrored the initial source of much of the music: the garage or bedroom. His early designs used Letraset, ransom-note lettering, cut-outs, photocopies, highlighter pens or Day-Glo inks and typewritten and hand-scrawled lyrics. Reid's first record cover for the Sex Pistols, for the single "Anarchy in the UK" of 1976, featured his graphics, a torn Union Jack and ransom-style lettering held together by safety pins. The aesthetic shared with the clothing deliberate strategies of disfigurement. At the time of the Silver Jubilee of 1977 imagery abounded of the Royal Family and in particular Queen Elizabeth II. Reid enjoyed taking icons of the British establishment and mutilating them, the crudeness of the juxtaposition creating genuine shock.

A refusal to aestheticize distinguished Reid from other graphic designers associated with Punk, such as Malcolm Garrett, Peter Saville, Barney Bubbles and Russell Mills. Nor was he concerned with the professionalism of the later Adbusters (see pp238–9). In terms of a tradition Punk's espousal of mass-media strategies to disarm and dislocate can be compared with Dadaist manifestos. In 1983 the writer Jon Savage called Reid's use of collage and deliberate theft of ideas "the art of plunder".

Cover for record *Never Mind the Bollocks Here's the Sex Pistols*, 1977

NEVER MIND THE BOLLOCKS

HERE'S THE

Sex PiSTOLs

The cover of the Sex Pistols' album used fluorescent yellow ink, which was extremely difficult to print without importing impurities. The design caused controversy because it did not feature a picture, but the impact of the title was much greater. Three leading UK record shops which sold the album were charged with offences under the 1889 Indecent Advertisements Act and the 1824 Vagrancy Act.

Poster for single "Pretty Vacant", 1977

For this poster for "Pretty Vacant", released in July 1977, Reid derived the Situationist buses from his earlier work for *Suburban Press*. The cover of the single featured a smashed empty picture frame into which he inserted the title.

Cover for *Suburban Press*, no. 5

Jamie Reid, Jeremy Brook and Nigel Edwards set up *Suburban Press* at a time when community politics and direct action were considered to be viable alternatives to mainstream culture. Six issues appeared between 1970 and 1975.

DESIGN IN THE DIGITAL ERA

DESIGN IN THE DIGITAL ERA

In the late twentieth century the foundations of graphic design changed with the digitization of typography brought about by computers. For its entire history typography had been a physical activity, initially based on the arrangement of metal typefaces for letterpress printing, and after 1960, on the preparation of camera-ready artwork for offset lithographic printing. With computerization, the design process was dematerialized into electronic form and graphic design was radically altered.

Working with computers did away with many of the activities that were previously an essential part of the graphic designer's work, notably manual processes that employed the physical materials of the craft. At the same time computers increased the scope of the work and the speed at which it could be produced. Desktop-publishing software brought the means of production into the studio, making it easier for designers to continue to work in small groups and to avoid the need for constant expansion. Traditional job definitions were called into question, and flexible multi-tasking became widespread as computers blurred the distinctions between studio and office and between office and home.

The Apple Macintosh computer, the most successful of the micro-computers, was introduced in 1984. Its system ran on the principle of windows, icon, mouse and pull-down menus (WIMP). From the start "Mac" software was oriented towards designers. However, while computer technology brought about a substantial shift, it would be misleading to suggest that computers alone determined the nature of design changes after about 1980. In fact many of the characteristic stylistic ideas had been developed before their extensive introduction in electronic form, making it clear that broader ideas from culture, philosophy, fashion and "style" were just as important for graphic design.

"Design" became a key word in the late twentieth century, and "designer" was used as a prefix for a wide range of goods and cultural activities. Graphic design benefited from this increased exposure. A higher rate of design change was introduced into magazines, especially the style press, which depended on its readers' visual acuity to pick up references to previous design movements and to appreciate the nuanced graphic languages.

As multinational companies developed a global identity, consumers were made aware of the power of branding as manifest in graphic form. Designers such as Tibor Kalman and Adbusters took up questions formulated by writers on cultural studies, in order to expose corporate strategies of persuasion and media control. Many other designers expressed their reluctance to become the handmaiden of global corporations.

macromedia
AUTHORWARE 4
INTERACTIVE
STUDIO
The Leading Tools
for Web-based Multimedia
and Learning

macromedia

Neville Brody, a leading graphic designer associated with the new typography of the 1980s and 1990s, and himself a keen user of the latest computer technologies, was entrusted with the series design of web-based interactive software for Macromedia. The series design developed from the theme of the sunburst and hexagons, invoking computer science, the elements and space – a fusion of nature and technology.

Increasing ownership of computers spread an awareness of graphic design among the wider public, bringing the possibility of selecting typefaces and arranging text and images to them in their homes. The boundaries between professional and amateur design became blurred. Many designers were initially dismissive of the opportunities computers gave to typography and graphic design. Early exceptions, however, were Zuzana Licko and Rudy VanderLans, who formed the group Emigre in California in 1982. They chose not to imitate the quality of previous technologies. Calling themselves the New Primitives, they were attracted to the initial roughness of computer-derived type forms. Emigre's projects encapsulated the various possibilities of digitization. From the early 1980s the group published a magazine of international significance in the debate on graphic design in the digital age, ran a digital type foundry that made new typefaces available globally, and operated a recording studio.

Computers allowed the boundaries between print, film and television to be explored and further broken down. Additionally, the Internet encouraged on-line publication and graphic designers were as likely to be involved in web design as design for print media, as the examples of Why Not Associates, Jonathan Barnbrook, Neville Brody and David Carson indicate. The question they faced was whether the metaphor of the desktop was still appropriate or whether analogous forms of spatial organization, drawn from the fields of architecture or cartography, offered greater possibilities.

A growing interest in the relationship between technology and society not only challenged the idea that technology drives cultural change, but also modified an assumption that computer technology operates within an exclusively male context. The example of Muriel Cooper at the Media Laboratory at the Massachusetts Institute of Technology and April Greiman at the California Institute of Arts did much to dispel this notion.

By the end of the twentieth century there were notably more women involved in the practice of graphic design. Moreover, archival research by feminist design historians uncovered women designers from the earlier years who were "hidden from history", and important publications and exhibitions followed. At the same time the work of April Greiman, Sheila Levrant de Bretteville, Eiko Ishioka and Ellen Lupton indicated the many different ways in which women interpreted the activity of graphic designer and shaped its changing identity – through exhibitions and writing, site-specific design, art direction and multi-media applications. Such work contributed to a category redefinition in which graphic designers increasingly took responsibility for their professional activities. It helped to give graphic design renewed social significance while preparing it for the century to come.

APRIL GREIMAN

➔ 1948–
➔ American pioneer of computer-generated graphic design
➔ Studied graphic design at Kansas City Art Institute and pursued postgraduate studies at Allgemeine Gewerbeschule, Basle
➔ Work reflects interest in deconstructive typography and Eastern spiritualism
➔ Partner in Pentagram Los Angeles from 2000

April Greiman has been called the "doyenne of computer-generated design". She is renowned as a practitioner of experimental design which has tested the boundaries of legibility and accessibility in the pursuit of personally expressive ways of working.

Born in New York, Greiman studied graphic design at Kansas City Art Institute and pursued postgraduate studies with Wolfgang Weingart (see pp190–1) and Armin Hofmann at the Allgemeine Gewerbeschule in Basle. She worked for a period in New York, where she became involved with curatorial projects at the Museum of Modern Art in conjunction with Emilio Ambasz.

Greiman's early way of working predicted the techniques and ideas that computer-related design would allow. Like Weingart, she used the whole graphic field to arrange typeset fragments and small images. She extended his formal vocabulary by exploring the semiological interconnectedness of her imagery, often working in the area of self-referential reflection. Since the 1960s she had been attracted to the ideas of Carl Jung and Eastern religion, and these informed her use of colour, myth and symbol.

In 1976 Greiman moved to Los Angeles, bored with what she saw as the predictability of much graphic design and its stress on form over content. California offered new inspirations: she became interested in the contemporary colours of Hollywood's popular culture, while also responding to the beauty of the vegetation, the vastness of the desert and the area's ancient history.

In 1982 Greiman became Director of Communications at the California Institute of Arts, which offered her the chance to work with advanced computer systems and video and computer graphics. Subsequent work has shown how important this period was for her, allowing interdisciplinary research which brought together Swiss-style graphics, the experience of California and the early possibilities of multi-layering with computers.

A personal landmark, which also had a major impact on the international graphic design world, was the publication in 1986 of "Does it Make Sense?" This, Greiman's contribution to a special issue of *Design Quarterly*, was a fold-out sheet of nearly two by six feet showing a digitized life-size self-portrait with a wide range of superimposed type, images and ideograms. Dispensing with conventional paste-up, it was composed as a single document, rendered digitally. As well as mixing graphic design languages and recent social and political history, Greiman here indicated the direction that computer-aided design could take.

In 1990 Greiman published *Hybrid Imagery: the fusion of technology and graphic design*, a review of her previous 13 years of graphic design. She received a Medal for Innovation from the American Institute of Graphic Arts in 1998.

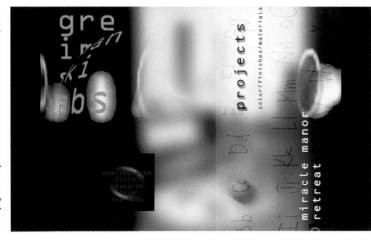

Home page from April Greiman's website Greimanski Labs, 2001

Greimanski Labs is the studio in California of April Greiman, who has always embraced new technologies with enthusiasm and flair. In 2000 she became a partner in the Los Angeles office of the design group Pentagram.

Poster for South California Institute of Architecture, 1991

An early poster (above) for SCI-ARC (South California Institute of Architecture) reflected on the design process in ways reminiscent of modernist design of the 1920s. Greiman subsequently designed the identity, signage, publications, print materials and website for the school.

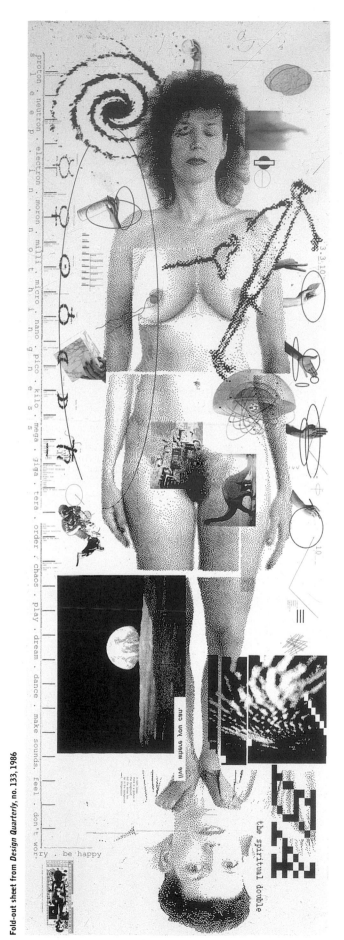

Fold-out sheet from *Design Quarterly*, no. 133, 1986

This fold-out sheet "Does It Make Sense?", for *Design Quarterly*, published by the Walker Art Center, Minneapolis, was Greiman's early contribution to computerized image making. A self-portrait, composed of digitized images, it was output by a low-resolution printer on to standard paper.

STYLE MAGAZINES

A magazine's appearance depends on design decisions about the format, cover, internal pace and arrangement of articles, as well as the choice of typefaces and deployment of images on individual pages. Art direction, the coordination of all these elements, was born as a separate activity in the United States, where as early as 1920 the Art Directors Club was formed in New York in recognition of the specialized division of labour that was customary there in design for publication.

Modern magazine design reached a high point with the New York style of the 1950s and 1960s. But by the end of the century the global picture of magazines was much more diverse and this was just one among many styles that could be imitated. Style magazines of the past 20 years have contributed to these changes by challenging assumptions about design and content. They emerged as a reaction to mainstream magazines, which were seen as dominated by advertising sponsorship. In their first years many style magazines flouted convention to attract a younger, specialist readership who understood the terms of reference and were in tune with the editorial selection and overall outlook. A new category of "info-tainment", they invited readers to browse for connoisseurial knowledge of music, clothes, design, film and sport. To retain their identity they turned away advertising that did not suit their readers' interests or the title's image.

The most famous style magazines were *The Face* and *i-D*, both started in London in 1980. These represented a break from the conventional music and fashion magazines. Ian Logan, editor of *The Face* – in Mod slang "Face" meant "trendsetter" – had previously worked on the music magazine *Smash Hits* and established the new title with £5000 and the help of two journalists. Early on Logan appointed Neville Brody (see pp222–3) as art editor, a move that immediately determined its distinctive style. Headlines consisted of Brody's invented display typefaces, used from one issue to another. The overall treatment of typography, photography and graphic symbols made for a modern, abrasive and highly energized style. In 1983 *The Face* was honoured as Magazine of the Year in Britain's annual Magazine Publishing Awards and a year later its circulation had reached 80,000.

Logan recognized that *The Face* could appeal to young men as well as to the expected female readership of fashion titles. In doing so he identified a new kind of male consumer who was as interested in fashion as he was in more traditionally masculine subjects, and this led him to establish a second magazine in 1986. *Arena* was aimed directly at men and was again designed by Brody.

Terry Jones, co-editor and art director of *i-D*, left British *Vogue* to set up the new magazine as an independent title. It was part of a movement to take young style and culture seriously. The magazine covered dress, music, film, exhibitions and dance, initially giving space to Punk, post-Punk and the new Romanticism. At a time when Margaret Thatcher's Conservative government was antagonistic towards young, creative ideas and the country was experiencing high youth unemployment, *i-D*'s "do-it-yourself" aesthetic made it clear that its readers were not dependent on high fashion for their style. The first issues profiled individuals photographed in the street.

iD's title derived from the standard abbreviation for identity and the inverted masthead became its logo, coupled with the formula of the model with the winking eye and smiling face. The first covers were printed in

Cover by Neville Brody for magazine *The Face*, no. 59, March 1985

One of the more unusual designs for an *i-D* cover took the smiling-face symbol from Ibiza's "summer of love" of 1987 and adapted it to accommodate the winking eye used on all the other covers for the magazine.

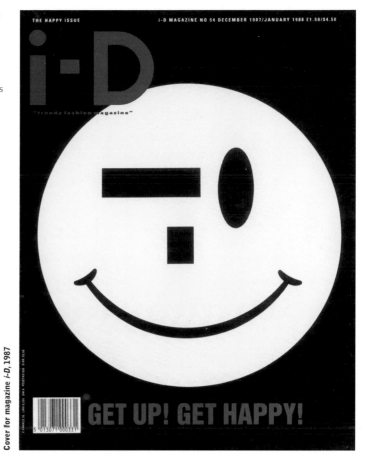

Cover for magazine *i-D*, 1987

Arena's graphic style, like that of its predecessor *The Face*, was created by Neville Brody and continued many of the conventions he established in the earlier title. But while section headings in *Arena* were hand-drawn, other headings were in Helvetica and reflected a cooler approach.

In this cover (opposite) by Neville Brody, with photography by Jamie Morgan and styling by Ray Petri, the striking image of the child star Felix was used to interpret the contemporary Buffalo style in music and fashion. The masthead includes *The Face*'s distinctive dropped triangular "A".

Cover by Neville Brody for magazine *Arena*, no. 4, 1987

207

Cover by M&Co. for magazine *Interview*

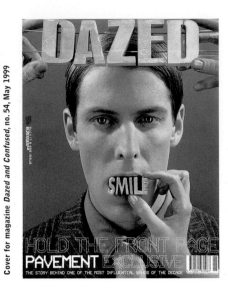

Cover for magazine *Dazed and Confused*, no. 54, May 1999

Cover for magazine *Studio Voice*, vol. 299, no. 11, November 2000

The studied informality of *Interview*'s masthead belongs to a graphic convention. To suggest speech, or the "interview", the word is presented in calligraphy. The design was by the eminent American partnership M&Co., headed by Tibor Kalman.

The creation of a cover for a style magazine is often the work of a large team. In addition to art direction by Matt Roach, among the skills involved here were photography, styling, hair, make-up, clothing design and post-production.

This issue examined "orgonic design". The term "orgonic" came from the psychoanalyst Wilhelm Reich and referred to an excess of sexual energy. Here it was applied to architecture and design that combined organic form and technological futurism.

fluorescent inks, and had a stapled landscape format, although this changed to perfect binding and a more conventional vertical format to facilitate display in shops. Attention to fashion remained central and the magazine was dubbed "the ultimate fashion victim's Bible". Jones pushed layouts to the brink of legibility. His hallmark style embraced stencilled lettering and typewriter script, montage, reportage-effect photography, photocopies, block type as headings, video and film stills, Polaroid camera shots and computer-type distortions. Claiming to be of the "make it up as you go along" school, Jones acted as a catalyst for the team of stylists, designers and photographers he had assembled around him.

As *The Face* and *i-D* matured, their "deconstructive" style of abrupt juxtaposition of type and image gave way to a cooler revival of modernism. In the process they spawned a host of imitators. If the early 1980s were years of innovation and invention for the two magazines, the subsequent period saw consolidation and professionalization as they became mainstream titles.

A second generation of magazines attempted to test boundaries further and to present new fashions for the next group of young readers. Style magazines were circulated internationally, and subsequently, during the 1990s, new titles appeared in many countries, marking the coming of age of style culture. Their impact was felt by mainstream titles, which responded to the challenge of the younger upstarts by revising their own approaches. A number of designers and journalists from style magazines joined their more established counterparts.

Specialization within the sector also occurred. For example, in the mid-1990s a huge interest in design for the home was reflected in a clutch of new titles on interiors that challenged journalistic conventions in much the same way as the fashion magazines had done a decade earlier. Among these was the quarterly *Nest*, launched in New York in 1997. The art director and editor-in-chief, Joseph Holtzman, experimented with layout, pictures were framed by decorative textiles, pull-outs were inserted and unusual formats with die-cut wavy or angular edges were published. Holtzman pushed the limits of design journalism by inviting film-makers, authors and scientists, as well as established journalists, to contribute, raising the quality of the writing and broadening the visual interpretation of subjects.

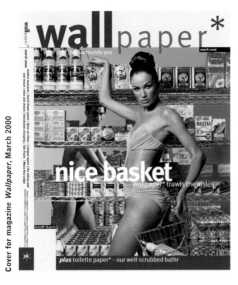

Cover for magazine *Wallpaper*, March 2000

The brainchild of Tyler Brule, *Wallpaper**
covers interior design and architecture,
as well as acting as a style guide to
travel, fashion and other cultural forms.
For this cover, Richard Spencer Powell
was the art director and Joachim Daldauf
the photographer

Spread from magazine *Nest*, Summer 2000

In this spread from *Nest*, a magazine
both art-directed and edited by Joseph
Holtzman, a die-cut angled format and a
chequerboard border give a striking
appearance to an article on the NhEW
house in Copenhagen, Denmark.

Page from magazine *Vanidad*, September 2000

A pastiche of previous graphic styles,
combined with the exaggerated colour
produced by new print technology, gave
Vanidad an edge when it first appeared.
Here the designer was Lucía Fernández
Muñez, the stylist Clarita Spindler and
the photographer Sophie De La Porte.

Spread from magazine *Dazed and Confused*, no. 54, May 1999

In his last issue as art director of *Dazed
and Confused*, Roach illustrated a feature
on the pop producer William Orbit with a
reference to the Surrealist paintings of
Magritte, and created a disturbing image
with a mixture of black, white and flesh
tones. The photographer was Rankin.

Poster for Barcelona Olympic Games, 1992

Barcelona'92 — Jocs de la XXVa Olimpiada Barcelona 1992 / Juegos de la XXV Olimpiada Barcelona 1992 / Jeux de la XXVe Olympiade Barcelona 1992 / Games of the XXV Olympiad Barcelona 1992

Mariscal designed the mascot Cobi in 1988 and used it in this poster for the next Olympic Games, held in Barcelona. The humanoid dog provoked controversy among the people of his adopted city.

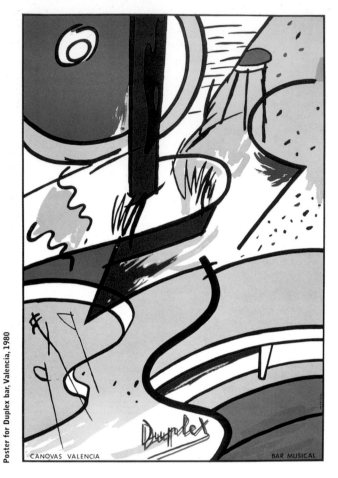

Poster for Duplex bar, Valencia, 1980

CANOVAS VALENCIA   BAR MUSICAL

In addition to this work, Mariscal designed the bar itself and developed the Duplex bar stool featured in the poster. In reality the stool has a more exaggerated zigzag leg.

210

➔ 1950–
➔ Major figure in Spanish design of 1980s–1990s
➔ Studied philosophy at Valencia University
➔ Designs, illustrations and TV animation key elements in Barcelona's rebirth as design centre

Javier Mariscal has long maintained a reputation as an *enfant terrible* of the new Spanish design. A witty and unconventional designer, he has worked in furniture, interiors, fashion and textiles, as well as graphic design, cartoons, illustration and television. Although Mariscal is not a native of Barcelona, he is nevertheless regarded as a key figure in placing design at the centre of the city's revitalized identity.

Mariscal was born in Valencia and studied philosophy at the city's university from 1967 to 1970 before moving to Barcelona, where he continued his studies at the Escuela de Grafismo Elisava between 1971 and 1973. His student years coincided with an unsettled period when a youthful counterculture was spreading

widely across Europe. At the same time the last years of General Franco's dictatorship were being played out, and even though Spain is an advanced industrial country, the possibilities for an avant-garde or experimental design culture to emerge were limited. In response to this situation many designers formed small partnerships and took on small, private commissions rather than large-scale assignments. This embryonic period was crucial for the resurgence of cultural activity after the death of Franco in 1975 and the transition to democracy.

At this time Mariscal specialized in cartoons, strongly influenced by the American tradition of Robert Crumb and subversive, humorous underground magazines. His artistic style derived from a distinctive range of forms, colours and attitudes to material. Using a live, elastic, organic line and quirky figures, he progressed from two

Animated film for television, *Twipsy*, 1999

Twipsy, written by Patty Marx and
produced by Haffa Diebold, marked
Mariscal's move into animated film. Made
for television in 26 half-hour episodes, the
series tells of the adventures of human
and cyberspace characters.

to three dimensions with agility – animating furniture
and ceramics as well as his graphic designs.

Mariscal had powerful childhood memories of the
rebuilding of Valencia after a serious flood in the late
1950s, and the architectural design language, colours
and surfaces of that era were a consistent inspiration.
Similar references to Italian vernacular design were made
by members of the Milan-based design group Memphis.
Famed for its strength in design, Milan was a crucial
model for Mariscal, and he joined Memphis to take on
furniture designs. Working across genres of design with
specialist manufactures, many in the Barcelona area, he
quickly gained international recognition.

As the capital of Catalonia, Barcelona benefited from
a regional distribution of wealth within Europe in the
1980s and 1990s – a period when the city dissociated

itself from Madrid. Its tradition was urban, with a distinct
imagery, small-scale furniture-making, clients frequenting
design studios and a public eager for design filling the
refashioned city's bars, cafés and restaurants. Barcelona's
cultural climate recalled the Modernismo movement that
flourished there at the turn of the twentieth century.

Like the cartoonist Saul Steinberg, whose drawings
built a graphic identity for New York, Mariscal helped to
define Barcelona's image through a series of drawings.
First he broke up the name "Bar Cel Ona' (Bar – Sky –
Wave in Catalan) in a 1984 design for a poster, later
applied to T-shirts. Two years later he devised Abecedari
Barcelona, an alphabet drawing on landmarks of the city,
and most famously, he personified the Barcelona Olympic
Games of 1992 in the character of Cobi at a time when
the city won recognition as a world design capital.

VAUGHAN OLIVER

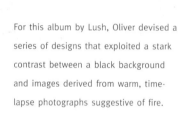

Poster and catalogue for exhibition "Vaughan Oliver", 1990

Oliver received international recognition through this exhibition, which opened in Nantes in 1990 and went to Paris the next year. He derived the image of a shattered knife from his reading of Jung's *Memories, Dreams and Reflections*.

For this album by Lush, Oliver devised a series of designs that exploited a stark contrast between a black background and images derived from warm, time-lapse photographs suggestive of fire.

Cover for record *Gala*, 1990

212

➔ 1957–
➔ Key figure in new British graphic design
➔ Studied graphic design at Newcastle Polytechnic
➔ Interested in Surrealist collage and juxtaposition
➔ Specializes in image making for record industry

The British designer, art director, illustrator and typographer Vaughan Oliver built his reputation on work for the independent record company 4AD. By experimenting with covers, posters and lyric booklets he devised poetic interpretations that aspired to be the equivalents of music. It has been suggested that Oliver's work is too emotional to be considered postmodern. In its search for an ethereal quality, it lacks the self-conscious aspect of parody and disinterest.

Oliver studied graphic design from 1976 to 1979 at Newcastle Polytechnic. On moving to London he joined Benchmark and then the Michael Peters Group, specialists in packaging design. This experience opened him to the possibilities of mixing typefaces in the applied context of packaging design within a highly successful design group. By 1983 he had left Michael Peters to specialize in work for 4AD, developing graphic identities for the bands the Cocteau Twins, This Mortal Coil, the Pixies, Lush and Ultra Vivid Scene. He worked with the photographer Nigel Grierson as a self-sufficient unit that called itself 23 envelope. In 1988 Grierson left and Oliver set up V23, collaborating with the designer Chris Bigg and the photographers Simon Larbalestier and Jim Friedman. As well as record companies, clients included Picador Books, the furniture designer Ron Arad, the fashion designer John Galliano and the Spanish television company Documania.

The graphic context of Oliver's arrival in London was that of post-Punk. Style magazines such as *The Face* and *i-D* emerged as important vehicles for the rapid transfer of visual ideas. The formation of various independent

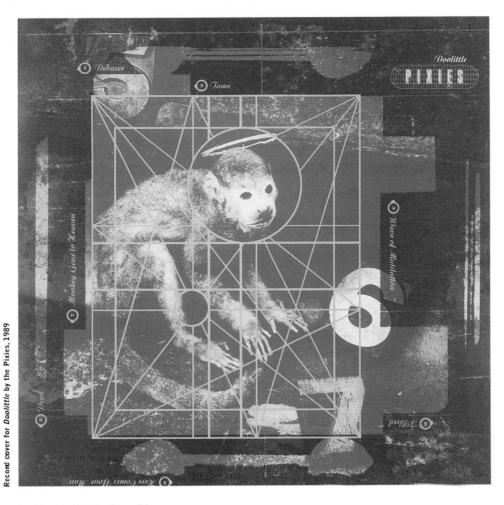

Record cover for *Doolittle* by the Pixies, 1989

A grid connecting the titles of the songs covers the image, photographed by Simon Larbalestier and printed in sepia tone and overprinted with a copper tone. The record came with a lyric booklet with photographs by Larbalestier.

record companies freed designers to work creatively, not bound by the usual mainstream tradition of promoting personalities. Unlike Neville Brody (see pp222–3), Peter Saville and Malcolm Garrett, who occupied similar positions in graphic design, Oliver's inspiration was not the "new typography" of the 1920s. He was drawn to the esoteric and poetic rather than the explicit, objective rhetoric of Constructivism.

Oliver found resonance in the strategies of the Surrealist André Breton, who, in the "First Surrealist Manifesto" of 1924, had celebrated the potential of convulsive beauty in chance encounters between dissimilar inanimate objects. Like Surrealist painters and photographers, Oliver explored the disquieting impact of juxtaposition through collage and photography, finding pleasure in the esoteric, the sexually suggestive or

ambiguous with an established vocabulary of hair, teeth and other body parts, knives and creatures.

The success of the 4AD formula depended on a mutual understanding between Oliver and its director, Ivo Watts-Russell. The latter gave Oliver a free rein, sparing no expense in the quality of printing, the use of metallic inks and a general tendency towards luxury. The work depended on multi-layered imagery and sensitivity towards colour, patina, paper quality and surface, all of which contributed to the atmosphere created by mixing photographically derived imagery. In terms of typography, Oliver was drawn to elegant solutions and the incorporation of complex calligraphy. Before computers this required a combination of skill, experience and chance, while the 1990s brought the further possibility of exploring the huge potential of Quantel Paintbox.

CRANBROOK ACADEMY OF ART

Blauvelt's poster announcing Cranbrook's printmaking programme indicates a close interest in semiology and structuralism at the school. Among the images he assembled is Magritte's painting *Ceci n'est pas une Pipe*. This alerted viewers to a central premise of semiology – the separation of the signifier and signified.

Poster by Andrew Blauvelt, "Cranbrook Printmaking", 1987

Under the direction of Michael and Katherine McCoy, joint professors of the Department of Design from the mid-1970s, the Cranbrook Academy of Art, in Michigan, became one of the most important seedbeds for postmodern graphic design in the United States.

The McCoys arrived at a time when international design was in stasis. Katherine McCoy took charge of the two-dimensionsal visual communications teaching, while her husband directed furniture, product and interior design.

The "Cranbrook discourse", as it came to be called, resulted from influences from both within and beyond the design world. Among these were the early writings of postmodernism, recently available translations of semiology and structuralism and the design experiments of Wolfgang Weingart (see pp190–1) in Basle, Switzerland.

In particular, Robert Venturi and Denise Scott Brown's *Complexity and Contradiction in Architecture* of 1966 and *Learning from Las Vegas* of 1972 (with Steven Izenour) changed how design in the urban environment was understood. Replacing the reductive vocabulary of late modernism, they interpreted the signs of everyday life in America, such as shopping centres, neon signs and the vernacular tradition, as an enrichment of architecture. At Cranbrook the recognition of the power of popular idioms

in design coincided with an interest in French linguistic philosophy. The writings of, for example, Roland Barthes offered ways of interpreting the iconography of industrial products and mass culture, seeing them as powerful ideological messages and the result of complex processes of signification. For the McCoys the relationship between designer and audience was no longer a matter of problem-solving or a strictly one-way process of communication. Instead they introduced scepticism about meaning.

Cranbrook graphic design became anti-formal, embracing vernacular design as a source, looking beyond sans-serif universal typefaces and adopting the multi-layered approach to word and image which had already been identified as a hallmark of postmodernism. One of the first manifestations was a special issue of the journal *Visible Language* (1978) which challenged much typographic convention.

At first the Cranbrook approach was seen by others in the design community rather than by the wider commercial world. For example, projects in which students were asked to interpret figures from the history of graphic design in poster form became known through exhibition and review articles. Among the most noted designs is Allen Hori's "Typography as Discourse" poster, an advertisement for a 1989 lecture by Katherine McCoy which took as its source a communication theory diagram.

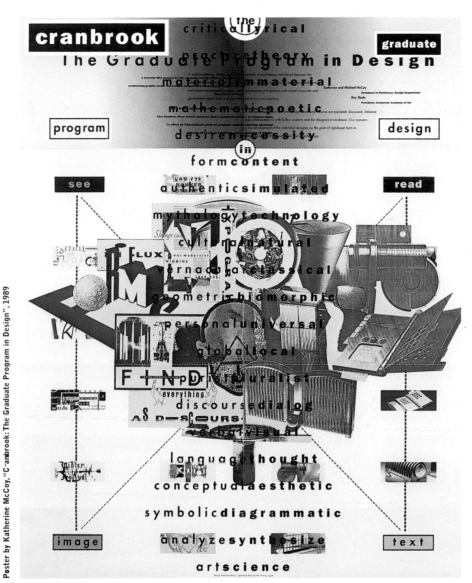

McCoy was head of graduate studies in Graphic Design at Cranbrook. Her poster shows a communication model interrupted by key terms used in analysis and criticism, taken from the design teaching curriculum at the school.

215

Cranbrook had a well-established position in the history of design and architecture teaching and this was celebrated with a fiftieth-anniversary exhibition and publication. Allen Hori's poster captured both the contemporary enthusiasm for deconstructive typography and the lyrical beauty of the school's location.

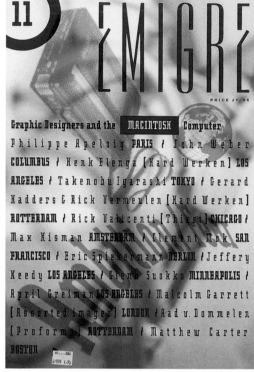

Cover by Rudy VanderLans with typeface design by Zuzana Licko for *Emigre* magazine, no. 11, 1989

In this issue of *Emigre* magazine contemporary designers spoke of their use of the Apple Macintosh computer. In three levels of visual information the shadowy words "Ambition/Fear", a computer and a globe add a commentary.

Cover by Rudy VanderLans with typeface design by Zuzana Licko for *Emigre* magazine, no. 23, 1992

The title of issue 23 of *Emigre* referred to the leading article, written by Dutch designer Gerard Unger. At the height of the international enthusiasm for deconstructive typography, distortion, layering and complexity, the piece explored questions of legibility.

⊕ Rudy VanderLans, 1955–
⊕ Zuzana Licko, 1961–
⊕ Started working together 1982
⊕ Pioneered graphic design in digital era
⊕ Formed influential *Emigre* magazine and digital type foundry

Emigre, which has been described as "the magazine that ignores boundaries", was internationally recognized as one of the most important graphic design journals of the last 15 years of the twentieth century. It was established by two Europeans resident in California, who gave a generation a forum in which the excitement and scepticism about digital typography could be explored.

Rudy VanderLans grew up in The Hague, in the Netherlands, where he studied graphic design at the Royal Academy of Fine Art. He found the Dutch modernist tradition too restrictive and turned instead to the American expressive graphic design of Milton Glaser (see pp152–7) and Herb Lubalin (see pp156–7), admiring their informality. Nevertheless, he gained experience at

Total Design, Vorm Vijf and Tel Design before going to the United States to study photography at the University of California at Berkeley. There he met Zuzana Licko, his future wife.

Licko was born in Bratislava, Czechoslovakia, but her family settled in the United States when she was seven. Initially she studied architecture, but changed to Visual Studies at Berkeley. She had grown up with computers and showed an early fascination with adapting their use to experimental typography. Licko was interested in working on typefaces within the constraints of the computer's grid and modulation, to develop an aesthetic impact rather than an exact science. The combined design experience of Licko and VanderLans led to the founding in 1982 of a magazine, a font workshop and a recording company, all trading under the name Emigre.

Cover by Rudy VanderLans with typeface design by Zuzana Licko for *Emigre* magazine, no. 43, 1997

This was the first issue of *Emigre* to include advertisements as a way to secure the revenue needed to continue to publish. Aware that they might be accused of "selling out", VanderLans addressed the theme in his editorial and commissioned articles that explored the relationship between designers, the market and ethics.

The first issue of *Emigre* was published in 1983 in Berkeley with a layout of xeroxed images and typewriter script. After a move to Sacramento, it became a twice-yearly publication. In 1984 the Apple Macintosh computer became available. Many established designers regarded its possibilities negatively; they had doubts about how amateur designers would take charge of their own work but were also dismissive of the qualities it offered professionals. By contrast, VanderLans and Licko accepted the limitations of the "Mac". Their designs were made to look good on a coarse-resolution printer, in the belief that they should work with the computer instead of forcing it into pre-established standards.

The first of Licko's bitmapped fonts, Emigre, Oakland, Universal and Emperor, were shown in the second issue of *Emigre*, while the third issue saw their application to the design. At this point Emigre Fonts was formed as a digital type foundry for the distribution of graphic software: first Licko's typefaces and then examples by an international range of designers.

Instead of the New York model of art direction, which stressed a clean, modernist approach, *Emigre* was pluralistic. An early important inspiration came from the Dutch design group Hard Werken (see pp186–7). No two issues looked the same: the format changed according to editor and subject matter. Guest editors were invited from many countries, including the United States, Britain, the Netherlands, Switzerland and Germany. Mainly mid-career professional graphic designers, they tackled themes of legibility, cultural theory, deconstructive typography and graphic authorship at the same time as introducing their own designs to a worldwide readership.

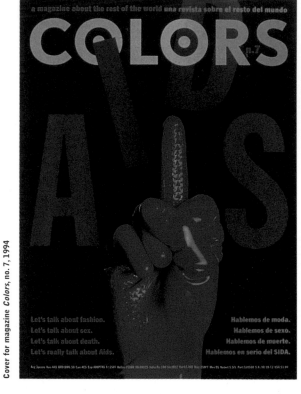

Cover for magazine *Colors*, no. 7, 1994

This issue of *Colors* sought to dispel myths about AIDS. The cover visualized shockingly the expression "giving the finger", with its reference to anal intercourse and latex protection.

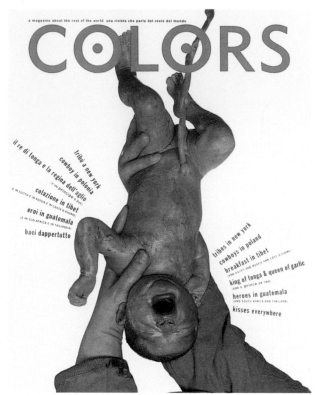

Cover for magazine *Colors*, 1991

It has been suggested that the image of the newborn baby on the cover of the first issue of *Colors*, which was also used in a billboard campaign, was the most censored picture in history.

⊕ 1949–99
⊕ Hungarian-born graphic designer and art director
⊕ Studied journalism at New York University
⊕ Founded M&Co. 1979
⊕ Editor-in-chief of Benetton magazine *Colors*

Tibor Kalman had a reputation as a dissenting voice among graphic designers. In the 1980s, when the booming economy in Western countries allowed design to become preoccupied with lifestyle and consumerism, he demanded social responsibility. Through his editorial design he prompted discussion about the global power of imagery. In 1989 he co-chaired with Milton Glaser (see pp152–5) the Dangerous Ideas conference, organized by the American Institute of Graphic Arts to encourage designers to re-evaluate the social implications of their work.

Kalman was born in Budapest and his parents moved to the United States when he was a child. He studied journalism at New York University in 1968 and, in a period of radicalized student politics, dropped out after two years. He then worked for the Barnes and Noble bookstore before it became a hugely successful national chain. He was responsible for window displays and publicity, recruiting younger designers and learning their trade from them.

By 1979 he was ready to set up the design group M&Co., named after his wife Maira, in New York. It soon became a fashionable studio, gaining commissions from David Byrne of the group Talking Heads and from the New York-based journal *Art Forum*. Among other early clients was Florent Morellet, who ran the New York restaurant Florent. Reacting against the conspicuous design of many restaurants during the "designer decade" of the 1980s, Morellet turned to Kalman, who applied his interest in vernacular design to the job.

what if..?
e se..?

Spread from magazine *Colors*, no. 4, 1992

ⓒCOLORS

Colors explored racial prejudice in this issue. The article "What If...?" showed internationally recognizable figures in photographs computer-manipulated to change racial characteristics. The Pope appeared Chinese, Michael Jackson and Spike Lee were white with blue eyes and Queen Elizabeth II was black.

Kalman's approach to the design of press advertisements, menu cards, postcards and matchboxes for this restaurant was discreet and low-key, displaying a dry humour. It was also often self-reflexive about the process of dining.

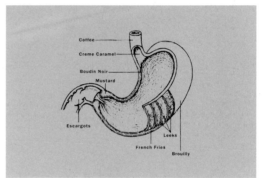

Card for restaurant Florent, New York, c.1992

219

On noticing Kalman's work as the creative director of *Interview* magazine, Oliver Toscani, Benetton's advertising director, asked him to work on a proposal for a new magazine, *Colors*, for the international clothing chain. The Italian-based company had already provoked controversy with its "United Colors of Benetton" advertising campaign. The way photography could be read on different levels laid it open to accusations of using pictures of human suffering to sell its goods. *Colors* contributed to this debate by further exploring the nature of issue-related imagery.

Kalman became editor-in-chief of *Colors* in 1991. Of his new role he said: "I felt that around the world there were young people who were progressive, and closer in spirits to each other than to their parents or cultures. This is the audience I wanted to reach with *Colors*." He

called it "the first magazine for the global village", developing the influential idea first outlined by Marshall McLuhan in 1968 in his book *War and Peace in the Global Village*. McLuhan's idea was that, through technologies of modern visual communication, similar communities of interest can form in all parts of the world. Accordingly Kalman ran issues on racism, AIDS and ecology, as well as on cultural ideas that were less controversial, such as Heaven, Miracles and The Street.

Kalman closed M&Co. in 1993 and moved to Rome to continue his involvement with *Colors*. While there he was found to be suffering from cancer. He returned with his family to New York, where he re-established a leaner version of M&Co., taking on only those clients and campaigns for which he had a direct sympathy. He died in Puerto Rico in 1999.

⊕ 1947–
⊕ Prolific designer, typographer and writer
⊕ Studied English and Art History in Berlin
⊕ Co-founder of MetaDesign in Berlin 1979; branches in London and San Francisco
⊕ Specializes in typography and information design for complex systems
⊕ Author of *Rhyme & Reason: A Typographic Novel* and *Stop Stealing Sheep (And Find Out How Type Works)*

220

Towards the end of the twentieth century momentous events changed the cultural and political map of the Western world. As a Berlin-based designer and head of the internationally successful MetaDesign, Erik Spiekermann felt the impact more than many graphic designers and he subsequently contributed to the transformation of the city, from the emblem of Cold War division to the new capital of a unified Germany.

Spiekermann was born in Hanover, but moved to Berlin, a city with a distinctive status and culturally vibrant identity, where he studied English and Art History at university and set up a press. In 1973 he transferred to London and worked for the design groups Wolff Olins, Henrion Design (see pp120–1) and Pentagram (see pp176–9), as well as teaching at the London College of Printing.

Gradually, Spiekermann has changed the face of German typography. He is not only the designer of several widely acclaimed typefaces but also adviser on historical typefaces for the Berthold type foundry. In association with Neville Brody (see pp222–3) in London, he opened FontShop Berlin, a mail-order company supplying typeface designs for computerized PostScript printers.

Spiekermann comments on typography by using metaphor and wit. He has written two typographic books: the first dates from 1982 and was published in English in 1987 as *Rhyme & Reason: A Typographic Novel*, while *Stop Stealing Sheep (And Find Out How Type Works)*, a collaboration with E.M. Ginger, appeared in 1993. Avoiding the dry approach of much earlier writing on typography, Spiekermann encourages the reader by showing how design decisions relate to a wide range of issues of taste and imagination.

While committed to the social role of design as effective communication, Spiekermann dissociated himself from what he perceived as the over-rational German design tradition. It was in this spirit that he designed the Meta typeface as an alternative to Helvetica, the ubiquitous typeface for information design in most parts of Europe and America in the 1960s and 1970s. He responded to what he saw as Helvetica's blandness by developing Meta for a similar range of uses but with exaggerated features such as curves and pseudo-serifs, intended to give the design more character. His other typefaces include ITC Officina (1988–90), FF Info, a signage information face first employed at Düsseldorf Airport in 1996 and then in Glasgow in 1999, when the city was UK City of Architecture and Design.

Spiekermann's career is inseparable from the development of MetaDesign, the design group he co-founded in Berlin in 1979. At first MetaDesign tackled design problems for local companies but it soon grew, accepting national design work on corporate identities and information systems. With the opening of a new office in Berlin's Potsdamer Platz in 1990 it began to take on international assignments, and by 2000 it had 150 staff in Berlin, 50 in San Francisco and 27 in London.

Typeface Meta, 1985

abcdefghijklmnopqrst
uvwxyzßABCDEFGHIJKL
MNQPRSTUVWXYZ(/·:·
1234567̓890&
abcdefghijklmnopqrst
uvwxyzßABCDEFGHIJKL
MNQPRSTUVWXYZ(/·:·
1234567̓890&
abcdefghijklmnopqrst
uvwxyzßABCDEFGHIJKL
MNQPRSTUVWXYZ(/·:·
1234567890&

Initially commissioned for use by the Bundespost (German Post Office), Meta – seen here early in its development – was taken up for a great number of alternative uses and became a hallmark typeface of the 1990s.

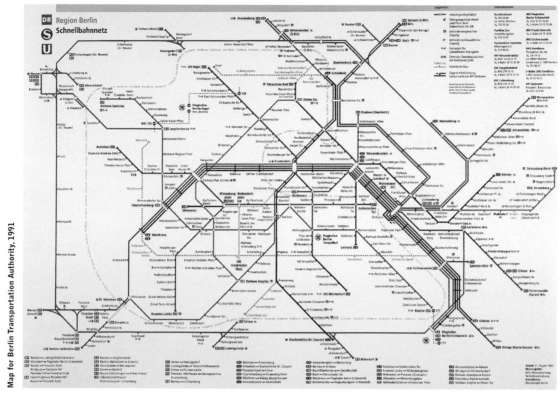

An important symbol of Germany's reunification in the early 1990s was the project MetaDesign undertook for the Berlin Transportation Authority (BVG). West Berlin and East Berlin had different transport systems and this map sought to resolve the inconsistencies.

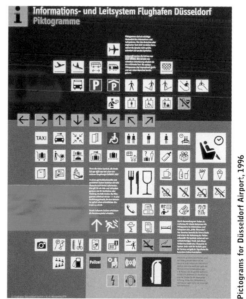

221

In this scheme Spiekermann and MetaDesign differentiated between directional and service signs through a change in background colour. Green was used to distinguish Düsseldorf from other German international airports.

After a fire at Düsseldorf Airport in 1996, Spiekermann and MetaDesign, Berlin were commissioned to devise a new signage system. While conforming broadly to international standards, it provided an opportunity to question assumptions about information design.

In the early 1980s Neville Brody contributed to a defining moment in British graphic design. When many established names were considered to have joined the mainstream or lost their interest for younger designers, Brody represented a heady mix of fashion, graphics, music and style culture. He re-energized graphic design by bringing together, in a new way, sources from the edges of youth style and commercial culture.

⊕ 1957–
⊕ Designer associated with defining moment of British graphic design in 1980s
⊕ Studied at London College of Printing
⊕ Designer of style magazine *The Face*
⊕ Highly influential approach to layout
⊕ Moved into digital typography and multimedia design in 1990s

While a student of graphic design at the London College of Printing from 1976, Brody became enthusiastic about the history of avant-garde art of the early twentieth century. Not for the first time in the century, Soviet Constructivist designers inspired a subsequent generation. Brody admired the work of El Lissitzky (see pp56–7), Rodchenko (see pp58–9) and others for their energetic readiness to work between editorial and commercial design. In the very different climate of post-Punk London, he took on work as a record designer for the labels Rocking Russian, Stiff Records and Fetish Records.

An important part of Brody's innovation was to turn to street style as a source for design. He was sensitive to the graphic languages of record labels of the 1950s and 1960s and more esoteric elements of American vernacular design. At a time when theory suggested eclecticism as a route out of the dead end of modernism, he offered a refined and highly edited version of this. Among his references were the writings of Jean Baudrillard and Paul Virilio on the systems of culture.

For more than six years Brody worked as art editor of *The Face*, the new style and culture magazine launched in 1980. There his work collapsed the conventional distinction between typeface and graphic symbol. Sometimes with the aid of the computer, but more often by hand, Brody devised many new alphabets for the headlines of the magazine's articles. Instead of offering immediate legibility, these designs intrigued the reader with a contemporary, nuanced feel that has been described as a set of "eccentric mannerisms".

222

Cover for magazine *The Face*, no. 42, October 1983

In the early days of *The Face*, Brodie's art direction stood out because of the title design, in which a triangle replaced the "A", photographic covers that captured the attention and the strong graphic feel of the magazine as a whole.

Initially through *The Face* and later through *Arena*, Brody's designs were celebrated by young designers and consumers around the world. Consolidating this reputation, two volumes of his work were published under the shared title *The Graphic Language of Neville Brody* in 1988 and 1994.

After leaving *The Face* in 1988 Brody worked for many international clients, among them Nike, Swatch, the Museum of Modern Art, New York, and the British fashion designer Katherine Hamnett. At the same time his interests as a type designer developed in collaboration with Erik Spiekermann (see pp220–1). Together they founded FontShop Berlin and FontWorksUK, specializing in the supply of typeface designs for computerized PostScript printers. As the world's first retailer of digital type the joint enterprise quickly developed to make some 3000 typeface designs available.

Spread from *The Face*, no. 59, March 1985

For the layout of an interview with Andy Warhol, Brody made reference to the American artist's interest in repetition, most famously in his screenprints, by reproducing six identical portraits. The title line was made up of Brodie's specially devised letters.

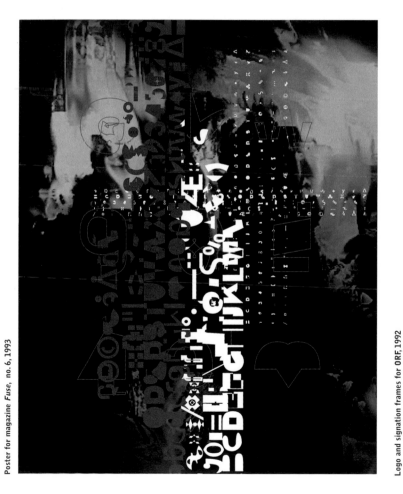

Poster for magazine *Fuse*, no. 6, 1993

Logo and signation frames for ORF, 1992

223

Throughout the 1990s Brody was an important figure in the promotion of ideas about digital typography. He published the digitized magazine *Fuse* and played a key role in the related series of typographic conferences.

Among Brody's multi-media designs in the 1990s was a corporate identity for the news programme of the Austrian television channel Österreichischer Rundfunk (ORF). Digitized type was phased and layered to create sequences.

⊕ Andy Altmann, 1962–
⊕ David Ellis, 1962–
⊕ Howard Greenhalgh, 1962–
⊕ Founded 1987 by Altmann, Ellis and Greenhalgh
⊕ Small and significant multi-media London-based design group
⊕ Designs for the book *Typography Now* and the Royal Academy of Art's catalogue *British Art Now*

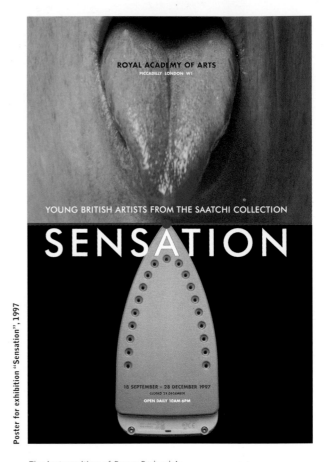

Poster for exhibition "Sensation", 1997

The juxtaposition of Rocco Redondo's photographs confronted the viewer and demanded a response, like the works on view in this controversial exhibition.

Why Not's design for an advertising campaign by Smirnoff in 1989–90 was unusual in making typography a central element. Three-dimensional letterforms of the brand name appeared on 48-sheet revolving billboards that were displayed on the London Underground.

The design partnership Why Not Associates came together in 1987, soon after the three founding members, Andy Altman, David Ellis and Howard Greenhalgh, graduated from the Royal College of Art in London. Altman and Ellis, the graphic designers in the group, had been students of Gert Dumbar (see pp184–5) at the College. Dumbar had encouraged them to explore the possibilities of image making which broke down the traditional boundaries between the personal and professional, the playful and the serious. In particular they understood how experimental photography could be combined with digitized type to produce exciting results in two and three dimensions.

On graduating the young designers realized they did not want to join one of the more established design groups in London. They saw their challenge as to define themselves as separate from the mainstream while not being ghettoized in the field of the style magazines (see pp206–9), a particularly lively area of work for graphic designers which had come to the fore a few years earlier in London. Their solution was to become "techno-friendly innovators". Operating one of the first multi-media design studios in London, they aimed to adopt a flexible approach to their partners while sustaining a variety of skills. This was made possible as their careers coincided with rapid improvements in computer-aided design. By using new technology they could remain a small company. The combination of their approach, technology and timing worked in their favour and they soon found

For an issue of the American cultural magazine *Plazm* devoted to the theme of the body, genetic engineering and science, Patrick Morrissey took quotations from Mary Shelley's book *Frankenstein* and overlaid them on images that alluded to the delicate boundaries of human nature.

Poster for magazine *Plazm*, 1995

IT WAS WITH THESE FEELINGS THAT I BEGAN THE CREATION OF A HUMAN BEING.

they were receiving commissions from high-profile clients. Greenhalgh led the film side, before leaving in 1993 to establish Why Not Films single-handedly. Others who worked for them include the British type designer Jonathan Barnbrook (see pp228–9), the photographer Rocco Redondo and the designers Chris Priest, Patrick Morrissey, Iain Cadby and Mark Molloy.

British graphic design has usually been defined as being concerned with the pragmatic rather than the theoretical, and Why Not Associates are no exception. While their designs often combine the characteristics of postmodern and deconstructionist typography, they do not articulate their interests through the vocabulary of American or Swiss design theory. Instead, while sharing with their counterparts elsewhere an interest in combining experimentation with new technologies, they

were comfortable in a commercial world, taking on work for advertising agencies, film and television companies and galleries and museums. They explained the success of their work as quite simply satisfying the client.

Commentators often referred to their dependence on humour, popular culture and football, a particularly British mix, as well as to graphic design "with attitude". Altman, for example, was quoted as saying that his interest is in "typography as entertainment". If this was the case, then it was not at the expense of pushing boundaries in the approach to style and technique.

Why Not's formula proved remarkably successful and very soon they were asked to work for major commercial and cultural clients. Their work became known to a much wider audience than much experimental graphic design when they designed the mail-order catalogue for

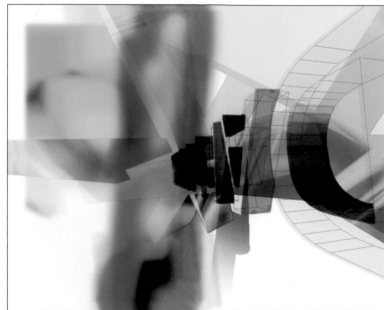

Still from video for Virgin Records, 2000

Why Not were commissioned to produce an hour-long film for the Virgin Records international conference in 2000. To mark the sections between the sequences of music, they developed typographic dividers exploring the possibilities of dimensional typography, in this case for the band Daft Punk.

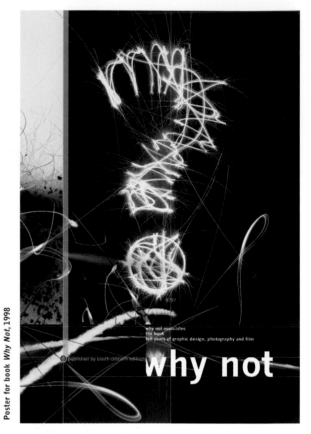

Poster for book *Why Not*, 1998

A profile of Why Not, with an essay by Liz Farrelly, was published in 1998. The design of the book and the accompanying graphics revealed the group's characteristic virtuosity.

the British clothing company Next in 1990, introducing their designs of multi-layered, fragmented type and image fields to many households. Other commissions came from Smirnoff, Nike, Marcatré and the Royal Mail.

Two commissions in particular linked the group with defining moments in British cultural history of the 1990s. The first was when they collaborated with Edward Booth-Clibborn and Rick Poynor on *Typography Now – the next wave* in 1991. Poynor, the design critic and founding editor of *Eye* magazine, compiled a selection of contemporary design which he believed represented a significant break with tradition. Many examples came from the Cranbrook Academy of Art (see pp214–15), California Institute of the Arts and representatives of the new wave in Switzerland and the Netherlands, as well as

from London. Why Not's design exemplified the message of much of the book's content – that typography was "aiming towards multiple meanings rather than fixed readings, to provoke the reader into becoming an active participant in the construction of the message".

The second example of the group's contribution to a key moment in cultural life came in 1997, when they were selected to design the poster for the controversial exhibition "Sensation: Young British Artists from the Saatchi Collection", shown at the Royal Academy of Arts in London and then at Brooklyn Art Museum, New York. These commissions identified Why Not as among the most important of the young designers who were marking a generational shift in the cultural map of Britain at the end of the twentieth century.

martinique
tobago
womenswear collection
jamaica
tahiti
eveningwear

Catalogue for Next, *Next Directory 5*, 1987–8

227

One of Why Not's early high-profile
commissions was the *Next Directory*, for
the British clothing company Next. This
introduced new-wave typography and
computer-generated imaging, initially
associated with avant-garde graphic
design, to a much broader public.

→ 1966–
→ British graphic designer and typographer
→ Studied at St Martin's College of Art and Design and Royal College of Art, London
→ Designed many digital typefaces
→ Associated with Young British Artists and designed Damien Hirst's book *I Want to Spend the Rest of My Life Everywhere with Everyone, One to One Always Forever, Now*

Jonathan Barnbrook became identified as the single most important graphic designer in Britain in the late 1990s through his association with the rise of the Young British Artists movement and, in particular, Damien Hirst. He is a graphic designer, film-maker and font designer who has chosen to stay a small company rather than expand and take on the larger commissions of corporate design. His design identity has been characterized as a mixture of idealism and cynicism, irony and self-deprecatory humour.

Barnbrook studied graphic design in London, at St Martin's College of Art and Design from 1985 to 1988 and the Royal College of Art from 1988 to 1990. He then worked with Why Not Associates (see pp224–7) before becoming a freelance designer. His interest in typographic design is rooted as much in the history of typeface design and the English lettering tradition as in Futurist experiment and contemporary cultural practice. For example, he produced a series of machine-cut inscriptions in stone that make ironic commentary on the legacy of Eric Gill (see pp30–1). At the same time his design has been used to make some of the most contemporary visual statements.

His interest in developing the relationship between typeface design and language is reflected in the names of his typeface designs. Since 1990 these have included Prototype (1990), Exocet (1991), Mason, Mason Sans and Patriot (1994), Nylon (1996), Draylon, Drone, Apocalypso, Bastard, Prototype, Delux, False Idol, Nixon Script, Patriot and Prozac (1997), Newspeak (1998) and Moron (2000). Barnbrook uses association a great deal in selecting witty and direct names. The analogies he makes between type form and wider cultural or social forces flow from his belief that designers should make objects from the materials that surround them. This approach to naming depends on the wider popular awareness of typeface design among a generation of young readers – by no means all professional designers, but nonetheless informed by design for the Apple Macintosh and the place of typefaces in style culture.

Barnbrook chose the name Prozac, for example, at the design stage; the abstract shapes reminded him of pharmaceuticals at a time when the new drug was in the news. In the case of Mason, the name was changed from Manson, chosen for its link with the serial killer, when the American design community found such an association unacceptable. Mason and Exocet were released by Emigre (see pp216–17) Fonts in Los Angeles, while the rest were made available through the designer's own type manufacturer, Virus, and sold through Fontworks.

Committed to innovation in type use, Barnbrook also pioneered new ways of incorporating type on film title sequences by using stop-frame animation The technique was used by the director Tony Kaye in a series of advertisements for clients such as Vidal Sassoon, Lloyd's, Volkswagen and Mazda.

Cover for Damien Hirst's book *I Want to Spend....1997*

Breaking the mould of the familiar format of many artists' monographs in which the book cover is used to illustrate a single work, Barnbrook's design for this book, published by Booth-Clibborn Editions, interpreted the subject's interests. An operating theatre is overlaid by chemical formulae, making reference to Damien Hirst's exploration of the boundaries between art, science and medicine.

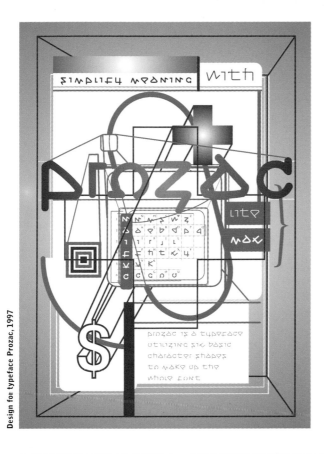

Design for typeface Prozac, 1997

The typeface Prozac, seen here in the font catalogue *Welcome to the Cult of Virus*, was named after the new anti-depressant drug. Barnbrook's idea was to use the minimum number of characters possible to generate a typeface, with individual shapes being rotated to provide other characters.

Spread from Damien Hirst's book *I Want to Spend...*, 1997

A spread from Hirst's book shows two works from a series of cage installations made by the artist in 1994. Barnbrook set off the photographs with simple grids and single colour blocks.

An offset poster for the department store Parco posed the American actress Faye Dunaway, photographed by Kazumi Kurigami, as a Japanese Bodhissatva with two child temple servers. The clothes were designed by Issey Miyake.

This spread is from a 10-page article entitled "Iki Ikite kasanete iki iku" (Go Go and Go Go Go), inspired by the theme "My Image of Fashion". Eiko Ishioka was the art director and Bishin Jumonji took the photographs.

230

⊖ 1939–
⊖ Acclaimed Japanese art director who opened Japanese design to international influences
⊖ Studied design at Tokyo National University of Fine Arts and Music
⊖ Art director for Parco department store

Eiko Ishioka has been called Japan's greatest art director. In a period when consumerism had reached its height she worked across cultures to define a global system of representation. Her approach was to use highly professional photography of models whom she directs, combining ideas from theatre and fine art. Her images confront attitudes towards gender, sexuality, beauty, the body, nationality and race.

The daughter of the renowned graphic designer Tomio Ishioka, Eiko studied from 1957 in the Design Department at the Tokyo National University of Fine Arts and Music, graduating in 1961. She then worked in the advertising division of Shiseido, Japan's oldest and largest cosmetics company. A pioneer designer in many

respects, she was the first woman to be elected to the Tokyo Art Directors' Club in 1971 and the first Japanese designer to take a photographic shoot abroad when she went to Hawaii in 1961.

The first stage of modern graphic design in Japan in the 1950s and 1960s had primarily involved integrating Western ideas in a national tradition. Ishioka and her generation, including her friend the fashion designer Issey Miyake, recognized that Japanese ideas, presented in new ways, could be taken to the United States and the rest of the world. She resisted cultural assumptions about Japanese style which were often based on a fusion of Buddhism and modernism. Instead, while still aware of these possibilities, she embraced the full impact of media, film, TV, pop music and the fashion world. She interpreted the role of art director broadly, staging

Sakikio Arai, a dancer friend of Ishioka,
was photographed by Noriaki Yokosuka
making figurative shapes in a blue
stretch-fabric bag to provide the main
motif for this offset poster advertising an
international design competition.

professional models in imaginary scenarios, evoking sexuality, exoticism and risk.

In many cases the work engaged with sexual politics, not to find a feminist political correctness but to challenge assumptions. The 1975 campaign titles reveal this: "A Model is More than Just a Pretty Face", "Don't Stare at the Nude; Be Naked", "A Woman Can Feel a Foreign Country" and "Girls Be Ambitious!".

Much of Ishioka's international acclaim came from her work for the innovative department store Parco, where she was art director. The first Parco opened in 1969 and mixed the functions of a cultural centre with a department store aimed at young people. Under the chairmanship of Seiji Tsutsumi of the Seibu Group, the chain grew into a prestigious shopping complex with 12 branches throughout Japan combining designer shops, restaurants, book stores, galleries and theatres. The profits of the stores were channelled into cultural projects, including the highly regarded but notorious advertising campaigns. Predicting the strategies of Oliviero Tosciano for the Italian clothing chain Benetton, the Parco advertisements made no direct reference to individual products sold at the stores. Instead, in newspaper and magazine advertising, posters, billboards, books, exhibitions and theatrical productions, Ishioka made intriguing cultural allusions.

In the area of film Ishioka designed the posters for the Japanese screening of Francis Ford Coppola's *Apocalypse Now* (1979). She also designed the posters, sets and costumes for Paul Schrader's *Mishima* (1985), a study of the Japanese poet Yukio Mishima, winning an award at Cannes for the best artistic contribution to a film.

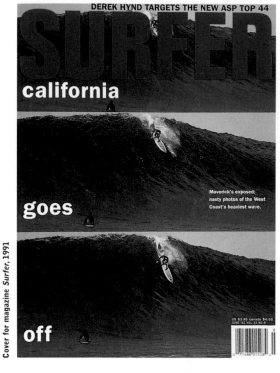

Cover for magazine *Surfer*, 1991

Cover for magazine *Raygun*, no. 17, 1994

Moving from the experimental magazine *Beach Culture* (1989–91), Carson was asked to redesign the more established *Surfer*. A top professional surfer himself, he approached the task armed with an intimate knowledge of the subject.

As art director of *Raygun* Carson helped give this new magazine an innovative design. Covering music and the beach scene, it became a respected voice in the popular fine arts. The photographer for this cover was Melanie McDaniel.

232

⊕ 1957–
⊕ American designer, art director, lecturer and writer
⊕ Fuses interests in surfing, beach culture and graphic design
⊕ Associated with deconstructive typography

David Carson is an internationally acclaimed designer who has reinterpreted the role of graphic designer, teacher, writer and art director as one of virtuoso performer. In 1995 fellow designer Jeffrey Keedy nicknamed Carson the "Paganini of type" – a title that encapsulated his ability to combine enthusiasm for new techniques with a highly complex and intricate artistic language.

Originally a sociologist and lecturer in higher education, Carson began working as a graphic designer when he re-styled the specialist magazine *Transworld Skateboarding*. Carson was a professional surfer, ranking eighth in the world at the time, and working on a boarding publication such as *TWS* fulfilled two of his fundamental criteria: to work on a subject of interest

and to have the opportunity to create an experimental layout that avoided traditional graphic conventions. He continued this approach with the design and art direction of the magazines *Beach Culture* (1989–91) and *Surfer* (1991–3), before launching his own publication, *Raygun,* in 1992.

Carson's career coincided with the growing awareness of the impact of digitalization in typeface design. His great interest in typography, modern European philosophy, film and music, and his passion for the beach, were in tune with the interests of a generation of readers who were also experimenting with design on the Apple Macintosh. The potential of someone who could embody the interests of young consumers was soon noticed by advertisers. In ten years, Carson moved from designing high-profile but specialist

Spread from article "Hots for Teacher", *Raygun*, 1994

For the opening page of an article on rock stars' crushes on their former teachers, Carson deconstructed the headline, making a full-page arrangement of type, symbols and images.

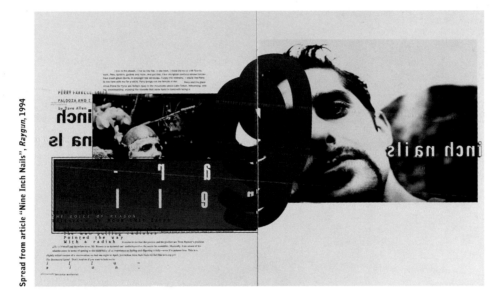

Spread from article "Nine Inch Nails", *Raygun*, 1994

Carson recognized that he had a committed readership who would be prepared to spend longer than average on a text because of their fascination with the integration of subject matter and style. He was concerned that neither element should dominate his designs.

233

magazines to undertaking major commissions from some of the world's largest companies including Levi's, Pepsi Cola, American Express, Citibank, Coca-Cola, Apple Macintosh, National Bank and Nike.

Greatly indebted to the work of Wolfgang Weingart and the Cranbrook Academy (see pp214–15), Carson, who studied graphic design only briefly in Rapperswil, Switzerland, in 1983, belongs to the tradition of deconstructive typography. Countering the modernist position that "form follows function" or that the designer is the expert who should solve a client's communication problem, he uses layout to explore meaning. The typographic form is expected to represent ideas actively, rather than present a transparent medium.

The hallmarks of Carson's approach are the manipulation or distortion of type, and visually driven arrangements of text. These extend expression and in many respects can be viewed as illustrating the earlier ideas of the Canadian sociologist Marshall McLuhan about the potential of the medium to be the message in contemporary global communication.

Throughout his career Carson has been an important catalyst for design change, running many workshops for graphic design students in universities around the world. He has incorporated the results of some of the projects under his supervision into his books *The End of Print* and *Grafik Design After the End of Print*. Some critics have accused him of distorting type to the point of illegibility. In his defence Carson has suggested that this view underestimates the capabilities of the enthusiastic reader or viewer and that work of a multi-layered nature stimulates both the imagination and interest of readers.

⊖ Nicolaus Ott, 1947–
⊖ Bernhard Stein, 1949–
⊖ Modernist graphic
design partnership
founded 1978
⊖ Both studied graphic
design at Hochschule
der Künste, Berlin
⊖ Combine interest in
functional typography
with image making
⊖ Important cultural
commissions, including
posters for theatrical
productions, concerts
and exhibitions

In contrast with the vibrant and versatile graphic design of Britain, the USA and the Netherlands in the 1980s, much German design was stable but uninspiring. Information design was one strength, however, with the rational approach of Ulm and Swiss typography still making an impact on public design schemes, but otherwise graphic design was dominated by international advertising. An exception was the partnership of Nicolaus Ott and Bernhard Stein, which was formed in 1978 in West Berlin. Their posters and publications contributed to the visual character of the city as they appeared on poster columns and at major cultural venues.

Both designers were trained as modernists at Berlin's Hochschule der Künste. Ott studied under Herbert Kapitzki, formerly of the Hochschule für Gestaltung in Ulm, where systems design and analytical approaches to visual communication had been taught. Until the Wall fell in 1989, Berlin attracted less major commercial investment than other West German cities. But even though industrial clients were not readily available, Ott + Stein built up a reputation with cultural projects. By 1990 they had designed over 200 posters and over 100 catalogues for Berlin's many concert halls, galleries and museums.

The two collaborate on each design. Ott has been described as seeking beauty and the perfect solution; Stein is interested in word play and looks for the distinctive ingredient. Their posters have what has been called a "tectonic structure", a method of composition that leads the eye across the page, where clusters of type and image are presented in a non-hierarchical format. German san-serif typefaces are predominantly used for "hard" information – names, addresses, opening times and other important details. The designs often depend on a central motif, either a deconstructed word or single image, set against a strongly contrasting colour field. Words may be broken up into elements such as curves, diagonals, verticals and horizontals. At other times they are arranged so that they have associations. Hand-rendered, they become equivalents to faces (as in the "Foto" poster) and buildings (as in the "Diseño" poster), or resemble people and things. These permutations transform the designs from being straightforwardly modernist solutions, but neither are they overtly postmodern. At a time when much design aspired to irony, their work appeared playful yet serious. It betrays what has been called "an enlightened manipulation of language and typography", driven by ideas rather than purely visual thinking.

Ott + Stein's approach has been compared to the work of Müller-Brockmann (see pp124–5), Glaser (see pp152–5) and Pentagram (see pp176–9). Their stress on the poster as an important cultural intervention also recalls the Polish poster tradition of Tomaszewski (see pp142–3) and others.

234

Poster for exhibition "Design from Catalonia", 1989

Strong colours and playful lettering give a Spanish inflection and evoke Miró, whose work was popular among Catalan artists at the time of the exhibition. A tiny silhouette of Gaudí's Calvet chair reinforces the illusionistic sense of scale.

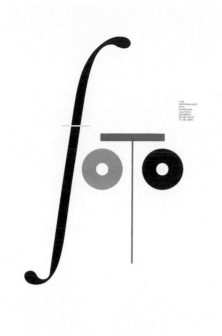

This design depends on the pure typographical elegance of the letterforms. The central element resembles a face, but in addition, without seeking to achieve direct resemblance or representation, the letters "O" and "T" hint at the technical aspects of photography.

Poster for exhibition "Foto", 1990

ARCHIV-VISUM

Poster for opera *The Rake's Progress*, 1987

235

Before the fall of the Wall in 1989, major commissions for designers in Berlin came from cultural institutions. This opera poster has the colourful directness associated with designers of the Polish poster school such as Tomaszewski.

→ 1940–
→ Graphic designer, teacher, writer and feminist artist
→ Studied graphic design at Yale University, where she now directs graduate programme in graphic design
→ Works engage with feminist history; some are site-specific and incorporate multi-media

The last 30 years of the twentieth century saw a marked growth of interest in the idea of typography as discourse. According to this new outlook, typography could create active responses in its viewers, posing questions rather than resolving them as the designer as problem-solver had previously done. Sheila Levrant de Bretteville is a major contributor to the principles of typography as discourse in her work as educator and professional designer.

A student on Yale University's graphic design graduate programme in the early 1960s, de Bretteville returned in 1991 as its newly appointed director. For the previous ten years she had led the department of communication art and design at the Otis Art Institute of Parsons School of Design in Los Angeles, combining this with designing for corporate clients in her own studio.

De Bretteville takes a feminist perspective in her work and she has been an important figure in establishing a gender critique of the international style in graphic design. Dissatisfied with the nature of the clients and the tendency towards homogeneity in late modernism, and as part of a wider radicalization of design at the time, she created the first design programme for women at the California Institute of Arts in 1971. In particular she aligned her strategies of deconstructivist critique with the architectural criticism of Robert Venturi and Denise Scott Brown, who acknowledged that the vernacular design of the street offered a rich set of references from which architecture could benefit.

In her teaching de Bretteville has consistently encouraged students to work on issue-related projects that engage with their community. The method she uses is, in her words, "asking, listening, reflecting, suggesting, and sustaining". She recommends that form making should be delayed until the exact content has been established through discussion with the users, clients or an audience, whom she regards as co-participants.

236

Part of installation "Hear Us", 1999

In this work, made of marble and bronze with a newspaper substrate, the first women to be represented in the Massachusetts State House, in Boston, are set against a wall of legislative documents regarding the issues that they worked to change.

De Bretteville shares strategies with other feminist artists. She designed two books which documented Judy Chicago's *Dinner Party* of 1978, an installation to celebrate women's history. The idea of commemoration also runs through de Bretteville's works. Many take the form of public artworks which combine research into the community and an engagement with local history. The work is multi-media, with significance attributed to the architectural setting of inscriptions. One example, *Biddy Mason, Time and Place*, dating from 1989, was an artwork dedicated to the life of a Los Angeles woman. Each panel contains a text that relates the woman's life through letters, photographs, maps and historic documents. In this work de Bretteville reclaimed the use of the heroic monumental tradition, which is often associated with patriarchy, to explore new and previously overlooked subjects.

An installation at the site of her home paid tribute to the former slave and midwife Biddy Mason by recounting her history and that of her city. The work, made of concrete, slate, granite and steel, took the form of a wall divided into the decades of the subject's life. The photography was by Annette del Zoppo.

Installation, *Biddy Mason: Time and Place*, Los Angeles, 1989

Shrink-wrapped poster, "not enough", Los Angeles, 1970

When the new School of Design opened at the California Institute of Arts, this poster, with photography by Roger Conrad, was used to attract appropriate students. Shrink-wrapped in clear plastic, it incorporates a printed circuit, a jack and a fir cone.

ADBUSTERS

Adbusters, or Adbusters Media Foundation and Powershift Advocacy Agency, to give it its full name, was established by Kalle Lasn, a self-proclaimed postmodern revolutionary. After the direct political struggles of earlier in the twentieth century and the gender and environmental campaigns of the 1970s, Lasn suggested that it was time to find a strategy for a critique of global advertising.

Lasn was born in Estonia in 1942 and the family emigrated to Australia when he young. He studied mathematics at university before starting to travel. He then settled in Japan and established his own company, taking on work for McCann Erickson and the Japanese Hakuhodo advertising agencies. This experience led Lasn to the opinion that professionals working in the advertising industry were frequently forced into a position of neutrality in relation to the messages they were employed to promote. Disillusioned, he left for Vancouver in Canada to become an independent film-maker.

Lasn's transition to media activist was partly prompted by a major TV network's refusal to broadcast one of his films. In 1989 he made a film that criticized a promotional film about the logging industry in north-west Canada. Lasn's counter-film showed what was, in his view, the true character of the industry's mismanagement. After it was rejected he made accusations of injustice until the company also withdrew the original film from screening.

His subsequent activities have been inspired partly by the example of the Situationist International, a group of radical philosophers and cultural activists who initially had formed in 1958 in Paris. Like them, Lasn turned to the magazine as an effective format for spreading ideas of dissent, and founded the publication *Adbusters* with Chris Dixon as art director. He aimed his messages at designers and educationalists, most of whom are readers of the magazine, whose circulation has grown to 60,000.

The principle was to promote strategies of "culture jamming". Concerned about the saturation of people's lives, especially children's, by advertising, Lasn devised the tactic of disrupting expectation through "uncommercials" – television advertisements that promote ideas rather than sell products. The text for one of the most prominent ran: "The average North American consumers five times more than a Mexican, ten times more than a Chinese person and 30 times more than a person from India. We are the most voracious consumers in the world – a world that could die because of the way we North Americans live."

Another strategy has been in "subvertising", in which spoof advertisements in the printed media undermine established messages. These campaigns are aimed in particular at the domination achieved by global brands, and they attack Nike, Absolut, Calvin Klein and the tobacco company Philip Morris. Subvertisements depend for their impact on technically accurate reconstructions. Professionals in the advertising industry help Adbusters to achieve this by offering their advice anonymously.

Adbusters fits into the tradition of deconstructing the media, alongside the photomontages of John Heartfield or the juxtaposition of text and image by the contemporary artist Barbara Kruger. Nevertheless, Lasn has been criticized by some commentators on the Left for using the very means he is intending to expose rather than finding an alternative visual language.

The effectiveness of this spoof magazine advertisement derives from its accurate reconstruction of the photographic style, advertising copyline and typography used in the well-known campaign for a fashion house's perfume.

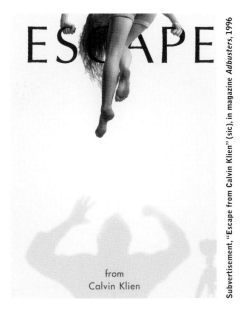

ESCAPE

from
Calvin Klien

Subvertisement, "Escape from Calvin Klien" (sic), in magazine *Adbusters*, 1996

This subvertisement relies on the recognition of the genre of soap-powder advertisement aimed at female audiences who are traditionally promised happiness through using the product. The subvertisement's double edge is that it exposed advertising strategies while commenting on the new anti-depressant drug Prozac.

Subvertisement, "New Improved Prozac Mood Brightener – Wash Your Blues Away", in magazine *Adbusters*, 1997

239

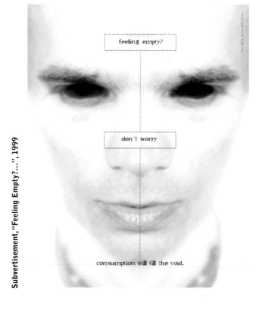

Subvertisement, "Feeling Empty?...", 1999

A more abstract design challenges the assumption that in modern life shopping can act as a form of "retail therapy". The form, which is not based on a specific product, echoes the many advertisements that do not explain themselves but leave the viewer to puzzle out their meaning. The work appears in Kalle Lasn's *Culture Jam: How to Reverse America's Suicidal Consumer Binge: and Why We Must*, published in 2000.

⊖ Ellen Lupton, 1963–
⊖ J. Abbott Miller, 1963–
⊖ Partnership founded
in New York 1985
⊖ Important contributors
to "typography as
discourse" movement
in United States
⊖ Designs break
boundaries between
form and content
⊖ Many exhibition and
publishing projects

Design/Writing/Research was founded in 1985 by Ellen Lupton and J. Abbott Miller. This design group became a vital element in the movement for typography as discourse that emerged in the United States in the closing decades of the twentieth century. In a range of projects it collapsed the distinction between designer and author. Combining critical theory and design practice, it made major contributions to design and culture through publications and exhibitions. The British design writer Rick Poynor said of Lupton and Miller: "They have turned critical reflection into a viable form of everyday practice."

Lupton and Miller graduated from the design programme at New York's Cooper Union art school in 1985. Their education coincided with an increasing engagement with critical theory, semiotics and post-structuralism in art teaching. Establishing the design group provided an after-hours focus for collaboration outside paid work. At the Cooper Union's Herb Lubalin Study Center for Design and Typography, Lupton was appointed to work on exhibitions and related publications. She curated monographic exhibitions on Vignelli (see pp136–7), Silverstein, Chermayeff (see pp134–5) and Casey, interpreted the non-phonetic visual language of Otto Neurath, and extended the boundaries of graphic design history with thematic and national studies.

She collaborated with Miller on many publications. For example, The ABCs of ▲■●: The Bauhaus and Design Theory, from Pre-School to Post-Modernism (1991) interpreted the design school for the next generation, using the design of the text to exemplify their critique of modernism.

In 1992 Lupton was appointed Curator for Contemporary Design at the Cooper Hewitt National Museum of Design, New York, where she broadened her range to include all genres of design, often working on the design of the exhibitions themselves. Her book Mechanical Brides (1993) engaged with recent feminist design history, exploring the relationship between women and technology in the home and the office.

240

Spread by Lupton from Mechanical Brides, 1993

As writer and designer (with Hall Smyth) of Mechanical Brides, published by Princeton Architectural Press, Ellen Lupton used graphic ephemera to show how the representation of women changed during the twentieth century.

"Mixing Messages, Graphic Design in Contemporary Culture", a review of the previous 15 years of American graphic design, was shown at the Cooper Hewitt Museum in 1996 and brought up to date an earlier project, "Graphicizing Design in America, a Visual Language History", at the Walker Art Center, Minneapolis, in 1989, to which Lupton and Miller had contributed. In 1993 they were jointly awarded the Chrysler Design Award.

Throughout the 1990s they contributed extensively to design journalism in Emigre and Eye, among other magazines. In 1995 Miller became director of Kiosk, a small publishing division of Princeton Architectural Press. The two designers were made joint professors at Maryland College, Baltimore, in 1998, and the following year Miller became a partner in Pentagram (see pp176–9), New York.

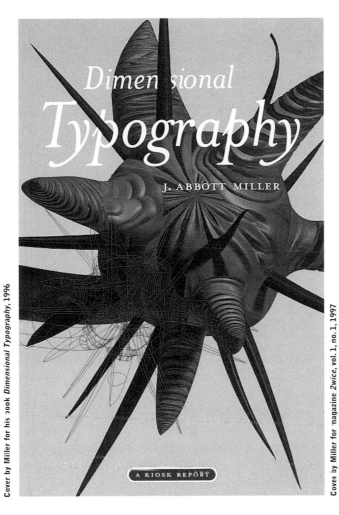

Written and designed by J. Abbott Miller and published by Kiosk Books in 1996, *Dimensional Typography* examines the design possibilities for letters in virtual environments and the sculptural or three-dimensional forms of individual letters.

The first issue of *2wice* was devoted to the theme of "Feet". An interdisciplinary project, edited and art-directed by Miller, *2wice* concentrates on themes that cross the boundaries between various cultural practices and performance.

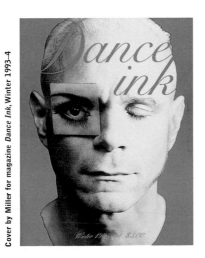

Published from 1990 to 1996, the quarterly magazine *Dance Ink* was an innovative collaboration between designers, under art director J. Abbott Miller, photographers and performance artists. Its founder and publisher, Patsy Tarr, established a serious and imaginative forum for the interpretation of the New Dance movement of Merce Cunningham, Paul Taylor, Twyla Tharp, Trisha Brown, Mark Morris and others.

- Daniela Haufe, 1966–
- Detlef Fiedler, 1955–
- Susanne Bax, 1973–
- Design group based in Berlin
- Cultural projects for former German Democratic Republic
- Acclaimed posters for Bauhaus concerts
- Experiments in digital imagery
- Work with poets, dancers, musicians and visual artists
- Teaching at Leipzig Academy of Visual Arts

Detlef Fiedler and Daniela Haufe founded the graphic design group Cyan in the Mitte district, Berlin's historical centre, in 1992. Fiedler came from an architectural background, having studied in Weimar, while Haufe trained as a compositor before becoming a publication designer. Cyan's distinctive identity has evolved through their commitment to revive the experimental avant-garde of the 1920s – a period closed to most designers during the four decades of the German Democratic Republic.

The situation for East German designers was complex when the Berlin Wall fell. Between 1948 and the collapse of the GDR in 1989 the state controlled a design industry fashioned on the Soviet model. A free-market economy with a design and publication industry based on competition, highly expensive techniques and promotional culture were not a part of the GDR's experience. But now, graphic design, like all other industrial and commercial sectors, faced open competition from Western equivalents. Many cultural figures in East Germany resisted the West German multi-national companies.

One of the first major projects that Cyan took on was for the magazine *Form + Zweck* (Form + Purpose), the official publication of the East German Council of Industrial Design. Since its formation in 1956 the Council had advocated functionalism and rationality in design. Working closely with editors Angelika and Jörg Petruschat, Cyan revived the magazine to create a twice-yearly themed publication that explored design and its relationship to the environment and history. Most significantly, at a point when much design journalism elsewhere was preoccupied with lifestyle, the new *Form + Zweck* did not become consumer-driven.

Cyan's work is largely a combination of experimental typography and poetic photography, drawn from either archives or their own work. They blend text, image and paper through the medium of print. Although they use computers in all of their work, they were trained in the hand-setting of type, as well as in darkroom techniques and calligraphy, and these skills help them in their aim to produce inexpensive and effective design solutions.

Cover for Scardanelli's book *Tod Versuche Mich*, 1999

Tod Versuche Mich (Death Seeks Me) was the second book by Scardanelli to be published by Cyan Press. The young Berlin poet and musician is well known for performances on the city's club scene.

Most of Cyan's assignments have been in the cultural sector, and include a prestigious commission to redesign the programmes for the state opera house on Unter den Linden and the publicity for Leipzig's cultural office. They applied their distinctive approach to a set of eight posters for chamber concerts held at the Bauhaus in Dessau in 1992. The series simply used two colours and photographs, largely from the Bauhaus archives. Space, form and shadow conveyed the nature of the music. Aware of the constant drive for expendability and rapid succession of print, Haufe has suggested that new technologies have superseded posters in terms of information value. This leaves room to interpret the poster as something that can last, either displayed in the street or kept and valued privately.

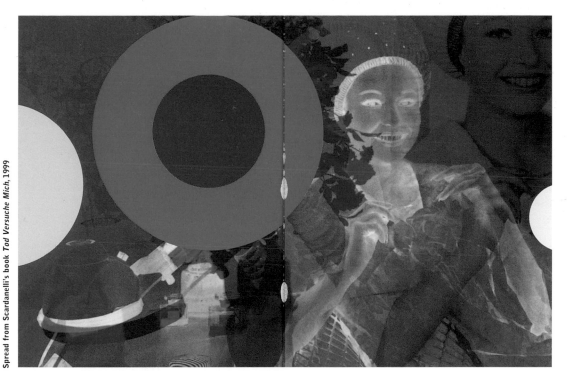

Spread from Scardanelli's book *Tod Versuche Mich*, 1999

Fluorescent inks and the layering of found images which had a distinctively period quality marked a new direction for Cyan. Using computers to manipulate found photographs of 1960s consumer society, they made the images comment on Scardanelli's poems.

Poster, "Kammerkonzert am Bauhaus", 1994

This poster is one of a series for concerts held at the former Bauhaus in Dessau. The designers adapted their own photographs and historical photographs, largely from the 1920s. The layering of images suggests the duration of musical sound and the vibration of the violin.

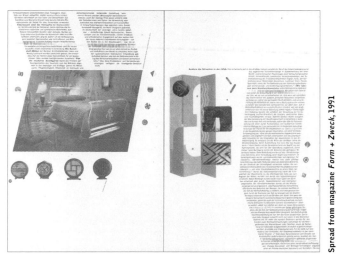

Spread from magazine *Form + Zweck*, 1991

The design magazine *Form + Zweck* (above) was published by the East German Design Council. For this article on the theme of ecology, Cyan explored the relationship between text and image by arranging the blocks of type overtly to respond to the pictorial material.

243

BIBLIOGRAPHY

GENERAL

Amstutz, Walter (ed.), *Who's Who in Graphic Art*, vol. 2, De Clivo Press, Dübendorf, 1982

Aynsley, Jeremy, *Graphic Design in Germany, 1890–1945*, Thames & Hudson, London, 2000

Bierut, Michael, William Drenttel, Steven Heller and D.K. Holland (eds), *Looking Closer, Critical Writings on Graphic Design*, Allworth Press, New York, 1994

Bierut, Michael, William Drenttel, Steven Heller and D.K. Holland (eds), *Looking Closer 2, Critical Writings on Graphic Design*, Allworth Press, New York, 1997

Bierut, Michael, Jessica Helfand, Steven Heller and Rick Poynor (eds), *Looking Closer 3, Classic Writings on Graphic Design*, Allworth Press, New York, 1999

Friedl, Friedrich, Nicolaus Ott and Bernard Stein, *Typography when, who, how*, Könemann, Cologne, 1998

Friedman, Mildred, *Graphic Design in America: A Visual Language History*, Walker Art Center, Minneapolis and Harry N. Abrams, Inc., New York, 1989

Heller, Martin, Toshiro Katayama, Helmut Langer and Trix Wetter, *Who's Who in Graphic Design*, Benteli-Werd Verlag, Zurich, 1994

Heller, Steven and Seymour Chwast, *Graphic Style: from Victorian to Post-modern*, Harry N. Abrams, New York, 1988

Heller, Steven and Karen Pomeroy, *Design literacy, understanding graphic design*, Allworth Press, New York, 1997

Heller, Steven and Karen Pomeroy, *Design literacy (continued), understanding graphic design*, Allworth Press, New York, 1999

Hollis, Richard, *Graphic Design, a Concise History*, Thames & Hudson, London, 1994

Jobling, Paul and David Crowley, *Graphic Design, reproduction and representation since 1800*, Manchester University Press, Manchester, 1996

Kinross, Robin, *Modern Typography: an essay in critical history*, Hyphen Press, London, 1992

Labuz, Ronald, *Contemporary Graphic Design*, Van Nostrand, New York, 1989

Lewis, John, *The Twentieth Century Book*, Studio Vista, London, 1967

Livingston, Alan and Isabella Livingston, *Encyclopaedia of Graphic Design and Designers*, Thames & Hudson, London, 1992

Lupton, Ellen, *Mixing Messages, graphic design in contemporary culture*, Cooper Hewitt Museum, New York and Princeton Architectural Press, 1996

Lupton, Ellen and J. Abbott Miller, *Design, Writing, Research: Writing on Graphic Design*, Phaidon Press, London, 1999

Marchand, Roland, *Advertising the American Dream, making way for modernity 1920–1940*, University of California Press, Berkeley, 1985

Meggs, Philip, *A History of Graphic Design* (third edn.), John Wiley, New York and Chichester, 1998

Owen, William, *Magazine Design*, Laurence King, London, 1991

Poynor, Rick, *Design without Boundaries: visual communication in transition*, Booth-Clibborn Editions, London, 1998

Remington, Roger R. and Barbara J. Hodik, *Nine Pioneers in American Graphic Design*, MIT Press, Cambridge, Mass., 1989

Thomson, Ellen M., *The Origins of Graphic Design in America*, Yale University Press, New Haven and London, 1997

A NEW PROFESSION

Peter Behrens
Buddensieg, Tilmann (ed.), *Industriekultur: Peter Behrens and the AEG*, MIT Press, Cambridge, Mass., 1984

Windsor, Alan, *Peter Behrens, architect and designer 1868–1940*, The Architectural Press, London, 1981

Schwartz, Frederic J., *The Werkbund, design theory and mass culture before the First World War*, Yale University Press, New Haven and London, 1996

Henry van de Velde
Sembach, Klaus-Jürgen, *Henry van de Velde*, Thames & Hudson, London, 1989

Will Bradley
Hornung, Clarence P., *Will Bradley, his graphic art*, Dover Publications, New York, 1974

The New Poster
Margaret Timmers (ed.), *The Power of the Poster* (exhibition catalogue), V&A Publications, London, 1998

Ades, Dawn, *The 20th Century Poster: Design of the Avant-Garde*, Abbeville Press, New York, 1984

Graphics for Retail
Opie, Robert, *The Art of the Label, designs of the times*, Simon and Schuster, London, 1987

Strasser, Susan, *Satisfaction Guaranteed, the making of the American Mass Market*, Pantheon Books, New York, 1989

The Suffrage Movement
Tickner, Lisa, *The Spectacle of Women, imagery of the suffrage campaign 1907–14*, Chatto and Windus, London, 1987

Eric Gill
Harling, Robert, *The Letterforms and Type Designs of Eric Gill*, Eva Svensson, Westerham Press, 1976

MacCarthy, Fiona, *Eric Gill*, Faber and Faber, London, 1989

Wiener Werkstätte
Schweiger, Werner J., *Wiener Werkstätte, design in Vienna 1903–1932*, Thames & Hudson, London, 1982

Fahr-Becker, Gabriele, *Wiener Werkstätte, 1903–1932*, Taschen Verlag, Cologne, 1995

Charles Rennie Mackintosh
Crawford, Alan, *Charles Rennie Mackintosh*, Thames & Hudson, London, 1995

Kaplan, Wendy (ed.), *Charles Rennie Mackintosh* (exhibition catalogue), Glasgow Museums, Glasgow, 1996

THE NEW DESIGN AND ARTISTIC EXPERIMENT

Italian Futurism
Apollonio, Umbro, *Futurist Manifestos*, Thames & Hudson, London, 1973

World War I Posters
Darracott, Joe and Belinda Loftus, *First World War Posters*, Imperial War Museum, London, 1981

E. McKnight Kauffer
Haworth-Booth, Mark, *E. McKnight Kauffer, a designer and his public*, Gordon Fraser, London, 1979

A.M. Cassandre
Mouron, Henri, *Cassandre*, Thames & Hudson, London, 1985

De Stijl
Friedman, Mildred (ed.), *De Stijl: 1917–1931, Visions of Utopia* (exhibition catalogue), Walker Art Center, Minneapolis and Phaidon Press, London, 1982

El Lissitzky
El Lissitzky, 1890–1941 architect, painter, photographer, typographer (exhibition catalogue), Municipal Van Abbemuseum, Eindhoven, 1990

Lissitzky-Küppers, Sophie, *El Lissitzky: Life, Letters, Texts*, Thames & Hudson, London, 1968

Alexander Rodchenko
Lodder, Christina, *Russian Constructivism*, Yale University Press, New Haven and London, 1983

Alexander Rodchenko, 1891–1956 (exhibition catalogue), Museum of Modern Art, Oxford, 1979

Bauhaus
Brüning, Ute, *Das A und O des Bauhauses*, Bauhaus-Archiv, Edition Leipzig, 1995

Wingler, Hans M., *The Bauhaus, Weimar, Dessau, Berlin, Chicago*, MIT Press, Cambridge, Mass., and London, 1978

László Moholy-Nagy
Passuth, Krisztina, *Moholy-Nagy*, Thames & Hudson, London, 1985

Herbert Bayer
Droste, Magdalena (ed.), *Herbert Bayer, das künstlerische Werk, 1918–1938*, Bauhaus Verlag, Gebr. Mann, Berlin, 1982

Neumann, Eckhard (ed.), *Herbert Bayer: Kunst und Design in Amerika, 1938–1985*, Bauhaus Verlag, Gebr. Mann, Berlin, 1986

Cohen, Arthur, *Herbert Bayer: The Complete Work*, MIT Press, Cambridge, Mass., 1984

Jan Tschichold
McLean, Ruari, *Jan Tschichold – Typographer*, Lund Humphries, London, 1975

Tschichold, Ruari, *The New Typography*, trans. Ruari McLean with an introduction by Robin Kinross, University of California Press, Berkeley, c.1995

The Ring
Rasch, Bodo and Heinz Rasch, *Gefesselter Blick*, Wissenschaftlicher Verlag Dr Zaugg, Stuttgart, 1930; reprinted, Lars Müller Verlag, Baden, Switzerland, 1996

Photomontage
Ades, Dawn, *Photomontage*, Thames & Hudson, London, 1976

Teitelbaum, Matthew (ed.), *Montage and Modern Life: 1919–1942*, MIT Press, Cambridge, Mass., and ICA, Boston, 1992

Alexey Brodovitch
Grundberg, Andy, *Alexey Brodovitch*, Harry N. Abrams, New York, 1989

Art Deco
Escritt, Stephen and Bevis Hillier, *Art Deco Style*, Phaidon, London, 1997

Hillier, Bevis, *The World of Art Deco*, Dutton, New York, 1971

Duncan, Alistair, *Art Deco*, London, 1988

Studio Boggeri
Bruno Monguzzi, Lo Studio Boggeri, 1933–1981 (catalogue), Cinisello Balsamo, Pizzi, 1974

Waibl, Heinz, *The Roots of Italian Visual Communication*, Edition Mascal, Castellarano, 1998

Karel Teige
Devetsil, Czech Avant-garde Art, Architecture and Design of the 1920s and 30s (exhibition catalogue), Museum of Modern Art, Oxford, and Design Museum, London, 1990

Dluhosch, Erich and Svácha, Rostislav, *Karel Teige, 1900–1951, L'Enfant Terrible of the Czech Modernist Avant-Garde*, MIT Press, Cambridge, Mass., 1999

Ladislav Sutnar
Sutnar, Ladislav, *Visual Design in Action – Principles, Purposes*, Hastings House, New York, 1961

Sutnar, Ladislav, "Ladislav Sutnar: Visual Design in Action", *Print*, vol. 15, September 1961, pp.52–6

Hendrik Werkman
hot printing by hendrik nicolaas werkman (catalogue), H.N. Werkman Foundation and Stedelijk Museum, Amsterdam, 1963

National Identity
Kaplan, Wendy (ed.), *Designing Modernity, the arts of reform and persuasion, 1885–1945* (catalogue), Thames & Hudson, London, 1995

Art and Power, Europe under the Dictators 1930–45 (exhibition catalogue), Hayward Gallery, London, 1996

MID-CENTURY MODERN

Hermann Zapf
Hermann Zapf and his Design Philosophy, Society of Typographic Arts, Chicago, 1987

Max Bill
Staber, Margit, *Max Bill*, Erker Verlag, St Gallen, 1971

Fleischmann, Gerd, Hans Rudolf Bosshard and Christoph Bignens, *max bill, typografie, reklame, buchgestaltung*, Verlag Niggli, Zurich, 1999

Herbert Matter
Matter, Herbert, *Foto-Grafiker Sehformen der Zeit*, Schweizerische Stiftung für die Photographie, Verlag Lars Müller, Baden, Switzerland, 1995

"Herbert Matter", *Graphis*, no. 212, Graphis Press, Zurich, May–June 1981

Saul Bass
Friedman, Mildred, *Graphic Design in America: A Visual Language History*, Walker Art Center, Minneapolis, and Harry N. Abrams, Inc., New York, 1989

Paul Rand
Heller, Steven, *Paul Rand*, Phaidon Press, London, 1999

Cipe Pineles
Scotford, Martha, *Cipe Pineles: a Life of Design*, W.W. Norton, New York, 1999

Lester Beall
Remington, Roger R., *Lester Beall: Trailblazer of American Graphic Design*, W.W. Norton, New York, 1996

Leo Lionni
Lionni, Leo, *Between Worlds, the autobiography of Leo Lionni*, Alfred A. Knopf, New York, 1997

Bernard Villemot
Allner, W.H., "Villemot", *Graphis*, no. 18, Graphis Press, Zurich, 1947, pp.96–8

François Stahly, "Villemot", *Graphis*, no. 57, Graphis Press, Zurich, 1955 pp.30–9

Abram Games
A. Games, 60 years of Design (exhibition catalogue), Howard Gardens Gallery, South Glamorgan Institute of Higher Education, 1990

Games, Abram, *Over My Shoulder*, Studio Books, London, 1960

F.H.K. Henrion
FHK Henrion Five Decades a Designer (exhibition catalogue), Flaxman Gallery, Staffordshire Polytechnic, Stoke-on-Trent, 1989

Design Magazines
Spencer, Herbert (ed.), *The Liberated Page, an anthology of major typographic experiments of this century as recorded in Typographica magazine*, Lund Humphries, London, 1987

Josef Müller-Brockmann
Lars Müller (ed.), *Josef Müller-Brockmann*, Lars Müller Verlag, Baden, Switzerland, 1994

Bruno Munari
Tanchis, Aldo, *Bruno Munari, from futurism to post-industrial design*, Lund Humphries, London, 1987

Munari, Bruno, *Design as Art*, Penguin Books, Harmondsworth, 1971

Olle Eksell
Marie-Louise Bowallius, *Swedish Graphic Design* (unpublished MA dissertation), V&A/RCA History of Design, London, 1999

Design for Transportation
Baines, Phil, "Kinneir, Calvert and the British road sign system", *Eye*, vol. 8, no. 34, 1999

Ivan Chermayeff
"Chermayeff and Geismar", *Idea* (special issue), Japan, April 1981

Chermayeff, Ivan, "Some Thoughts on Modernism: past, present and future", reprinted in *Looking Closer, Critical Writings on Graphic Design*, Michael Bierut, William Drenttel, Steven Heller and D.K. Holland (eds), Allworth Press, New York, 1994, originally in *AIGA Journal of Graphic Design*, vol. 5, no. 2, 1987

Massimo Vignelli
Vignelli, Massimo, *design: Vignelli*, Rizzoli, New York, 1981

Robert Brownjohn
Mendel, Hortense, "Brownjohn, Chermayeff & Geismar", *Graphis*, no. 87, Graphis Press, Zurich, 1960

Homans, Katy, "Robert Brownjohn", *Eye*, no. 4, 1991

Yusaku Kamekura
Bayer, Herbert and Masaru Katsumi, *The Graphic Design of Yusaku Kamekura*, Weatherhill/Bijutsu Shuppan-Sha, New York and Tokyo, 1973

Yusaku Kamekura (exhibition catalogue), National Museum of Modern Art, Tokyo, 1996

Henryk Tomaszewski
Dydo, Krzysztof (ed.), *100th Anniversary of Polish Poster Art (100 lat polskiej sztuki plakatu)* (exhibition catalogue), Galeria Plakatu, Cracow, 1993

Jazz Covers
Kinross, Robin, "Cool, Clear, Collected", *Eye*, vol. 1, no. 1, 1990

Mukoda, Naoki, *Jazzical Moods, Artwork of Excellent Jazz Labels*, Bijutsi Shuppan-Sha, 1993

POP, SUBVERSION AND ALTERNATIVES

Massin
Facetti, Germano, "Massin", *Typographica*, new series 11, June 1965

Hollis, Richard, "Massin: Language unleashed", *Eye*, vol. 4, no. 16, 1995

Push Pin Studio
Chwast, Seymour and Steven Heller (ed.), *The Left-Handed Designer*, Booth-Clibborn Editions, Paris, 1985

Glaser, Milton, *Graphic Design*, Penguin Books, Harmondsworth, 1973

Glaser, Milton, *Art is Work*, Thames & Hudson, London, 2000

Heller, Steven and Seymour Chwast, *Graphic Style, from Victorian to Post-Modern*, Thames & Hudson, London, 1988

Herb Lubalin
Snyder, Gertrude and Alan Herb Peckolick, *Lubalin, art director, graphic designer and typographer*, American Showcase, Inc., New York, 1985

Pop in the High Street
Harris, Jennifer, Sarah Hyde and Greg Smith, *1966 and All That, design and the consumer in Britain, 1960–1969*, Whitworth Art Gallery, Manchester and Trefoil, London, 1986

Whiteley, Nigel, *Pop Design: Modernism to Mod*, The Design Council, London, 1987

Psychedelic Graphics
Whiteley, Nigel, *Pop Design: Modernism to Mod*, The Design Council, London, 1987

The Underground Press
Roszak, Theodore, *The Making of a Counter Culture, reflections on the technocratic society and its youthful opposition*, Faber and Faber, London, 1970

Poynor, Rick, "The Magazine as Theatre of Experiment, Oz" [1993], reprinted in *Design Without Boundaries*, Booth-Clibborn Editions, London, 1998

Chinese Graphic Design
Minck, Scott and Jiao Ping, *Chinese Graphic Design in the Twentieth Century*, Thames & Hudson, London, 1990

Fairbank, John K., Edwin O. Reischauer and Albert M. Craig, *East Asia, Tradition and Transformation*, George Allen & Unwin, London, 1973

Roman Cieslewicz
Rouard-Snowman, Margo, *Roman Cieslewicz*, Thames & Hudson, London, 1993

Cuban Posters
Cubaanse Affiches (exhibition catalogue), Stedelijk Museum, Amsterdam, c.1970

Sontag, Susan, "Posters: advertisement, art, political artifact, commodity", in Dugald Stermer, *The Art of Revolution: 96 Posters from Cuba*, Pall Mall Press, London, 1970

Grapus
Held, Ursula, "Reputations. Gérard Paris-Clavel", *Eye*, vol. 7, no. 27, Spring 1998.

Heller, Steven, "Grapus", *Graphis*, vol. 44, no. 257, September–October 1988

Poynor, Rick, "Pierre Bernard", *Eye*, vol. 1, no. 3, Spring 1991

LATE MODERN AND POSTMODERNISM

Pentagram
Pentagram: the work of five designers, Lund Humphries, London, 1972

Gorb, Peter, *Living by Design*, Lund Humphries, London, 1978

Pentagram, The Compendium, Phaidon Press, London, 1993

Pentagram Book V, Monacelli Press, New York, 1999

Wim Crouwel
Crouwel, Wim, *Kunst & Design*, Editor Cantz, 1991

Staal, Gert and Hester Wolters (eds.), *Holland in Vorm, Dutch Design 1945–1987* (exhibition catalogue), Stichting Holland in Vorm 's-Gravenhage, 1987

Jan van Toorn
van Toorn, Jan (ed.), *design beyond Design*, Jan van Eyck Akademie Editions, Maastricht, 1998

Forde, Gerald, "The Designer Unmasked", *Eye*, vol. 1 no. 2, Winter 1991

Gert Dumbar
Poynor, Rick, "Function and Pleasure, Studio Dumbar", in *Design without Boundaries*, Booth-Clibborn Editions, London, 1998

Hard Werken
Staal, Gert and Hester Wolters (eds.), *Holland in Vorm, Dutch Design 1945–1987* (exhibition catalogue), Stichting Holland in Vorm 's-Gravenhage, 1987

Muriel Cooper
Abrams, Janet, "Muriel Cooper's Visible Wisdom", *ID*, New York, vol. 41, September–October 1994

Cooper, Muriel, "Computers and Design", *Design Quarterly*, no. 142 (special issue) MIT Press, Cambridge, Mass., 1988

Wolfgang Weingart
Weingart, Wolfgang, *My Way to Typography, Retrospective in Ten Sections (Wege zur Typographie, Ein Rückblick in zehn Teilen)*, Lars Müller Publishers, Baden, Switzerland, 2000

Dan Friedman
Friedman, Dan with essays by Jeffrey Deitch, Steven Holt and Alessandro Mendini, *Dan Friedman: Radical Modernism*, Yale University Press, New Haven and London, 1994

Bruno Monguzzi
Boffa, Valentina, "Reputations: Bruno Monguzzi", *Eye*, vol. 1, no. 1, 1990

Nunoo-Quarcoo, Franc, *Bruno Monguzzi, A designer's perspective*, University of Maryland Press, Baltimore, 1998

Ikko Tanaka
Calza, Gian Carlo, *Tanaka Ikko, graphic master*, Phaidon Press, London, 1997

Jamie Reid

Savage, Jon, *The Incomplete Works of Jamie Reid*, Faber and Faber, London, 1987

Gray, Christopher, *Leaving the 20th Century, The Incomplete work of the Situationist International*, Free Fall Publications, London, 1974

DESIGN IN THE DIGITAL ERA

April Greiman

Farrelly, Liz, *April Greiman, Floating Ideas into Time and Space*, Thames & Hudson, London, 1998

Style Magazines

Leslie, Jeremy, *Issues: New Magazine Design*, Laurence King, London, 2000

Hebdige, Dick, *Hiding in the Light*, Routledge, London, 1988

Jones, Terry, *Catching the Moment*, Booth-Clibborn Editions, London, 1997

Javier Mariscal

Dent Coad, Emma, *Javier Mariscal, Designing the New Spain*, Fourth Estate Ltd, London, 1991

Julier, Guy, *New Spanish Design*, Thames & Hudson, London, 1991

Vaughan Oliver

This Rimy River, Vaughan Oliver and his graphic works, 1988–94 (exhibition catalogue), Murray Feldman Gallery, Los Angeles, 1994

Poynor, Rick, *Vaughan Oliver, visceral pleasures*, Booth-Clibborn Editions, London, 2000

Cranbrook Academy of Art

Aldersey-Williams, Hugh, *Cranbrook Design, The New Discourse*, Rizzoli, New York, 1990

Lupton, Ellen, "The Academy of Deconstructed Design", *Eye*, vol. 1 no. 3, Spring 1991

Emigre

VanderLans, Rudy and Zuzana Licko with Mary E. Gray, *Emigre (The Book), Graphic Design into the Digital Realm*, a Byron Preiss Book, Van Rostrand Reinhold, New York, 1993

Tibor Kalman

Hall, Peter and Peter Bierut (eds.), *Tibor Kalman, Perverse Optimist*, Booth-Clibborn Editions, London, 1998

Erik Spiekermann

Sweet, Fay, *Meta Design, Design from the World Up*, Thames & Hudson, London, 1999

Neville Brody

Wozencroft, Jon, *The Graphic Language of Neville Brody*, Thames & Hudson, London 1988

Wozencroft, Jon, *The Graphic Language of Neville Brody 2*, Thames & Hudson, London 1994

Why Not Associates

Farrelly, Liz, *Why Not Associates*, Booth-Clibborn Editions, London, 1998

Rick Poynor, "Type as Entertainment", *Eye*, vol. 2 no. 7, 1993

Jonathan Barnbrook

Rick Poynor, "Design is a Virus. Jonathan Barnbrook", in *Design without Boundaries: visual communication in transition*, Booth-Clibborn Editions, London, 1998

Eiko Ishioka

Eiko Ishioka, *Eiko by Eiko: Japan's Ultimate Designer*, Jonathan Cape, London, 1990

David Carson

Blackwell, Lewis, *The End of Print: the Graphic Design of Print*, Laurence King, London, 1995

Blackwell, Lewis, *David Carson: 2nd Sight: grafik design after the end of print*, Laurence King, London, c.1999

Ott+Stein

Friedl, Friedrich, "Ott + Stein", *Novumgebrauchsgraphik*, 81, August 1992

"'Berlin Design' Guus Ros in conversation with Ott + Stein", *Affiche*, no. 7, September 1993

Sheila Levrant de Bretteville

'Profile: Sheila Levrant de Bretteville', Lupton, Ellen, *Eye*, no. 8, 1993

Bretteville, Sheila Levrant de, essay in *design beyond Design*, edited by Jan van Toorn, Jan van Eyck Akademie Editions, Maastricht, 1998

Adbusters

Lasn, Kalle, *Culture Jam: How to Reverse America's Suicidal Consumer Binge: and Why We Must*, Quill, 2000

Poynor, Rick, "Kalle Lasn: Ad Buster", *Graphis*, vol. 55, no. 323, September–October 1999

Design/Writing/Research

Lupton, Ellen and Abbott Miller, *Design Writing Research Writing on Graphic Design*, Kiosk, New York, 1996 and Phaidon Press, London, 1999

Cyan

Daupe, Michele-Anne, "Form and Purpose", *Eye*, no. 17, 1995

Petruschat, Jörg, "Graphisches Büro Cyan", *Novumgebrauchsgraphik*, vol. 65, February 1994

MUSEUMS AND DESIGN COLLECTIONS

AUSTRALIA

The Powerhouse, Sydney

Flinders University Art Museum, Adelaide

Queensland Art Gallery, South Brisbane

AUSTRIA

Albertina, Vienna

Museum für Angewandte Kunst, Vienna

BELGIUM

Musées Royaux des Beaux-Arts de Belgique

Musée de La Vie Wallonne, Liège

Musée Plantin, Antwerp

BRAZIL

Museu Nacional de Belas Artes, Rio de Janeiro

CANADA

Oakville Galleries, Oakville

CZECH REPUBLIC

Decorative Arts Museum, Prague

DENMARK

Danske Kunstindustrimuseet, Copenhagen

FINLAND

Poster Museum, Lahti

FRANCE

Bibliothèque Nationale, Paris

Musée Carnavalet, Paris

Musée de la Publicité, Paris

GERMANY

Bauhaus Archiv, Museum für Gestaltung, Berlin

Buch und Schrift Museum, Leipzig

Hessisches Landesmuseum, Darmstadt

Kleines Plakatmuseum, Bayreuth

Klingspor Museum, Offenbach am Main

Kunstbibliothek am Kulturforum, Berlin

Museum für Angewandte, Cologne

Museum für Kunst und Gewerbe, Hamburg

Deutsches Plakatmuseum, Essen

Stadtmuseum, Munich

HUNGARY

National Gallery of Art, Budapest

ITALY

Biblioteca de Storia Moderna e contemporanea, Rome

JAPAN

National Museum of Modern Art, Tokyo

Musashino Art University Museum, Tokyo

Museum of Modern Art, Toyama

Kyoto Institute of Technology, Kyoto

THE NETHERLANDS

Museum Boymans Van Beuningen, Rotterdam

Stedelijk Museum, Amsterdam

Stedelijk van Abbemuseum, Eindhoven

POLAND

Muzeum Narodowe w Warszawie, Warsaw

Muzeum Plakata w Wilanowie, Warsaw

RUSSIA

Gosudarstvennaia biblioteka SSR imeni V.I. Lenina (Lenin Library), Moscow

SPAIN

Biblioteca de Catalunya, Barcelona

Biblioteca Nacional de Madrid, Madrid

IVAM Centre, Valencia

SWEDEN

Uppsala University Library, Stockholm

SWITZERLAND

Kunstgewerbemuseum der Stadt, Zurich

Museum für Gestaltung, Zurich

UNITED KINGDOM

British Library, London

British Museum, London

Design Museum, London

London Transport Museum, London

Imperial War Museum, London

National Library of Scotland, Edinburgh

National Railway Museum, York

Public Record Office, London

St Bride's Printing Library, London

Victoria and Albert Museum, London

UNITED STATES

American Institute of Graphic Arts, New York

Cooper-Hewitt National Museum of Design, New York

Herbert Bayer Collection and Archive, Denver Art Museum, Denver

International Dada Archive, University of Iowa, Iowa City

Library of Congress, Washington D.C.

Metropolitan Museum of Art, New York

Museum of Modern Art, New York

Rochester Institute of Technology, Rochester

Smithsonian Institute, Washington D.C.

Wolfsonian Foundation Library, Miami Beach

GLOSSARY

Affichiste

A French term derived from the word for poster (*affiche*) and applied to the designers of strongly individualized posters. Characteristically, this tradition depended on the lithographic printing process, with its ability to reproduce the desinger's marks. Although the term was initially associated with the French designers Jules Chéret and A.M. Cassandre, by the 1950s, when graphic design had become a product of sophisticated division of labour, there was a renewed interest in *affichistes* such as Villemot and Tomaszewski.

Art Deco

The term applied retrospectively to describe the architecture, decorative arts and design associated with the Exposition Internationale des Arts Décoratifs et Industriels Modernes held in Paris in 1925. In graphic design the style was particularly associated with posters, magazine covers and packaging for luxury goods, notably perfumes, cosmetics and fashionable clothing. Although a modern style, Art Deco is distinguished from modernism by its greater interest in ornament and its eclectic sources.

Art Nouveau

The style associated with the Exposition Universelle held in Paris in 1900 and, more generally, in many European centres from the 1890s. It was characterized by stylized curvilinear designs and reference to nature in ornament. In graphic design Art Nouveau coincided with the rise of the artistic poster and many exponents of the style contributed stunning examples of these, as well as book, catalogue and magazine designs. The German and Scandinavian version of Art Nouveau was known as Jugendstil, while in Austria the work of the Vienna Secessionists and the Wiener Werkstätte represented a more geometric and more stylized version.

Collage

A term derived from the French word *coller* ("to stick") and used to describe the technique of sticking found printed matter (including newsprint, coloured papers and tickets) on to the picture surface. In Cubist painting (1908–14) the idea was developed primarily by Braque and Picasso. For graphic designers collage became a useful way to juxtapose contrasting elements within a design and was used to striking effect by, for example, Paul Rand.

Constructivism

In 1917 Russia experienced a Communist revolution that led to the founding of the Soviet Union. Artists, designers and architects worked together to develop a new visual style for this progressive society, building on the ideas of Cubism and Futurism and non-figurative art. The idea of the designer as "constructor" drew an analogy with engineering. In graphic design the style depended on using typography and photography in a way that evoked the machine, as in El Lissitzky and Rodchenko's designs. Through congresses and publications Constructivism became an international movement in the 1920s and 1930s, a time when links were formed with the De Stijl movement in the Netherlands and the Bauhaus in Germany.

Deconstruction

The movement associated with postmodern typography and post-Structuralist philosophy. The French philosopher Jacques Derrida developed the theory in *Of Grammatology* (1967). A central premise was that cultural artefacts could be interpreted as being polyvalent, or having a multiplicity of meanings rather than a single meaning. Major exponents of deconstructive typography included members of the Cranbrook Academy of Art and Wolfgang Weingart and his followers.

Eclecticism

A term used to define an approach to design that draws references from a wide range of sources, styles and tastes, whether from history or other places. In graphic design the most eclectic stages in the twentieth century are Pop and postmodernism.

Historicism

A term used to define reference to and use of previous historical styles of art, design and architecture. Most twentieth-century graphic design attempted to avoid historicism, although exceptions were Art Deco and postmodernism.

Modernism

Used to describe the dominant movement of the twentieth century, modernism is a wide-ranging term that covers various stylistic developments in the visual arts from Art Nouveau, through Cubism, Futurism, Constructivism and Surrealism, to the Minimalism of the late 1960s. The development of graphic design is intimately bound up with modernism. Many graphic designers believed that radical modernist experiments in painting, sculpture and architecture could inform their work. The desire to create something new, using abstraction, primary colours, sans-serif typefaces and asymmetry was felt most strongly in Europe in the 1920s. Many graphic designers subsequently took their ideas to the United States, where the New York Style of the 1940s–1960s epitomized the triumph of modernism in this area of design. Forceful challenges to modernism came with the rise of the counterculture in the 1960s. This was followed by the pronouncement of the "death of modernism" by some cultural critics, philosophers and historians, who further asserted that postmodernism had superseded it. Nevertheless, modernist influences were still being felt in the late twentieth century and modernism remained the most influential movement in graphic design of the century.

New photography

In the 1920s the "new photography" (from the German "*die neue fotografie*") developed in parallel with the "new typography". It reflected a rebirth of interest in the visual language of the photograph and a move away from pictorialism and the idea that photography should aspire to imitate painting. Instead, the new photography placed emphasis on the properties of the photograph itself, and to this end it embraced experiments in photograms (camera-less photographs), abstract photography, close-ups, aerial photography and photomontage.

New typography

A product of the 1920s, the "new typography" represented the striving to define the modern in contrast to academic tradition or neoclassicism. The German designer Jan Tschichold described the approach comprehensively in his book *Die Neue Typographie* (1928). The main elements were the use of sans-serif typefaces, asymmetrical layout, photography for illustration, primary colours and geometry. In the late 1920s a spate of publications and exhibitions celebrated the new typography.

New York School

By the 1940s modern graphic design had been displaced from Europe by the traumatic impact of totalitarian politics and world war. The new home to which graphic designers gravitated was the United States, and in particular New York. Here many émigré designers joined forces with resident Americans to introduce modernist ideas in art direction, advertising and graphic design. The New York School was more sophisticated than its European counterpart and became allied to American corporate industry. Art directors involved with the movement include Alexey Brodovitch and Henry Wolf, and among the most celebrated designers are Paul Rand, Leo Lionni and Ivan Chermayeff.

Postmodernism

The term postmodernism was adopted in order to define a change in cultural sensibility during the 1970s and 1980s. Among the most prominent of the philosophers who described the impact of the condition on culture were Jean Baudrillard and J.F. Lyotard. In graphic design postmodernism may be seen as a stylistic reaction against what were perceived as the dogmatic principles of modernism. It celebrated all that had been considered inappropriate – decoration, associative colour, narrative content and eclecticism. In place of a search for the rational, functional and simple, postmodern graphic designers preferred a style that stressed the playful and the complex and that made reference to earlier styles.

Sans-serif

A term used to describe a typeface characterized by letters without terminal strokes (serifs) at top and bottom of letterforms and with a consistent thickness. In the twentieth century such typefaces were seen as the most suitable for international communication as they were thought to avoid national or regional inflections. Among the most successful were Futura by Paul Renner (1926–8), Gill Sans by Eric Gill (1928), Univers by Adrian Frutiger (1956) and Helvetica by Max Meidinger and Edouard Hoffman (1957).

Swiss typography

After 1930 Switzerland became an important centre for the development of graphic design. As it was a trilingual, politically neutral country, many designers moved there at a time of increasingly difficult political tensions. The design schools in Zurich and Basle built up a significant reputation. Swiss typography, promoted through the journals *Graphis* (1944–) and *Neue Graphik* (1958–65), became the international standard for modern design from the 1940 to the 1960s.

249

A

Absolut 238
Abstract Expressionism 144
Adbusters 11, 198, 202, 238, *238–9*
AEG 7, 16, 17
Agha, Dr Mohamed F. 110, 112
Aicher, Otl 100, 196
Air Canada 130
Air France 117
Die Aktion 86
Albers, Anni 114
Albers, Josef 62, 114, 160
Alliance Graphique Internationale (AGI) 97
Alloway, Lawrence 158
Altman, Andy 224–5
Ambasz, Emilio 204
American Express 233
American Institute of Graphic Arts (AIGA) 7, 11, 107, 218
American Type Founders Co. 20, 21
Anspach Grossman Portugal Inc. *193*
Apollinaire, Guillaume 54, 86, 149
Apparel Arts 106
Apple Macintosh computers 185, 202, *216*, 217, 228, 232, 233
Arai, Sakikio 231
Arbeiter Illustrierte Zeitung 76, *77*
Arena 206, *207*, 222
The Ark 164
Arp, Hans 97, 100, 107
Arp, Sophie 100
Art Deco 41, 80–2, *80–3*, 164
Art Directors Club 7, 206
Art Forum 218
Art Grafiche Nidasio *194*
Art Nouveau 15, 20, 32, 37, 80, 160
Artists' Suffrage League 28, *29*
Arts and Crafts movement 14–15, 16, 20, 22, 30, 32, 60, 158
Arts et Métiers Graphiques 8, *52*, 78, 102, 112
Atelier de Création Graphique 170
Atlantic Records 144, 145
Au Bucheron 50
Aulenti, Gae 195
Avant-garde 157, *157*
Avedon, Richard 78
Ayer, N.W. & Co. 52

B

Baader, Johannes 74
Bachollet, Jean-Paul 170

Baker, Arthur *156*
Baldauf, Joachim 209
Balet, Jan 111
Balla, Giacomo 42, 126
Ballmer, Theo 84, 100
Bally, *116*, 117
Banham, Reyner 158
Barnbrook, Jonathan 7, 11, 203, 225, 228, 228–9
Barringer, Wallis and Manners Ltd 27
Barthes, Roland 175, 214
Bass, Elaine 105
Bass, Saul 96, 104–5, *104–5*, 196
Batista, Fulgencio 168
Baudrillard, Jean 222
Bauhaus 7, 19, 40, 60–2, *60–3*, 64, 66, 84, 86, 100, 114, 175, 182, 188, 242, *243*
Baumeister, Willi *71*
Bax, Susanne 242, *242*
Bayer, Herbert 10, 41, 54, 60, *61*, 62, *62*, 64, 66, *66–7*, 84, 122, 140, 196
Beall, Lester *93*, 96, 112–13, *112–13*
Beardsley, Aubrey 20, 36
Beck, Henry 130, *131*
Beddington, Jack 46–8, 118
Behrens, Peter 7, 15, 16, *16–17*
Beltrán, Félix 168, *169*
Benchmark 212
Benetton 219, 231
Bergasol 117
Berkel 54
Berlewi 122
Berlin Transportation Authority (BVG) *221*
Berliner Illustrierte Zeitung 93
Bernard, Pierre 170, *170*
Bernard, Walter 154
Bernbach, Bill 107
Bernhard, Lucien *25*
Biba *160*
"The Big Five" 160
Bigg, Chris 212
Bill, Max 97, 100, *100–1*, 122, 124
Bing, Samuel 18
Birkhäuser 68
Black Dwarf 162
Blackie & Son 37
Blauvelt, Andrew *214*
De Blauwe Schuit 90
Blok *166*
Blue Note 144, *144–5*
Boccioni, Umberto 42

Boggeri, Antonio 84, *194*
Bonnard, Pierre 21, 22
Booth-Clibborn, Edward 226
Boots 27
Bowater 121
Bradley, Will 7, 15, 20–1, *20–1*
Brangwyn, Frank *45*
Braque, Georges 50, 74
Brassaï 78
Brecht, Bertolt 76
Breton, André 78, 213
Breuer, Marcel 62, *62*
British Airways 132, *133*
Brodovitch, Alexey 41, 78, *78–9*, 112
Brody, Neville 203, *203*, 206, *206–7*, 213, 220, 222, *222–3*
Brownjohn, Robert 134, 138–9, *138–9*
Brule, Tyler 209
Bubbles, Barney 198
Burchartz, Max 72, *73*
Burns, Aaron 156, 157
Bütler, Heinz *194*

C

Cadby, Iain 225
Cahiers d'Art 78, 112
Calder, Alexander *103*, 114, 126
California Institute of Arts 237
Calvert, Margaret 132, *132*
Campaign for Nuclear Disarmament (CND) *121*
Campari 126
Campo Grafico 84, 127
Candler, Asa 27
Canis, Johannes 72
Cappiello, Leonetto 24, *24*
Carlu, Jean 24, 50, 81
Carnaby Street 158, *158–9*
Carnase, Tom 157
Carolus Duran 18
Carrà, Carlo 42
Carroll, Lewis 29
Carson, David 203, 232–3, *232–3*
Cartier-Bresson, Henri 78
Casey 240
Cassandre, A.M. 24, 41, 50–2, *50–4*, 97, 102, 116
Castro, Fidel 168, *169*
CBS 144
Ceci, Vincent 152
Centre Georges Pompidou, Paris *167*

Chagall, Marc 56
Charm 110, 111
Chase Manhattan Bank 134
Chéret, Jules 21, 22
Chermayeff, Ivan 7, 96, 134, *134–5*, 240
Chermayeff, Serge 134, 138
Chicago, Judy 236
Chinese graphic design 164, *164–5*
Churchill, Winston 135
Chwast, Seymour 7, 152–4, *152–4*, 156, 162
Cieslewicz, Roman 166, *166–7*
Cinzano 127
Citibank *193*, 233
Clarks 178
Cobden-Sanderson, T.J. 14–15
Coca-Cola 27, 132, 233
Cohen, Henry 150
Cole, Henry 14
Colin, Paul 24, 50, 116, 120
Colors 218–19, 219
Commerce Japan 140
computers 202–3
Condé Nast 110
Conrad, Roger *237*
Constructivism 48, 56, 58, 60, 64, 68, 86, 88, 113, 124, 140, 166, 168, 213, 222
Container Corporation of America 52, 66, 96, 114
Contempora Ltd 110
Cooper, Muriel 188–9, *188–9*, 203
Corcos, Lucille 111
Council of Industrial Design 158
Cracow Academy 166
Crafts Council 178
Cranach Press 19
Cranbrook Academy of Art 184, 185, 214, *214–15*, 226, 233
Crosby, Theo 176, 178
Crouwel, Wim 180, *180–1*, 182
Crumb, Robert 210
Cuban posters 168, *168–9*
Cubism 42, 46, 50, 56, 74, 80
Cutex 27
Cyan 242, *242–3*
Czeschka, Carl Otto 32, 34

D

Dada 40, 70, 74, 90, 126
Daily Herald 48
Dance Ink 241
Danziger, Lou 194–5

Dazed and Confused 208, 209
de Bretteville, Sheila Levrant 11, 203, 236, *236–7*
De Chirico, Giorgio 154
De La Porte, Sophie *209*
Deberny & Peignot 52, 102
Depero, Fortunato 42, *43*
Design and Industries Association 130
design magazines 122, *122–3*
Design Processing International 98
Design Quarterly 204, *205*
Design Research Unit 132, *132*
Design/Writing/Research 240, *240–1*
Deste Foundation for Contemporary Art, Athens 193
Deutsche Werkbund 17, *72*, 70, 130
Devetsil 86
digital design 202–3
Direction 106
Dixon, Chris 238
Documania 212
Doesburg, Theo van 54
Domela, Cesar 72, 74
Domus 84
Dorfsman, Lou 194–5
Dorland Agency 66
Dorn, Marion 48
Doyle Dane Bernbach 139, 157
Drees, Willem 182
Dresser, Christopher 20
Driade 192
Druzsterni-Práce 88
Dubonnet 51
Dubuffet, Jean 180
Duchamp, Marcel 154
Dumbar, Gert 184–5, *184–5*, 224
Düsseldorf Airport 220, 221
Dutch Art + Architecture Today 182, 183
Dwiggins, William Addison 6

E
Eames, Charles and Ray 102
East German Council of Industrial Design 242, *243*
Einaudi 84
Eisenstein, Sergei 57, 58
Eksell, Olle 128, *128–9*
Elektra 153
Elementarism 56
Elenga, Henk 186
Elle 166

Ellis, David 224
Ellis, Estelle 110
Emigre 9, 10, 203, 216–17, *216–17*, 228, 240
Engelhaard, J.U. 45
English, Malcolm *159*
English, Michael 160, 162, *163*
Erni, Hans 124
Eros 157
Esquire 106, 154
Evolution Records *198*
L'Express 154
Expressionism 60, 142, 166
Eye 9, 226, 240

F
Faber & Faber 48, 178, *178*
The Face 206, *206*, 208, 212, 222, *222–3*
Fact 157
Farm Security Administration 76
Fascist Party 92, *93*
Fawcett, Millicent 28
Federico, Gene 194–5
Feininger, Lyonel 60
Ferrier, Louise *149*
Festival of Britain (1951) 118, *119*, 120
Fetish Records 222
Fiedler, Detlef 242, *242*
Le Figaro 42
Flagg, James Montgomery 44
Fletcher, Alan 139, 176, *176–7*
Florent *50*
Fluxus 184
FontShop Berlin 220, 222
FontWorksUK 222
Forbes, Colin 176–8
Fordism 174
Form 128
Form + Zweck 242, *243*
Formek, Jan 86
Fortune 41, 52, 66, 88, 114, *115*
"Fosso" *162*
Fotografia 84
4AD 212, 213
François, André 116
Fretz, Gebrüder 102, *102*
Freud, Sigmund 149
Friedman, Dan 175, 190, 192, *192–3*
Friedman, Jim 212
Frutiger, Adrien 97

Futurism 40, 41, 42, *42–3*, 46, 50, 56, 58, 74, 80, 84, 90, 92, 126, 149

G
Gallimard 7, 150–1, *151*
Games, Abram 118, *118–19*, 121
Gandalf's Garden 162
Garrett, Malcolm 198, 213
Gauguin, Paul 18
Gebrauchsgraphik 8
Geismar, Thomas 134, *134*
Geissbühler, Stefan 134
Gerstner, Karl 100, *133*
Gewerbemuseum, Basle *69*, 191
Gibbings, Robert 30
Gill, Bob 139, 178
Gill, Eric 7, 15, 30, *30–1*, 130, 228
Gillette 117
Ginzburg, Ralph 157
Gispen, W H 55
Glamour 110
Glaser, Milton 152–4, *152–5*, 156, 162, 216, 218, 234
Glasgow Four 32, 36–7
Goebbels, Joseph 92
Golden, William 144
Goodchild, Jonathan 162
Goudy, Frederic 15
Grady, John 134
Grange, Kenneth 176, 178
Graphis 8, 96, 122, *129*
Grapus 11, 11, 170, *170–1*
Greenhalgh, Howard 224–5
Greiman, April 175, 190, 203, 204, *204–5*
Greimanski Labs *204*
Greyhound Bus 131
Grierson, Nigel 212
Griffin, Rick 160
Gropius, Walter 60, 62, 64
Grosz, George 74, 106
The Guardian 176, 178
Guevara, Che 168, *169*
Gugelot, Hans 100

H
Habitat 159
Hadders, Gerard 186, *187*
Hague, René 30, *31*
Hakuhodo 238
Hamilton, Richard 122, 158

Hapshash and the Coloured Coat 160
Hara, Hiromu 196
Hard Werken 186, *186–7*, 217
Haring, Keith 192
Harper's Bazaar 41, 52, 66, 78, *78–9*, 102
Haspel, Ton van den 186
Hauck, Fred 112
Haufe, Daniela 242, *242*
Hausmann, Raoul 74
Hayasaki, Osamu 141
Heartfield, John 11, 72, 74–6, *76*, *77*, 238
Henderson, Nigel 158
Henrion, F.H.K. 120–1, *120–1*, 180, 220
Herain, Karel *88*
Hillman, David *176*
Hirst, Damien 228, *228*, *229*
Hitchcock, Alfred 104–5
Hitler, Adolf 92
Höch, Hannah 74, *75*
Hoffmann, Edouard 97
Hoffmann, Josef 32, 35
Hofmann, Armin 190, 192, 204
Hohlwein, Ludwig 24, *25*, 93
Hollerbaum and Schmidt 24
Holtzman, Joseph 208, 209
Honeyman & Keppie 36
Hori, Allen 214, *215*
House and Garden 110
Huber, Max 84, *85*, 100, 136
Hulanicki, Barbara *160*
Huszar, Vilmos 54, *55*
Hyland, Angus *179*

I
i-D 206–8, *207*, 212
IBM 107, *109*, 124, 127, 178
Icograda 97, 180
Independent Group 158
Indiana, Robert 107
Inizio 186
Institute of Contemporary Arts (ICA) 158
Institute of Cuban Film Arts (ICAIC) 168, *169*
International Times (it) 162, *163*
International Typeface Corporation 156, 157
Internet 203
Interview 208
Ionesco, Eugene 150–1, *150*, 151
Ishioka, Eiko 203, 230–1, *230–1*

Ishizaki, Suguru *189*

Izenour, Steven 175, *189*, 214

J

Jakobson, Roman 86

Japanese Advertising Artists' Club 140

jazz covers 144, *145*

Jencks, Charles *175*

Johnston, Edward 15, 30, 98, 130

Jones, Owen 14, 20

Jones, Terry 206, 208

Jordan, Alexander 170

Jugendstil 16, 24, 34, 44

Jumonji, Bishin *230*

Jung, Carl 204

K

Kalman, Tibor 11, 202, 208, 218–19, *218–19*

Kamekura, Yusaku *9*, 140, *140–1*, 196

Kandinsky, Wassily 60, 66, 97, 107

Kapitzki, Herbert 234

Kars, Willem 186

Kauffer, Edward McKnight 41, 46–8, *46–9*, 97, 118, 130

Kaye, Tony 228

Keedy, Jeffrey 232

Keen, Graham *163*

Kelley, Alton 160

Kelmscott Press 15

Kenney, Annie 28

Kepes, Gyorgy 104

Kertesz, André 78

Kessler, Count Harry 19

King, Jessie M. 37

Kinneir, Jock 132, *132*

Kino Glaz. 59

Kitchener, Lord 44, *45*

Klee, Paul 60, 66, 97, 107, 127

Klimaschin 92

Klimt, Gustav 32

Kliros, Thea 79

KLM *120*, 121, 130

Klutsis, Gustav 74, *76*, 113

Knoll 96, 102, *103*, 137

Koch, Alexander *36*, 37

Koch, Rudolf 98

Kohn, Jacob & Josef *35*

Kok, Jan Willem de 186

Kokoschka, Oskar *32*, 34

Korda, Alberto 168

Kramer, Friso 180

Krauss, Karl 22

Kruger, Barbara 238

Kurlansky, Mervyn 176

L

Lang, Fritz *82*

Larbalastier, Simon 212, 213

Larisch, Rudolf von 32–4

Lasn, Kalle 11, 238, *239*

"late modern" 11, 174

Le Corbusier 51, 86, 100

Leavitt, George 152

Leering, Jean 182

Leete, Alfred 44, *45*

Lef 58, 59

Léger, Fernand 50, 51, 102

Lenin 92

Lepape, Georges *83*

Lethaby, W.R. 30, 60

Levi's 233

Lewis, Tim 152

Licko, Zuzana 203, 216–17, *216–17*

Lindinger, Herbert 100

Lindner, Richard 111

Lion, Alfred 144

Lionni, Leo 10, 96, 114, *114–15*

Lissitzky, El 10, 54, 56–7, *56–7*, 64, 71, 74, 90, 112, 122, 222

Lithographie und Cartonnage AG *125*

lithography 22

Lloyd's 228

Loewy, Raymond *27*, 131, *187*

Logan, Ian 206

Lohse, Richard P. 122

Lois, George 156

London College of Printing 220, 222

London Transport 46, *46*, 49, 118, 130, *130–1*

Loupot, Charles 24, 52

Lubalin, Herb 7, 156–7, *156–7*, 162, 168, 194–5, 216

Lumley, Savile 44

Lund Humphries 48

Lupton, Ellen 203, 240, *240*

Lush 210

Lustig, Alvin 134, 144

M

M&Co. *208*, 218, 219

McCann Erickson 139, 238

McConnell, John 160, 178

McCoy, Katherine 214, *215*

McCoy, Michael 214

McCullin, Don 189

McDaniel, Melanie *232*

Macdonald, Frances 36

Macdonald, Margaret 36

McHale, John 158

McInnerney, Michael 162

Mackintosh, Charles Rennie 32, 36, *36–7*

McLaren, Malcolm 198

McLuhan, Marshall 148, 219, 233

McMullan, James 152

MacNair, Herbert 36

Macromedia 203

Magazine of Art 22

magazines: design magazines *122–3*

   style magazines 206–8, *206–9*

Magritte, René 214

Les Maîtres de L'Affiche 8, 22

Maldonado, Tomas 100

Malevich, Kasimir 56, 58

Mallarmé, Stéphane 42, 86, 149

Manzoni, Piero 182

Mao Tse-tung 164

Marcatré 226

Marcuse, Herbert 149

Mari, Enzo 84

Marinetti, Filippo Tommaso 42, 42–3, 126

Mariscal, Javier 210–11, *210–11*

Martínez, Raúl 168, *168*

Marx, Roger 8

Massin 7, 122, 149, 150–1, *150–1*

Matisse, Henri 97, 107, 154

Matter, Herbert 41, 96, 102, *102–3*

Mayakovsky, Vladimir 56, 57, 58

Mazda 228

Meier-Graefe, Julius 18

Memphis 175, 192, 211

Mergenthaler Linotype 98

Merz 57

MetaDesign 37, 220, *221*

Meuse Pils *117*

Meyerhold, Vsevolod 57

Meynell, Francis 48

Meynell, Gerald 48

Michael Peters Group 212

Microsoft 132

Miedinger, Max 97

Miehe, François 170

Mies van der Rohe, Ludwig 60

Miles, Reid 144, *144–5*

Millais, John Everett 22

Miller, Henry 135

Miller, J. Abbott 240, *240–1*

Mills, Russell 198

MIT Press 188–9, *188*

Mite Corporation *112*

Miyake, Issey 230, *230*

Mobil 134, *134*

Model, Lisette 78

modernism 41, 152, 174

Moholy-Nagy, László 10, 41, 54, 60, 62, *62–5*, 64, 112, 118, 130, 138, 140

Molloy, Mark 225

Molzahn, Johannes *72*

Mondrian, Piet 54

Monguzzi, Bruno 84, 194–5, *194–5*

Monotype Corporation 30, 130

Montecatini 84

Moore, Henry *143*

Morandi, Giorgio 152

Morellet, Florent 218

Morison, Stanley 30

Morris, Talwin 37

Morris, William 14, 16, 18, 19, 20, 32, 60

Morrissey, Patrick 225, *225*

Moscoso, Victor 160, 161

Moser, Koloman 8, 32, *33–5*

Motta 84, 114

Mouse, Stanley 160

Movimento d'Arte Concrete 127

Mroszczack, Josef 142

Müller-Brockmann, Josef 97, 100, 122, 124, *124–5*, 140, 196, 234

Munari, Bruno 85, 126–7, *126–7*, 196

Muñez, Lucía Fernández *209*

Musée d'Orsay, Paris 195, *195*

Museum of Modern Art, New York 41, 48, 52, 66, 97, 114, 134, 204, 222

Mussolini, Benito 41, 92, 114

Muthesius, Hermann 19

N

National Bank 233

national identity 92, *92–3*

National Socialism (Nazis) 66, 74, 76, 90, 92, 96

National Society of Art Directors 157

National Union of Women's Suffrage Societies (NUWSS) 28, 29

NBC 134

Ne Pas Plier 170

Negroponte, Nicholas 189

Nest 208, 209

Neuburg, Hans 122

Neue Graphik 8, 96, 122, 123, 194

die neue linie 65, 66, 67

Neue Sachlichkeit 84

die neue typographie 64

Neurath, Marie 133

Neurath, Otto 133, 240

Neville, Richard 149, 162

New Primitives 203

New York School 96, 144, 168, 194–5, 206

New York subway 136, 137

New York University 134

Newell & Sorell 132, 133

Next 226, 227

The Next Call 90

NeXT Company 107, 108

Nezval, Vitezlav 86

Nietzsche, Friedrich 18, 19

Nike 185, 222, 226, 233, 238

Nikkei Design 179

Nikon 141

Nippon 140

Nippon Design Centre 140, 196

Nizzoli, Marcello 84

NKF 54

Nonesuch Press 48

Noorda, Bob 130, 136, 137

Nova 177

Novyi Lef 58

O

Odeon 86

Olbrich, Joseph Maria 32

Oliver, Vaughan 212–13, 212–13

Olivetti 84, 85, 96, 114, 114, 127, 178

Olympic Games 140, 141, 196, 196, 210, 211

Orangina 116, 117

Österreichischer Rundfunk (ORF) 223

Ott + Stein 234, 234–5

Oz 149, 160, 162, 163

Ozenfant, Amédée 51, 102

P

PAM 180

PanAm 130, 134

Pankhurst, Christabel 28

Pankhurst, Emmeline 28

Paolozzi, Eduardo 158

Paper Bag Machine Company 26

Parco 230, 231

Paris-Clavel, Gérard 170

Paris-Match 154

Pear's soap 22

Peignot, Charles 52

Peignot, Rémy 132

Pelikan 56, 70

Penfield, Edward 20

Penguin Books 30, 68, 68, 178

Penn, Irving 78

Pentagram 176–8, 176–9, 220, 234

Pepsi Cola 233

Perrier 117

Pet Shop Boys 178, 179

Philip Morris 238

Philips 185

Philishave 120

Phoebus Palast, Munich 68

photomontage 74–6, 74–7

Picador Books 212

Picasso, Pablo 50, 74, 97, 116, 128

Pick, Frank 46, 118, 130

Pieterson, Lex van 184, 185

Pineles, Cipe 96, 110–11, 110–11

Pirelli 84, 127, 177

Das Plakat 8, 22

Plank, George 81

Plazm 225

De Ploeg group 90

Poiret, Paul 80

Pop art 107, 148–9, 158, 158–9, 160, 168

Popova 58

Portfolio 79

Post-Impressionism 46

Post Office 118

The Poster 8, 22

posters 8, 22–4, 23–5

Cuban posters 168, 168–9

national identity 92, 92–3

World War I 44, 44–5

postmodernism 11, 152, 174–5, 185, 194, 214

Powell, Richard Spencer 209

Powolny, Michael 32

Poynor, Rick 226, 240

Prampolini, Enrico 126

Preminger, Otto 104, 105

Priest, Chris 225

Prinsen, Erik 187

Print 8, 114

Procter & Gamble 26

psychedelic graphics 160, 160–1

PTT 54, 180, 183, 184, 185

Punk 198, 206

Purism 50, 102

Push Pin Studio 134, 149, 152–4, 152–5, 156, 162

Q

Quant, Mary 158

Queen 158

Queneau, Raymond 150

R

Rand, Paul 96, 97, 97, 106–8, 106–9, 140

Rank Xerox 178

Rasch, Heinz and Bodo 71, 72

Ray, Man 78, 112

Raygun 232, 232–3

record covers 144, 145

RED 87

Redondo, Rocco 224, 225

Reid, Jamie 198, 198–9

Reuters 176, 178

Rhead 15

Rijksmuseum, Amsterdam 185

La Rinascente 84

The Ring 70–2, 70–3, 86

Rizzoli 136

Roach, Matt 208, 209

Rocking Russian 222

Rodchenko, Alexander 10, 58, 58–9, 74, 122, 175, 222

Rogers, Bruce 15

Roller, Alfred 32

Rondthaler, Edward 157

Roosevelt, Franklin D. 76, 92, 113

Rosskam, Edwin 77

Rostgaard, Alfredo 168, 169

Roszak, Theodore 162

Roth, Dieter 122

Rotterdam Art Foundation 186

Royal College of Art 185

Royal Mail 226

Royen, J.F. 185

Ruder, Emil 100, 190

Ruffins, Reynold 152

Rural Electrification Administration (USA) 112–13, 113

Ruskin, John 14–15, 18

S

Sachplakat (object poster) 24, 25

Sainsbury, J. 26

Salter, Tom 159

Sandberg, Willem 90, 122

Saturday Evening Post 157

Savage, Jon 198

Savignac, Raymond 116

Saville, Peter 198, 213

Scardanelli 242, 243

Schawinsky, Xanti 84, 85

Schiavone, Carmen 111

Schiele, Egon 34

Schleger, Hans 48

Schmidt, Joost 61, 62

School of Paris 166

Schuitema, Paul 54, 72, 122

Schulz-Neudamm, Heinz 82

Schwitters, Kurt 57, 64, 70, 70, 71, 72, 86

SCI-ARC 205

Scope 88, 112

Scott-Brown, Denise 175, 189, 214, 236

Scribner's Sons, 20

Secession 8, 15, 32–4, 44

Seibu Group 231

Seitlin, Percy 138

Senefelder, Alois 22

Serrano, Elena 169

Seventeen 110, 110

Severini, Gino 42

Sex Pistols 198, 199

Shahn, Ben 111

Shanghai style 164

Sharp, Martin 160, 161, 162

Shell 46–8, 47, 48, 118

Silverstein 240

Singer 26

Sironi, Mario 93

Situationist International 238

Small, David *189*

Smirnoff *224*, 226

Smithson, Alison 158

Smithson, Peter 158

Snow, Carmel 78

Socialist Realism 92, 142, 164, 166, 168

Société des Artistes-Décorateurs 80

Solzhenitsyn, Alexander 189

Sorel, Edward 152

Spear, Fred *44*

Spencer, Herbert 122, *123*, 138–9, 178

Spiekermann, Erik 7, 37, 130, 220, *220–1*, 222

Spindler, Clarita 209

Spruijt, Mart 183, *183*

Stalin, Josef 92

Stam, Mart 72, 182

Stankowski, Anton 124

Stedelijk Museum, Amsterdam 180, *181*

Stedelijk van Abbemuseum, Eindhoven 180, 182

Stein, Bernhard 234

Steiner, Albe 84

Steinlen, Théodore 21, 22, *23*

Stempel AG 98

Stephen, John 158

Stiff Records 222

De Stijl 54, *54–5*, 57, 60, 88, 185

De Stijl 40, 54

Stile Industria 84

Stone, Herbert 21

Stone & Kimball *21*

structuralism 175

The Studio 36

Studio Alchymia 175

Studio Boggeri 84, *84–5*, 122, 127, 194

Studio Dumbar 184–5, *184–5*

Studio H 120

Studio Voice 208

style magazines 206–8, *206–9*

Suburban Press 198, *199*

Suffrage Atelier 28, *28*

Suffrage movement 28, *28–9*

Suprematism 56

Surfer 232, *232*

Surrealism 41, 48, 52, 78, 86, 126, 142, 213

Sutnar, Ladislav 10, 41, 88, *88–9*

Swatch 178, 222

Swedish Association of Arts and Crafts 128

Swiss Automobile Club 124

Swiss Werkbund 100

Swissair *133*

Symbolism 15, 18, 160

Szemberg, Henryk 142

T

Tallents, Sir Stephen 118

Tanaka, Ikko 140, 196, *196–7*

Tatlin, Vladimir 58

Teige, Karel 10, 41, 86, *86–7*, 88

Tel Graphic Designs 184

Tempo 127

Teng Hsiao-p'ing 164

Téry, Margit *60*

Théâtre de l'Odéon, Paris *167*

Thompson, J. Walter 139

Tiemann, Walter 68

The Times 118

Tokyo International Lighting Fixtures Design Corporation *140*

Tomaszewski, Henryk 142, *142–3*, 166, 170, 234

Tonhalle, Zurich 124, *125*

Toorn, Jan van 175, 182–3, *182–3*

Toorop, Jan 36

Toscani, Oliver 219, 231

Total Design 180, 216

Toulouse-Lautrec, Henri de 21, 22, 116

Town 158

trademarks 108

transport 130–2, *130–3*

Tropon 18

Tschichold, Jan *41*, 48, 64, 68, *68–9*, 88, 112

Tsutsumi, Seiji 231

2wice 241

Typographica 8, 122, *122–3*, 139, 178

Typographische Mitteilungen 68

U

U&lc 156

underground press 162, *162–3*

Unger, Gerard 216

Unimark International Corporation 136

US Environmental Protection Agency 134

USSR in Construction 58

V

V23 212

Valentine, Helen 110

Van de Velde, Henri 18–19, *18–19*

VanderLans, Rudy 203, 216–17, *216–17*

Vanidad 209

Vanity Fair 42, 110

Vaughan, David 162

Venezky, Martin 184

Venturi, Robert 138, 175, 189, 214, 236

Ver Sacrum 32, *33*, 37

Vermeulen, Rick 186, *186*, 187

Victoria and Albert Museum, London 178, 196

Vignelli, Lella 136

Vignelli, Massimo 7, 130, 136, *136–7*, 240

Village Voice 154

Villemot, Bernard 116–17, *116–17*

Les Vingt 18

Virgin Records 226

Visible Language 214

Visible Language Workshop 188, 189, *189*

Visual Design Studio 195

Vivarelli, Carlo 84, 122

VKhUTEMAS 40, 58

Vogue 41, 81, *83*, 102, 110

Volkswagen 228

Vordemberge-Gildewart, Friedrich 72

Vorm Vijf 216

W

Wagner, Günter 70

Waibl, Heinz 84

Wallpaper 209

war posters 44, *44–5*

Warde, Beatrice 148

Warhol, Andy *223*

Wärndorfer, Fritz 32, 37

Watts-Russell, Ivo 213

Waymouth, Nigel 160, 162, *163*

Wayside Press 21

WBMG 154

Weil, Daniel *179*

Weingart, Wolfgang 175, 190, *190–1*, 204, 214, 233

Werkman, Hendrik 90, *90–1*, 122

Westinghouse Corporation 107, *107*

Westminster Press 48

Westwood, Vivienne 198

Why Not Associates 184, 203, 224–6, *224–7*, 228

Widmer, Jean 195

Wiener Werkstätte 32–4, *32–5*

Wilson, Wes 160, *162*

Windett, Peter *159*

Wingler, Hans Maria 188

Wissing, Benno 180

Wohnbedarf, 100, *101*

Wolff, Francis 144, *144*

Wolff Olins 220

Wolle, Francis 26

World War I 40, 44, *44–5*, 74

World War II 76, 97, 118, 120

Wright, Edward 122, *123*

Wydawnictwo Artystyczno-Graficzne (WAG) 142

Y

Yamashiro, Ryuichi 196

Yokusuka, Noriaki *231*

Young and Rubicam 52

Z

Zapf, Hermann 7, 41, 98, *98–9*

Zijeme 89

Zoom 166

Zoppo, Annette del *237*

Zwart, Piet 54, 72, *73*, 112, 122

ACKNOWLEDGMENTS

The author would like to thank staff and students on the joint Victoria and Albert Museum/Royal College of Art History of Design course, Barbara Berry at the Royal College of Art, Sarah Aynsley, and everyone at Mitchell Beazley, in particular Mark Fletcher, Claire Gouldstone, John Jervis, Hannah Barnes-Murphy and Richard Dawes. Julia Bigham offered her considerable expertise and generous assistance with the picture research.

Key

t top   b bottom   l left   r right   c centre

Back cover, c Library of Congress, Washington DC; **Back cover,** t Private Collection; **Back cover,** b Ikko Tanaka Design Studio; **7** AKG, London; **8** Art archive/Museum fur Gestaltung, Zurich; **9** Kamekura Yusaku Design Award Office; **10** Emigre; **11** Atelier de Creation Graphique/Grapus; **15** Library of Congress, Washington DC; **16** t EHG Elektroholding GmbH (DACS 2001); **16** b The Mitchell Wolfson Jr. Collection, The Wolfsonian-Florida International University, Miami Beach, Florida; **17** t Library of Congress, Washington DC (DACS 2001); **17** b EHG Elektroholding GmbH (DACS 2001); **18** left AKG, London; **18** t r Library of Congress, Washington DC; **18** b Archives d'Architecture Moderne; **19** AKG, London/Hilbich; **20** t l OPG Ltd/Dover Publications; **20** t r Bridgeman Art Library/Library of Congress, Washington DC; **20** b OPG Ltd; **21** AKG, London; **23** t AKG, London/Kestner Museum, Hannover; **23** b Christie's Images (ADAGP, Paris and DACS, London 2001); **24** l Advertising Archives (DACS 2001); **24** r Corbis UK Ltd/Bettmann; **25** t Jean-Loup Charmet/Bibliotheque des Arts Decoratifs; **25** b Art Archive/Museum f r Gestaltung, Z rich; **26** Sainsbury's Archive; **27** t The Boots Company; **27** t r Robert Opie; **27** b Robert Opie; **28** The Woman's Library; **29** t l Library of Congress, Washington DC; **29** t r The Woman's Library; **29** b r The Woman's Library; **30** t Hulton Getty Picture Collection; ; **30** b Wolseley Fine Arts/Estate of Eric Gill; **31** t Wolseley Fine Arts/Estate of Eric Gill; **31** b OPG Ltd/Estate of Eric Gill; **32** Fördererkreis Krefelder Kunstmuseen E.V. (DACS 2001); **33** Art archive; **34** AKG, London/Erich Lessing; **35** t The Mitchell Wolfson Jr. Collection, The Wolfsonian-Florida International University, Miami Beach, Florida; **35** b Fördererkreis Krefelder Kunstmuseen E.V.; **36** t Bridgeman Art Library/Private Collection; **36** b The Annan Gallery, Edinburgh; **37** l Hunterian Art Gallery, University of Glasgow/Mackintosh Collection; **37** r Hunterian Art Gallery, University of Glasgow/Mackintosh Collection; **41** Kunstbibliothek, Staatliche Museen zu Berlin - Preussischer Kulturbesitz, Berlin (West); **42** Art archive (DACS 2001); **43** t Estorick Collection (DACS 2001); **43** b The Mitchell Wolfson Jr. Collection, The Wolfsonian-Florida International University, Miami Beach, Florida; **44** Imperial War Museum, London; **45** t l Library of Congress. Washington DC; **45** t r Imperial War Museum, London; **45** b Imperial War Museum, London; **46** t Hulton Getty Picture Collection/Gordon Anthony; **46** b London Transport Museum; **47** t Christie's Images; **47** b Christie's Images; **48** l Courtesy of the Trustees of the Victoria & Albert Museum ; **48** r Christie's Images; **49** Christie's Images; **50** t l Private Collection (ADAGP, Paris and DACS, London 2001); **50** t r Christie's Images (ADAGP, Paris and DACS, London 2001); **50** b Roger-Viollet; **51** Jean-Loup Charmet (ADAGP, Paris and DACS, London 2001); **52** r AKG, London (ADAGP, Paris and DACS London 2001); **52** l Christie's Images (ADAGP, Paris and DACS, London 2001); **53** AKG, London (ADAGP, Paris and DACS London 2001); **54** Bridgeman Art Library/Haags Gemeentemuseum, Netherlands/DACS 2001/ADAGP, Paris and DACS, London 2001; **55** l Nederlands Architectuur instituut/Gispen Collection; **55** b AKG, London (ADAGP, Paris and DACS London); **56** t l David King Collection (DACS 2001); **56** t r David King Collection (DACS 2001); **56** b David King Collection; **57** Christie's Images (DACS 2001); **58** t David King Collection; **58** b David King Collection (DACS 2001); **59** t David King Collection (DACS 2001); **59** b David King Collection (DACS 2001); **60** Bauhaus-Archiv./Markus Hawlik; **61** t Bridgeman Art Library/Private Collection; **61** b AKG, London (DACS 2001); **62** l AKG, London (DACS 2001); **62** r Bauhaus-Archiv, (DACS 2001); **63** t Courtesy of the Trustees of the Victoria & Albert Museum (DACS 2001); **63** b The Mitchell Wolfson Jr. Collection, The Wolfsonian-Florida International University, Miami Beach, Florida (DACS 2001); **64** t AKG, London; **64** b AKG, London (DACS 2001); **65** t AKG, London (DACS 2001); **65** b Bauhaus-Archiv./Atelier Schneider, Berlin (DACS 2001); **66** t Bauhaus-Archiv,; **66** b Bridgeman Art Library/Private Collection/The Stapleton Collection (DACS 2001); **67** t Bauhaus-Archiv./Atelier Schneider, Berlin (DACS 2001); **67** b AKG, London (DACS 2001); **68** t Courtesy of Frau Tschichold; **68** b OPG Ltd/Penguin Books; **69** l Library of Congress, Washington DC; **69** b Museum Fur Gestaltung Zurich; **70** Christie's Images (DACS 2001); **71** t The Mitchell Wolfson Jr. Collection, The Wolfsonian-Florida International University, Miami

Beach, Florida (DACS 2001); **71** b AKG, London (DACS 2001); **72** The Mitchell Wolfson Jr. Collection, The Wolfsonian-Florida International University, Miami Beach, Florida; **73** t Private Collection (DACS 2001); **73** b Private Collection; **74** Kunstbibliothek, Staatliche Museen zu Berlin - Preussischer Kulturbesitz, Berlin (West); **75** Kunstbibliothek, Staatliche Museen zu Berlin - Preussischer Kulturbesitz, Berlin (West); **76** l David King Collection, **76** r AKG, London (DACS 2001); **77** t Corbis UK Ltd/Bettmann; **77** b AKG, London (DACS 2001); **78** t Magnum Photos/Henri Cartier-Bresson; **78** b Archives and Special Collections, Wallace Library, Rochester Institute of Technology, Rochester, New York/Courtesy of Harper's Bazaar; **79** t Archives and Special Collections, Wallace Library, Rochester Institute of Technology, Rochester, New York/Courtesy of Harper's Bazaar; **79** b Archives and Special Collections, Wallace Library, Rochester Institute of Technology, Rochester, New York; **80** OPG Ltd/Juliette Edwards/AJ Photographics; **81** t AKG, London (ADAGP, Paris and DACS, London 2001); **81** b Jean-Loup Charmet/Bibliotheque des Arts Decoratifs; **82** l The Ronald Grant Archive; **82** r The Ronald Grant Archive; **83** Jean-Loup Charmet/Bibliotheque des Arts Decoratifs (ADAGP, Paris, and DACS, London 2001); **84** t Courtesy of Bruno Monguzzi/Ugo Mulas Estate. All rs reserved; **84** c Courtesy of Bruno Monguzzi/Boggeri Archive/Antonio Boggeri; **84** b Courtesy of Bruno Monguzzi/Boggeri Archive; **85** t Courtesy of Bruno Monguzzi/Boggeri Archive; **85** b l Courtesy of Bruno Monguzzi/Boggeri Archive; **85** b r Courtesy of Bruno Monguzzi/Boggeri Archive; **86** t The Mitchell Wolfson Jr. Collection, The Wolfsonian-Florida International University, Miami Beach, Florida; **86** b The Mitchell Wolfson Jr. Collection, The Wolfsonian-Florida International University, Miami Beach, Florida; **87** t The Mitchell Wolfson Jr. Collection, The Wolfsonian-Florida International University, Miami Beach, Florida; **87** b l The Mitchell Wolfson Jr. Collection, The Wolfsonian-Florida International University. Miami Beach, Florida; **87** b r The Mitchell Wolfson Jr. Collection, The Wolfsonian-Florida International University, Miami Beach, Florida; **88** t Cooper Hewitt, NY; **88** b David King Collection; **89** t Archives and Special Collections, Wallace Library, Rochester Institute of Technology, Rochester, New York; **89** b Archives and Special Collections, Wallace Library, Rochester Institute of Technology, Rochester, New York; **90** t Stedelijk Museum, Amsterdam; **90** b Stedelijk Museum, Amsterdam; **91** t Stedelijk Museum, Amsterdam; **91** b Stedelijk Museum/Stedelijk Museum Amsterdam; **92** The Mitchell Wolfson Jr. Collection, The Wolfsonian-Florida International University, Miami Beach, Florida (DACS 2001); **93** t l Library of Congress, Washington DC/The Estate of Lester Beall Snr (DACS, London/VAGA, New York 2001); **93** t r Jean-Loup Charmet (DACS 2001); **93** b The Mitchell Wolfson Jr. Collection, The Wolfsonian-Florida International University, Miami Beach, Florida (DACS 2001); **97** OPG Ltd/Paul Rand; **98** t Courtesy of Hermann Zapf; **98** b Courtesy of Hermann Zapf; **99** t Courtesy of Hermann Zapf; **99** b Courtesy of Hermann Zapf; **100** t prolitteris CH-Zurich on behalf of Max, Binia + Jakob Bill Foundation, CH-Adligenswil; **100** b Museum Für Gestaltung Zurich (DACS 2001); **101** t Museum Für Gestaltung Zurich (DACS 2001); **101** b Library of Congress, Washington DC (DACS 2001); **102** t Knoll ; **102** b Courtesy of the Trustees of the Victoria & Albert Museum; **103** t Library of Congress, Washington DC; **103** b Knoll; **104** t l Corbis UK Ltd/Everett; **104** t r Library of Congress, Washington DC; **104** b The Ronald Grant Archive; **105** Library of Congress, Washington DC; **106** t l Courtesy of Mrs Paul Rand; **106** t r Courtesy of Mrs Paul Rand; **106** b Courtesy of Mrs Paul Rand/Sally Andersen-Bruce); **107** Courtesy of Mrs Paul Rand; **108** t l Courtesy of Mrs Paul Rand; **108** t c Courtesy of Mrs Paul Rand; **108** t r Courtesy of Mrs Paul Rand; **109** t Courtesy of Mrs Paul Rand; **109** b Courtesy of Mrs Paul Rand; **110** Archives and Special Collections, Wallace Library, Rochester Institute of Technology, Rochester, New York; **110** t l Archives and Special Collections, Wallace Library, Rochester Institute of Technology, Rochester, New York/Francesco Scavullo; **110** t r Archives and Special Collections, Wallace Library, Rochester Institute of Technology, Rochester, New York; **110** b Archives and Special Collections, Wallace Library, Rochester Institute of Technology, Rochester, New York; **112** t l Archives and Special

ACKNOWLEDGMENTS

Collections, Wallace Library, Rochester Institute of Technology, Rochester, New York/The Estate of Lester Beall Snr (DACS, London/VAGA, New York 2001); **112** t c r **3** Archives and Special Collections, Wallace Library, Rochester Institute of Technology, Rochester, New York/The Estate of Lester Beall Snr (DACS, London/VAGA, New York 2001)/Courtesy of Up John Company, 1948; **112** b Archives and Special Collections, Wallace Library, Rochester Institute of Technology, Rochester, New York; **113** Archives and Special Collections, Wallace Library, Rochester Institute of Technology, Rochester, New York/The Estate of Lester Beall Snr (DACS, London/VAGA, New York 2001); **114** t Archivio Storico of Olivetti, Ivrea, Italy; **114** b Archivio Storico of Olivetti, Ivrea, Italy; **115** t OPG Ltd; **115** b Archives and Special Collections, Wallace Library, Rochester Institute of Technology, Rochester, New York (Fortune Magazine © **1960** Time Inc. All rs reserved); **116** t l Christie's Images (ADAGP, Paris and DACS, London 2001); **116** t r Christie's Images (ADAGP, Paris and DACS, London 2001); **116** b Magnum Photos/Peter Marlow; **117** Christie's Images (ADAGP, Paris and DACS, London 2001); **118** t Estate of Abram Games; **118** b Estate of Abram Games; **119** t Estate of Abram Games/Crown Copyr; **119** b Imperial War Museum, London ; **120** t l Courtesy of Marion Wesel-Henrion; **120** t r Courtesy of Marion Wesel-Henrion; **120** c Courtesy of Marion Wesel-Henrion; **120** b Courtesy of Marion Wesel-Henrion; **121** Courtesy of Marion Wesel-Henrion; **122** OPG Ltd/Nigel Jackson/with thanks to Ric Poynor; **123** t OPG Ltd/Nigel Jackson/with thanks to Ric Poynor; **123** b l OPG Ltd/Nigel Jackson/with thanks to Ric Poynor; **123** b r OPG Ltd/Nigel Jackson/with thanks to Ric Poynor; **124** t The Estate of Josef M̦ller-Brockman; **124** b The Estate of Josef M̦ller-Brockman; **125** t l The Estate of Josef M̦ller-Brockman(DACS, London/prolitteris, Zurich 2001); **125** t r The Estate of Josef M̦ller-Brockman(DACS, London/prolitteris, Zurich 2001); **125** b The Estate of Josef M̦ller-Brockman (DACS, London/prolitteris, Zurich 2001); **126** t l OPG Ltd with thanks to Abitare, Milan; **126** t r OPG Ltd with thanks to Abitare, Milan; **126** b Miro Zagnoli; **127** The Mitchell Wolfson Jr. Collection, The Wolfsonian-Florida International University, Miami Beach, Florida ; **128** t Courtesy of Ruthell and Olle Eksell; **128** b Courtesy of Ruthell and Olle Eksell; **129** t Courtesy of Ruthell and Olle Eksell; **129** b Courtesy of Ruthell and Olle Eksell; **130** London Transport Museum; **131** t London Transport Museum; **131** b Corbis UK Ltd; **132** t l National Motor Museum; **132** t r Mile Post 92 1/2; **132** b Mile Post 92 1/2; **133** t Corbis UK Ltd/AFP; **133** c OPG Ltd; **133** b OPG Ltd/British Airways; **134** t l Ivan Chermayeff/ Chermayeff & Geismar Inc.; **134** c t Chermayeff & Geismar Inc.; **134** c b Chermayeff & Geismar Inc.; **134** b Chermayeff & Geismar Inc.; **135** t Ivan Chermayeff/ Chermayeff & Geismar Inc.; **135** b Ivan Chermayeff/ Chermayeff & Geismar Inc.; **136** t Vignelli Associates/Luca Vignelli; **136** b Vignelli Associates; **137** t Knoll; **137** b Vignelli Associates/Reven C. Wurman; **138** t l Robert Brownjohn/ Brownjohn, Chermayeff & Geismar; **138** t r Brownjohn, Chermayeff & Geismar ; **138** b Robert Brownjohn/ Brownjohn, Chermayeff & Geismar; **139** Robert Brownjohn/ Brownjohn, Chermayeff & Geismar; **140** t Kamekura Yusaku Design Award Office; **140** b Kamekura Yusaku Design Award Office; **141** t Kamekura Yusaku Design Award Office; **141** b Kamekura Yusaku Design Award Office; **142** t Sklep - Galeria PTTK/Erazm Ciolek; **142** b Sklep - Galeria PTTK (DACS 2001); **143** t Sklep - Galeria PTTK (DACS 2001); **143** b Sklep - Galeria PTTK (DACS 2001); **144** Blue Note/Capitol Records; **145** t OPG Ltd/Blue Note/Capitol Records; **145** b l OPG Ltd/Atlantic Recording Corporation; **145** b r Blue Note/Capitol Records; **149** OPG Ltd/Beat Books, London; **150** t l Editions Gallimard; **150** t r Editions Gallimard; **150** b Editions Gallimard/Jacques Sassier; **151** Editions Gallimard; **152** t l Pushpin Group Inc.; **152** t r Milton Glaser Inc; **152** b Pushpin Group Inc.; **153** t Pushpin Group Inc.; **153** b Pushpin Group Inc.; **154** r Milton Glaser Inc; **154** t Pushpin Group Inc.; **155** Milton Glaser Inc; **156** r The Herb Lubalin Study Center for Design and Typography, The Cooper Union, NY; **156** t l The Herb Lubalin Study Center for Design and Typography, The Cooper Union, NY; **156** c l The Herb Lubalin Study Center for Design and Typography,The Cooper Union, NY; **156** b The Herb Lubalin Study Center for Design and Typography, The Cooper Union, NY; **157** The Herb Lubalin Study Center for Design and Typography, The Cooper Union, NY; **158** Corbis UK Ltd/Bettmann; **159** t l OPG Ltd/Tim Ridley/Target Gallery; **159** t r The Manchester Metropolitain University; **159** b Hulton Getty Picture Collection; **160** Pentagram Design Limited/BIBA; **161** t OPG Ltd; **161** b Christie's Images; **162** OPG Ltd/Beat Books, London; **163** l OPG Ltd/Beat Books, London; **163** r OPG Ltd/Beat Books, London; **164** Minick +Jiao Design; **165** t Victoria & Albert Museum; **165** b Minick +Jiao Design; **166** t Chantal Petit Cieslewicz; **166** b Chantal Petit Cieslewicz (ADAGP, Paris and DACS, London 2001); **167** t Chantal Petit Cieslewicz (ADAGP, Paris and DACS, London 2001); **167** b Chantal Petit Cieslewicz (ADAGP, Paris and

DACS, London 2001); **168** International Instituut voor Sociale Geschiedenis; **169** t International Instituut voor Sociale Geschiedenis; **169** c r International Instituut voor Sociale Geschiedenis; **169** b International Instituut voor Sociale Geschiedenis; **170** t Atelier de Creation Graphique/Luc Perenon; **170** b Atelier de Creation Graphique/Grapus; **171** t Atelier de Creation Graphique/Grapus; **171** b Atelier de Creation Graphique/Grapus; **175** Courtesy of Jan Van Toorn (DACS 2001); **176** t Pentagram Design Limited; **176** b Pentagram Design Limited; **177** t l Pentagram Design Limited; **177** t r Pentagram Design Limited; **177** b l Pentagram Design Limited ; **177** b c Pentagram Design Limited; **177** b r Pentagram Design Limited ; **178** t Pentagram Design Limited; **178** b Pentagram Design Limited; **179** t Pentagram Design Limited; **179** b Pentagram Design Limited; **180** t Courtesy of Wim Crouwel; **180** b Courtesy of Wim Crouwel; **181** t Courtesy of Wim Crouwel; **181** b Courtesy of Wim Crouwel; **182** t l Courtesy of Jan Van Toorn (DACS 2001); **182** t r Courtesy of Jan Van Toorn (DACS 2001); **182** b Courtesy of Jan Van Toorn/Michel Boesveld; **183** Courtesy of Jan Van Toorn (DACS 2001); **184** t l Studio Dumbar/Lex van Pieterson; **184** t r Studio Dumbar/Lex van Pieterson; **184** b Studio Dumbar/Lec van Pieterson; **185** Studio Dumbar/Lex van Pieterson; **186** t Courtesy of Rick Vermeulen/Via Vermeulen; **186** b OPG Ltd/Rick Vermeulen/Via Vermeulen; **187** t OPG Ltd/Rick Vermeulen/Via Vermeulen; **187** b OPG Ltd/Rick Vermeulen/Via Vermeulen; **188** t l The MIT Press, Cambridge MA; **188** t r The MIT Press, Cambridge MA; **188** b Courtesy of Small Design; **189** t l Courtesy of Small Design; **189** t r Courtesy of Small Design; **189** b Courtesy of l Small Design; **189** b Courtesy of r Small Design; **190** t Courtesy of Wolfgang Weingart; **190** b OPG Ltd; **191** t OPG Ltd; **191** b OPG Ltd; **192** t Courtesy of Ken Friedman, Mill Valley, CA/Joe Coscia Jr; **192** b Courtesy of Ken Friedman, Mill Valley, CA/Tseng Kwong Chi; **193** t Courtesy of Ken Friedman, Mill Valley, CA/Artificial Nature edited by Jeffrey Deitch, photo by Joe Coscia Jr; **193** b Courtesy of Ken Friedman, Mill Valley, CA/Citibank/Anspach, Grossman, Portugal, Inc/Joe Coscia Jr; **194** t l Courtesy of Bruno Monguzzi; **194** t r Courtesy of Bruno Monguzzi; **194** b Courtesy of Bruno Monguzzi/Anna Boggeri; **195** Courtesy of Bruno Monguzzi; **196** t Ikko Tanaka Design Studio/Yasuhiro Ishimoto; **196** b Ikko Tanaka Design Studio; **197** t Ikko Tanaka Design Studio; **197** b Ikko Tanaka Design Studio; **198** t Jamie Reid **33** Productions Management; **198** b Jamie Reid **33** Productions Management; **199** t OPG Ltd/Jamie Reid; **199** b l OPG Ltd/Courtesy Stolpen/Wilson Collection; **199** b r OPG Ltd; **203** Research Studios / Neville Brody; **204** t Courtesy of April Greiman; **204** b Courtesy of April Greiman; **205** l Courtesy of April Greiman; **205** r Courtesy of April Greiman; **206** The Face, London; **207** t i-D Magazine, London; **207** b Arena, London; **208** l M&Co/Interview, NY; **208** c Dazed & Confused, London; **208** r OPG Ltd/Studio Voice, Japan; **209** t l Wallpaper, London; **209** t r OPG Ltd/Nest Magazine, NY; **209** b l OPG Ltd/Vanidad, Spain; **209** b r OPG Ltd/Dazed & Confused, London; **210** t l Estudio Mariscal; **210** t r Estudio Mariscal; **210** b Estudio Mariscal/Cote Cabrera; **211** Estudio Mariscal; **212** t l V(**23**); **212** t r V(**23**); **212** b V(**23**)/Michele Turriani; **213** V(**23**); **214** Cranbrook Academy; **215** Cranbrook Academy; **215** t Cranbrook Academy; **216** t l OPG Ltd/Emigre; **216** t r OPG Ltd/Emigre; **216** b Emigre; **217** Emigre; **218** t l M&Co; **218** t r M&Co; **218** b M&Co; **219** t M&Co; **219** b M&Co; **220** t Eric Spiekermann Meta Design; **220** b Eric Spiekermann Meta Design; **221** t Eric Spiekermann Meta Design; **221** b l Eric Spiekermann Meta Design; **221** b r Eric Spiekermann Meta Design; **222** t Research Studios / Neville Brody; **222** b The Face, London; **223** t OPG Ltd/The Face, London; **223** b l OPG Ltd; **223** b c r OPG Ltd; **224** t l Why Not Associates; **224** t r Why Not Associates; **224** b Why Not Associates; **225** Why Not Associates; **226** t l Why Not Associates; **226** t r Why Not Associates; **227** Why Not Associates; **228** t Courtesy of Jonathan Barnbrook; **228** b Courtesy of Jonathan Barnbrook; **229** t Courtesy of Jonathan Barnbrook; **229** b Courtesy of Jonathan Barnbrook; **230** t l Courtesy of Eiko Ishioka Inc; **230** t r Courtesy of Eiko Ishiokalnc; **230** b Courtesy of Eiko Ishioka Inc/Brigitte Lacombe; **231** Courtesy of Eiko Ishioka Inc; **232** t l David Carson Design; **232** t r David Carson Design; **232** b Laurence King Publishing; **233** t OPG Ltd; **233** b OPG Ltd; **234** t Courtesy of Ott + Stein/Ulf Erdmann Ziegler; **234** b Courtesy of Ott + Stein; **235** t Courtesy of Ott + Stein; **235** b Courtesy of Ott + Stein; **236** t Courtesy of Sheila Levrant de Bretteville; **236** b Courtesy of Sheila Levrant de Bretteville/Geoff Laurence; **237** t Courtesy of Sheila Levrant de Bretteville/Annette del Zoppo; **237** b Courtesy of Sheila Levrant de Bretteville/Roger Conrad; **238** Adbuster Media Foundation; **239** t Adbuster Media Foundation; **239** b Adbuster Media Foundation; **240** t Pentagram Design Inc; **240** b OPG Ltd; **241** t l Pentagram Design Inc; **241** t r Pentagram Design Inc; **241** b Pentagram Design Inc; **242** t Courtesy of Cyan; **242** b Courtesy of Cyan; **243** t Courtesy of Cyan; **243** b l Courtesy of Cyan; **243** b r Courtesy of Cyan